The Missouri Mormon Experience

The Missouri Mormon Experience

Edited by Thomas M. Spencer

University of Missouri Press
Columbia

University of Missouri Press, Columbia, Missouri 65211
Printed and bound in the United States of America

First paperback printing, 2018

ISBN 978-0-8262-2178-0 (paperback : alk. paper)

Library of Congress Cataloging-in-Publication Data

The Missouri Mormon experience / edited by Thomas M. Spencer.
p. cm.
Includes index.
ISBN 978-0-8262-1887-2 (cloth edition : alk. paper)
1. Church of Jesus Christ of Latter-day Saints–Missouri–History–19th century. 2. Mormon Church–Missouri–History–19th century. 3. Missouri–Church history–19th century. I. Spencer, Thomas M. (Thomas Morris), 1967-
BX8615.M8M57 2010
289.3'77809034–dc22
2009044294

∞™ This paper meets the requirements of the
American National Standard for Permanence of Paper
for Printed Library Materials, Z39.48, 1984.

Typefaces: Minion and Garamond

Contents

Acknowledgments

Like many scholarly anthologies, this volume had its genesis in a conference. In this case it was the Missouri Mormon Experience conference held at the Missouri State Capitol in September 2006. I have to thank the organizers of that conference, in particular Kenneth Winn of the Missouri State Archives, Jean Pry and Dale Whitman from the University of Missouri, and the Columbia, Missouri, Stake of the Church of Jesus Christ of Latter-day Saints. A few weeks after the conference, I received an e-mail requesting submissions for a conference anthology from Jean Pry. I sent my submission and the idea of this anthology was born.

During the summer of 2007, I was asked by Jean and Dale to become the editor for this project. I accepted their offer and have enjoyed the last two and a half years of working with these fine scholars of the Mormon-Missouri conflict of the 1830s to produce this volume.

I must also acknowledge the professionalism of the staff at the University of Missouri Press. Bev Jarrett, Dwight Browne, and Clair Willcox all provided ample support when called upon over the last three years. I also would like to thank Ann Youmans, our very capable copy editor, for the excellent job she did in preparing the manuscript for publication.

Not surprisingly, the greatest thanks must go to my nine fellow contributors. They kept the faith and submitted to two separate rounds of blind peer review and revision. Over the last three years, I have enjoyed getting to know them. We have met at conferences, and I am happy to call several of them my friends and all of them my colleagues. I am very pleased to present their excellent scholarship to the world via this volume. By publishing this volume on this cultural conflict of the 1830s, we are making an important contribution to the fields of Missouri and Mormon history.

The Missouri Mormon Experience

Introduction

"Persecution in the Most Odious Sense of the Word"

Thomas M. Spencer

Parley P. Pratt recalled that the Missouri wind during the winter of 1830-1831 blew "with a keenness that would almost take the skin off the face."[1] That winter was a particularly brutal one, called by pioneers in western Missouri the "Winter of the Deep Snow." Contemporaries living in the region claimed that the snow "seems to have continued for days, unabated—a wonder, at first, then a terror, a benumbing horror as it became a menace to life of men and animals."[2] One can imagine Pratt, the famous Mormon leader and fiery orator, hoping the weather was not a portent of troubles to come in Missouri.

Very soon after the birth of their faith, Mormon church members came to Missouri. According to a revelation received by Joseph Smith, Mormons asserted that a holy place, Zion, existed on the North American continent. Since Zion was to be, in the words of Smith, "on the borders of the Lamanites," most Mormons thought Zion was in the far western part of the continent. It was the faithless Lamanites who were to blame for the end of the holy civilization described in the Book of Mormon. Still, Book of Mormon prophets had asserted that the gospel, as restored by Joseph Smith, would be carried to Lamanite descendants. Smith, Pratt, and most Mormon leaders maintained that western North American Indians were Lamanite descendants in the 1830s and 1840s. Joseph Smith and many prominent Mormon leaders argued it was important for the sect to do all it could to redeem the Lamanite descendants centuries after their sin led to the end of the once holy and perfect civilization.

In the fall of 1830, less than a year after the church was founded, Joseph Smith had a revelation that he should send several missionaries, including the aforementioned Pratt, Oliver Cowdery, Peter Whitmer, and Ziba Peterson, "unto the land of Missouri, unto the borders of the Lamanites." After a harrowing trip of fifteen hundred miles through the inhospitable Midwest winter landscape, the Mormon missionaries arrived in Jackson County, Missouri, sometime in January 1831. Later during the summer of 1831, Joseph Smith would issue a revelation proclaiming that Independence, Missouri, a town on the very edge of the organized United States at the time, was the location of Zion and even suggested that the area to the north of Daviess County was the original location of the Garden of Eden. Since Jackson County originally included the present-day counties of Cass and Bates, the western "border of the Lamanites" was seventy miles long.[3] After the revelation from Joseph used the name, Mormon leaders even began to refer to Independence as the "New Jerusalem."

Like the Puritans of two centuries earlier (the ancestors of many of the original Mormons), the Mormons of the 1830s were decidedly millennialist in their outlook. They believed that the millennium would happen in their lifetime. Mormons believed that only those gathered in Zion would escape the violence and bloodshed of the end-times. Unusually for millenarians at the time, Mormons had not set a time frame for the second coming. However, they had decided upon a particular place where Christ would return and his true followers would be safe: Independence, Missouri.

After arriving in Independence in early 1831, two of the missionaries, Peterson and Whitmer, established themselves as tailors. The remaining missionaries went west across the Kansas River into Indian territory to meet with the Delaware and Shawnee tribes. Cowdery succeeded in convincing the Delaware chief, William Anderson, to promise he would build a house for the Mormon missionaries. Pratt would later claim that their successful visit made Indian agents and missionaries of other faiths envious. The reality was that the Mormon missionaries had not gotten the required federal permit to live in Indian territory. By the time Pratt returned to Kirtland, Ohio, in March 1831 to report on the activities of the missionaries, the church there had grown from a hundred to a thousand members during his absence.[4]

A small number of settlers moved to Jackson County during the spring and summer of 1831. Mormons began to buy large tracts of land in the county as early as July 1831. The Mormons also established the first newspaper in the county, the *Evening and Morning Star,* which published its first issue in June 1832. The newspaper, edited by William W. Phelps, was primarily concerned with detailed discussions of Mormon dogma. Little actual news made the pages of the *Star,* but the world news reported in its pages tended to focus on the cataclysmic in keeping with the widespread Mormon belief at the time that the Apocalypse was nigh. Non-Mormons in the county complained about the newspaper's content, complaining that it was "very distasteful to members and leaders of other religious denominations, the community being composed of Methodists, Baptists of two different orders, Presbyterians of two different orders, and Catholics, and a denomination calling themselves Christians."[5]

Mormon settlement in the area continued. By the end of 1832, 538 Mormons had moved to Jackson County. Eventually there developed a rivalry between the Mormon settlers in Missouri and those remaining in Kirtland, Ohio. By the middle of 1832 it was not clear which settlement was the church's headquarters—and Smith was not sending clear messages to his followers. Many in Jackson County began to wonder if Smith had doubts about Jackson County as the location of Zion. As the months passed, many in the area noticed that, despite his assurances he would do so, Smith had yet to move to Missouri to be with them. Eventually a rift developed and Smith would send a letter to Phelps warning him that "they who will not hear his voice, must expect to feel his wrath . . . Seek to purify yourselves, and also all the inhabitants of Zion, lest the Lord's anger be kindled to fierceness." Soon thereafter, church leaders in Missouri ceded control to the leaders Smith wished to have in control of church affairs in Missouri.[6]

Once Mormons moved to Jackson County, Joseph Smith proposed through an 1831 revelation a bold experiment in communitarianism. Those who chose to live in Zion, according to this revelation, were required to follow the law of consecration and stewardship. All members of the church in Zion were to deed over all property to the bishop of the church. Each bishop would then bestow an individual "inheritance" or "stewardship" on each member. Obviously this law, if followed, would lead to a radical redistribution of wealth among church members. The goal was for the male Mormon church member to be able to support his family and to eliminate the need for charity or support for the poor. If a surplus were produced, a farmer was to give it to the church leaders for redistribution to those who needed it. There has been much discussion about whether this approach arose from Smith's knowledge of prior utopian communitarian settlements in America. However, such a discussion seems moot. Despite Smith's pronouncements, few Mormon migrants to Zion complied with this law and most church members of means quietly acquired property in Missouri in their own name. Some of the wealthier Mormons even engaged in land speculation, thus demonstrating many were not committed to Smith's communitarian economic vision in any way, shape, or form. Eventually this law would be totally suspended by the church and the current law of tithing would take its place. While it was a bold idea for the time, it was not popular with the original Mormon settlers in Missouri and was eventually quietly dropped from church requirements. Even though contemporaries argued that Mormons in Missouri were mere pawns of Joseph Smith, this striking example of disobedience to the Prophet suggests otherwise.[7]

By the middle of 1833, there were twelve hundred Mormon settlers in Jackson County; perhaps a third of the county's population were saints. While there were a few settlers in Independence proper, most settlers were congregating in settlements along the Big Blue River to the west and southwest of the city. Along the Big Blue there were settlements named after their leaders or the geographic origin. These included the Whitmer Branch, the Prairie Branch, the Colesville Branch, and the Cincinnati Branch.[8] As Charles Brent Hancock, a Mormon settler, put it:

> We went to Jackson County and filled our mission preaching and baptizing when the door was opened. And viewing the land as it was very rich and productive abounding in much wild fruit and honey and game made it appear lovely and desireable for settlers. And it was considered by us a home for the Saints, a land of zion and a place of gathering . . . And we began to preach for the Saints to gather to Jackson County Missouri the land of Zion to learn more of the ways of the Lord.[9]

These industrious settlements were doing quite well, so well that some Missourians became envious of the Mormon settlers' improvements to their land.

Even though there had been episodes of property destruction and threatening language during the spring, things seemed to be going well for the Mormon settlers to the area by the early summer of 1833.[10] Disputes between themselves and the locals seemed to be dealt with and the situation in Jackson County was going to be all right—or so many in the area and the church leadership in Kirtland, Ohio, believed.

Unfortunately for the Mormons, many Missourians had begun to resent how the Mormon settlers believed the whole county would be theirs soon and seemed to enjoy pointing this out to the inhabitants of the area. The millennial vision of the Mormons convinced many of them that, because the end-times were near, the time of the other settlers living in Jackson County was drawing to end. In June 1833, Phelps contended in the *Evening and Morning Star* that

> the time is short for the Gentiles; not a moment should be lost. It is the time to save men's souls, and that too, by righteousness; and we do intreat men to behold for themselves, the great things that are passing before their eyes. See the sons of Joseph, [the Indians] gathered by Government; view the distress of nations; pray for deliverance while the destroying angel spreads

> the pestilence over the whole earth, and then mark the perfect man, for the end of that man is peace.[11]

These prophecies about the end of the world and contentions that God would give the Mormons the land of the gentiles rubbed many in the area the wrong way.

In July 1833, this short period of quietude came to an end. It began because of something W. W. Phelps wrote in the *Evening and Morning Star.* In the July issue of the paper, Phelps made a few statements about the laws of Missouri regarding free blacks that angered non-Mormons in the area. He quoted a state law that required free blacks to have written proof of citizenship from another state before being allowed to come to Missouri. It was a crime punishable by a five-hundred-dollar fine to bring a free black into Missouri without such a certificate. Phelps contended that "slaves were real estate" in Missouri and that the church must "shun every appearance of evil." Later in the same issue, Phelps said, "As to slaves we have nothing to say. In connection with the wonderful events of this age, much is doing towards abolishing slavery, and colonizing the blacks, in Africa." Missourians took this to mean that Phelps—and by extension all Mormons in the area—was in favor of abolishing slavery and perhaps of bringing free blacks to the state. Whether accurate or not, this led to unrest in the area. An "extra" was hurriedly published by Phelps on July 16, in which he claimed that he was in no way suggesting that the church would bring free blacks to the area. He even argued that he wished to prevent the church from admitting free blacks into membership. Phelps's statement in the extra was not an officially sanctioned statement of church doctrine. It was an attempt to ameliorate the immediate situation.

Phelps's desperate attempt to placate pro-slavery Missourians did not work. The day before Phelps's extra was published, a group of eighty prominent citizens of Independence signed a collection of assertions know as the "Secret Constitution." The signatories included many citizens who were directly involved in securing public safety: jailors, constables, judges, and justices of the peace. Also included among those who signed were others serving the county in an official capacity, including the county clerk, the deputy county clerk, and the local postmaster. The document also included the signatures of several local attorneys and merchants. Judging from those who signed it, the manifesto was more or less an official statement of the county's government at the time.

Frontier Missourians tended to be poor migrants from upper South states like Kentucky and Tennessee who, even though they seldom owned any slaves, supported the institution. These frontier Missourians viewed themselves as believers in individualism, although their persecution of the Mormons revealed how unwilling they were to defend their fellow Americans' civil liberties and religious liberties. Few among the Mormons were committed abolitionists and the Book of Mormon suggested that those with darker skins were considered inferior in the eyes of God. However, Missourians, like southerners during this period, were deeply suspicious of anyone who did not strongly support slavery. While there were few slaves in western Missouri at the time, an overwhelming majority of the settlers would have supported the institution, even though few frontier Missourians could afford slaves. The eighty Secret Constitution signers were of the mainstream if they thought the Mormon settlers threatened the future of good, decent, democratic, and slavery-based society in Jackson County.

In the Secret Constitution, Missourians contended that the Mormons were "deluded fanatics or weak and designing knaves" who came from the lowest possible social strata of the country. They accused the Mormons of "tampering" with the slaves in the county and attempting to convince them to revolt against their masters. There is no evidence that the Mormons ever did anything like this in Jackson County. Although many of the Mormons were openly ambivalent about slavery, they were in no way abolitionists. In fact, the Mormons—and those belonging to many other Christian sects at the time—believed that those with dark skins had been cursed by God and viewed those with dark skins as devious or evil. It was these sorts of views that had served to justify the existence of slavery in the first place. Phelps's response, while not official church doctrine, rings true and reflects the views of other Mormon church leaders at the time.

As Alex Baugh so memorably put it, the two groups, the Mormons and the Missourians, were like "oil and water" that "did not mix well."[12] Missourians in the early 1830s would have been suspicious of those with New England accents who moved to their area, although one should be careful in making the leap to suggesting that they would have viewed New Englanders as abolitionists. William Lloyd Garrison's abolitionist newspaper *The Liberator* was only a little over a year and a half old at the time of these events, and had fewer than four hundred subscribers even in a place as seemingly receptive as Boston. In 1833, abolitionism was a new idea in America—and one that would have had few adherents outside of Massachusetts.

If there is no evidence supporting this charge, then why did the writers include it in the Secret Constitution? The simplest answer seems to be that this was the most outrageous charge in the eyes of white Missourians. It allowed them to claim that the Mormons were a threat to the future of their society, that the Mormons wished to destroy it: "It manifests a desire on the part of their society to inflict on our society an injury that they know would be to us entirely insupportable, and one of the surest means of driving us from the county." In short, they included this baseless charge in order to incite as much anger as possible against the Mormons.

Worried about the future of Independence, the signers also believed that the Mormon identification of the area as Zion threatened their ability to raise their families and support them:

> They declare openly that their God hath given them this county of land, and that sooner or later they must and will have the possession of our lands for an inheritance, and in fine they have conducted themselves on many occasions in such a manner, that we believe it a duty we owe ourselves, to our wives and children, to the cause of public morals, to remove them from among us, as we are not prepared to give up our pleasant places, and goodly possessions to them, or to receive into the bosom of our families, as fit companions for our wives and daughters the degraded and corrupted free negroes and mulattoes that are now invited to settle among us.[13]

Again pushing the false charge that the Mormons were abolitionists, the non-Mormons contended that the Mormons threatened the racial order and thus were unworthy of remaining citizens of the county. The organization closed its manifesto by stating that a meeting would be held on July 20 to consider future actions against the Mormons.

Their appeal for a meeting was answered by between four hundred and five hundred Jackson Countians. A committee of prominent citizens was elected to draft a series of resolutions, a self-described "exposé" that the group released to the public. The group claimed that the document was the result of "cool deliberations." They argued that the situation was an "evil . . . that no one could have forseen and is therefore unprovided for by the laws." They claimed that they had to act rapidly and couldn't wait for the "delays of legislation." Additionally, the document claimed that the Mormons were poor and of very low social position. They once again expressed outrage that some Mormons were claiming that they would soon own most of the county. The Missourians raised the spectre of Mormon control of the county government:

> It requires no gift of prophecy to tell that is not far distant, when the government of the county will be in their hands, or persons willing to court their favor from motives of interest or ambition.
>
> What would be the fate of our lives and property in the hands of jurors or witnesses who do not blush to declare, and would not upon occasion hesitate, to swear that they have wrought miracles and supernatural cures; have conversed with God and his angels, and possess and exercise the gift of

> divination and of unknown tongues, and fired with the prospect of obtaining inheritances without money and without prices, may be better imagined than described.

In short, the group argued that mob action was necessary to "save" the county from Mormon control. They claimed (again sans evidence) that the Mormons were agitating among their slaves and that Phelps's paper had encouraged the settlement of free blacks in the area. The non-Mormons demanded that church leaders stop further Mormon settlement in the county and that those Mormons in the county should agree to leave very soon. They also demanded that Phelps cease publishing the *Evening and Morning Star* immediately. After the reading of the address and resolutions, they were approved by the group at large.[14]

Then a committee called upon the Mormon leaders to ask them to abide by the resolutions. They met with a group of prominent Mormons and informed them of their demands. The Mormons asked for more time, perhaps three months or at least ten days, to consider them. Phelps later claimed that the Missourians refused to give them more than fifteen minutes. When the Mormon leaders refused to comply with their demands, the committee returned to the larger group and told them that the Mormons would not answer and wanted too much time to consider the proposal.

After making sure the local sheriff had been locked in the back room of a local tavern, the larger group then voted to destroy Phelps's office and all of the associated Mormon businesses in the area. They destroyed the building that served as Phelps's residence and housed the printing press. Although the group broke into other businesses, the owners of these stores convinced the mob not to raze their properties as well. Another group took Mormon leader Edward Partridge and another Mormon, Charles Allen, and tarred and feathered them.

Three days later, on the morning of July 23, the mob of several hundred returned and forced the Mormon leaders to assemble in the public square. They demanded an answer to their proposal and threatened violence against them. The church leaders offered to sacrifice themselves if it would assuage the mob's anger towards the church. The mob refused and made further threats of violence. The church leaders agreed to leave the county and assented to a written agreement drawn up by the group to do so by the end of the year. Levi Jackman, a Mormon settler, contended that the "leaders of our people were trying to effect some treaty with the leaders of the mob, but it seemed like tempering with demons." Although some Mormons have insisted that Lilburn Boggs, who later issued the infamous "extermination order," was present and encouraging the mob, it is not clear that he was present. His son would later insist his father played no part in the anti-Mormon mob in Jackson County.[15]

Despite what some Mormons would later claim, not everyone in Missouri was pleased with this course of events. The editors of the *St. Louis Free Press* reacted with outrage when the news reached St. Louis in August. After recounting the story and stating that the editors were not familiar with Mormon doctrines, they went on to argue this was clearly an abridgment of religious freedom:

> We have no right to interfere with the religious creeds of our neighbors; and if their conduct towards us is regulated by the laws of the land, we can have no just cause of complaint. Had individuals of this sect, or even the whole body of it committed legal offenses, the civil tribunals of our country could have given sufficient redress; but to proceed against them as a religious body, not discriminating between the innocent and the guilty, must be considered persecution in the most odious sense of the word, and a disregard of the provisions of our Constitution.[16]

However, some in the state did argue that the ends justified the means. The editors of a competing paper in the same city, the *St. Louis Missouri Republican,* felt that while the actions were "wholly at war with the genius of our institutions," "perhaps, however, it was the only method which could have been effectually put in practice to get this odious description of [a] population out of the way."[17]

After signing the agreement, some brethren tried to move south into an area that would soon be Van Buren County, but they were soon driven back to their former homes by the same sorts of threats they had heard in Jackson County. As the months went by, Mormon settlers continued on as if little had changed. Ten high priests were appointed by the church leadership in Ohio to fill the pulpits in Jackson County.[18]

Meanwhile, Joseph Smith and the leadership of the church had decided to petition Governor Daniel Dunklin for assistance and protection. This was risky since the mob had threatened violence if they used the legal system in any way. In September, members of the church in Jackson County sent their petition to the governor. In it they recounted events and argued that their "situation was a critical one; we are located upon the western limits of the state, and of the United States; where desperadoes can commit outrages and even murder, and escape in a few minutes beyond the reach of process; where the most abandoned of all classes from almost every state may too often pass to the Mexican states, or to the most remote regions of the Rocky Mountains to escape the grasp of justice." Governor Dunklin replied three weeks later, in a letter dated October 19. He told the Mormons to seek redress through the courts and to sue for damages.[19]

By the time the Mormons received the governor's letter, they were debating whether or not they should arm themselves for self-defense. They began doing so. At the same time, the Mormons pursued their legal claims against the mob. They hired the firm of Doniphan, Atchison, Rees, and Wood for one thousand dollars. Predictably, the members of the mob responded negatively to this news. As Smith would later put it, "No sooner had this news spread among the mob, than they began to congregate and prepare for battle."[20]

In late October, as news spread that the saints sought redress through the courts and had hired a leading law firm in the area to represent them, a few vigilantes attacked the Mormon settlers. On October 31, the attacks began in earnest. First a mob attacked the settlement on the Big Blue River, west-southwest of Independence. They destroyed ten houses and threatened to do more. Many members of the settlement survived the night by hiding in a cornfield. Later they tried to get a peace warrant by going to the local magistrate. They read the governor's letter to him—especially the passage that suggested they first try local authorities. The magistrate insisted that he would do nothing about it. The Mormon settlers decided to create small groups of self-defense forces for each of the major settlements.

Every night in early November brought a new round of attacks on property from vigilantes upon the Mormons. On November 2, the Mormons responded by shooting one of the mobbers. Local magistrates still refused to grant peace warrants, some claiming they were fearful for their lives. Two Missourians and one Mormon were killed in a firefight near the Big Blue on November 4. On the same day, several prominent Mormons, including John Corrill and W. W. Phelps, were arrested for assault and battery. They had caught someone looting one of their businesses and had attempted to turn him over to the authorities. In other words, Mormons could not get the authorities to enforce the peace and protect their property but were themselves arrested for turning in someone they caught destroying their property. On the night of November 4, the church leaders in the jail agreed to vacate the county.

On November 5, the militia was assembled to "quell the mob," the action approved by Lieutenant Governor Lilburn Boggs, who was in Independence at the time. The militia was composed of many people who had also been taking part in the mob violence, thus making many Mormons nervous that the militia would engage in the same behavior. Eventually, the militia and a small Mormon force, with Boggs acting as an intermediary, negotiated a cease-fire and the Mormon force surrendered their arms. They were assured that no further violence would be perpetrated upon them.

However, the very next day, November 6, a systematic campaign of attacks began. Several groups of fifty to eighty men whipped Mormon settlers, fired upon them, chased them, and threatened to come back and massacre them. This caused much fear among the Mormons and they began to flee the county, most of them heading north into Clay County. Several heartrending stories exist about this period involving the violence and disorder, which resulted in the separation of families. On the night of November 13, there was a major meteor shower. Many Mormons believed that this was a sign that God would soon intercede on their behalf and they would be welcomed again into Zion. Many non-Mormons too feared that this was a sign that God's vengeance was at hand.

The citizens in Clay County behaved differently towards the Mormons. In the beginning at least, Clay Countians opened their homes to the Mormons and provided them with food, shelter, and employment. The Mormons slowly built temporary log homes and rented out land to farm. Mormon settlers were flabbergasted that they had been treated so unfairly. Many theorized that it was the right thing, that God would need to cleanse Zion of the unfaithful and sinful before they could again live there. They awaited word from the Prophet and bided their time.

Once again, the newspapers across Missouri spoke out against the actions of the mob in Jackson County. The *Missouri Intelligencer* maintained that "although we have always viewed these Mormons with abhorrence, we are not prepared to justify such outrageous proceedings on the part of the [county's] citizens." The editors of the *Intelligencer* also questioned the character of Jackson Countians: "Jackson County is situated at the very extremity of civilization on our western frontier, and the inhabitants have, we believe, the character (whether justly or injustly we do not know) of being very turbulent and lawless. The present occurrence is not calculated to remove that impression."[21]

The *St. Louis Missouri Republican*'s editors agreed, worrying that "the party opposed to the Mormons will think themselves placed so far beyond the pale of the law as to continue utterly regardless of it." Despite their tacit acceptance of the earlier attempt at expulsion, the *Republican*'s editors now asserted equal protection under the law, insisting, "There may be many worthless and intolerable members of the obnoxious sect; but the laws are equal to the punishment of all those who are guilty of violating them. The Mormons are as much protected in their religion, their property and person, as any other denomination or class of men. We think they acted perfectly right in offering the resistance which they did, and thus have the sympathy of this part of the community."[22]

Despite what many Mormons have said about Missourians, there was quite a bit of sympathy in eastern Missouri for the plight of the Mormons. The actions of Jackson Countians were simply not blithely accepted in the parts of the state that had been settled for much longer periods of time. In fact, the actions of these frontier Missourians were sharply criticized at the time by the intelligentsia in St. Louis and elsewhere in the state.

Almost a month after these events, and more than two weeks after he had received word of them, Smith finally sent instructions to Bishop Partridge. He told Partridge to retain the lands in Jackson County and that it was "not the will of the Lord for you to sell your lands in Zion." Later, he told the elders to seek redress with the courts first, then with the governor or, if that effort was unsuccessful, with the president. He told them to be careful, stating that "we must be wise as serpents, and harmless as doves."[23]

During November and December, Governor Dunklin seemed to be moving toward a state criminal inquiry into the actions of the mob in Jackson County. Dunklin wrote several sympathetic letters to the Mormon elders and stated that he would protect the Mormons if they wished to move back to Jackson County in a few months. In February 1834, the Liberty Blues were called out to protect several Mormon witnesses who were to be brought before the grand jury. On the morning of February 24, Amos Rees, attorney for the state court, and Robert Wells, state attorney general, visited the Mormons who were preparing to testify. Rees and Wells had decided "that all hope of criminal prosecution was at an end." They believed that the grand jury would not indict and a jury was unlikely to convict anyone associated with the mob violence. The Mormons decided not to pursue this avenue further. While Dunklin would later urge the legislature to pass legislation that would make such action illegal, nothing came of it. Thomas Pitcher, one of the leaders of the mob and a lieutenant colonel in the local militia, was arrested and held for a court-martial that convened in January. Ultimately, nothing came of this inquiry and no records apparently survived. Pitcher would later assert that the trial had taken "six or seven months, and cost the State over $30,000." Despite many promises to return weapons seized by Pitcher's militia, the local authorities never returned the weapons. Menacingly, the weapons were readily observed in the possession of the people in Independence by the early spring of 1834.

On April 10, the Mormons appealed directly to President Andrew Jackson to mobilize a detachment of the army to provide protection from the mob. Jackson, having just faced the nullification crisis in South Carolina, refused to interfere in a matter involving violations of state laws. Jackson's secretary of war, Lewis Cass, in a letter to the Mormons on May 2, summed up his case, stating, "The President cannot call out a military force to aid in the execution of the State laws, until the proper requisition is made upon him by the requisite authorities." The Congress would be petitioned several times in the following years by Mormons seeking redress for their grievances in Jackson County, to no avail. Congress generally responded as Cass had, that these acts were violations of state law, not federal law, and that redress should be sought through the courts of the State of Missouri.[24]

Smith and many prominent church leaders would make one attempt to "redeem Zion" in a failed Mormon military expedition called "Zion's Camp." Between February and early July 1834, a group of some 200 Mormons led by Joseph Smith marched from Kirtland, Ohio, towards Independence. Some have contended the expedition was an attempt to intimidate the Jackson County mobbers into giving the Saints back their lands. Others have contended it was an attempt to provide assistance to those Mormons in need in the area and to show Mormons in Missouri that church leaders still supported them. It is likely that both assertions are true. Regardless, Zion's Camp was, by these measures, an abysmal failure. As the group neared Jackson County, negotiations between the saints and their antagonists collapsed and a military conflict seemed likely in mid-June. Feelings were exacerbated when a ferry across the Missouri River carrying a few members of the Jackson County delegation to the negotiations sank on June 16. Many in Jackson County believed the boat had been sabotaged by the Mormons. This seems unlikely since there was no evidence of foul play and one of the supposed co-conspirators in the plot died in the calamity himself. A few days later, Zion's Camp was hurriedly disbanded after a cholera epidemic began to ravage the camp and several saints died. Smith interpreted the disease as God's vengeance upon them due to their unfaithfulness and decided that it would be best to return to Ohio.[25]

In 1836, the state government gave the Mormons a short reprieve by establishing Caldwell County in northwest Missouri as a haven for persecuted Mormons. Thousands of Mormon settlers, many of them recent converts from England and other parts of Europe, flooded into the area during the summer of 1838. However, tensions bubbled to the surface when Mormons began to settle in neighboring counties. "For a period of three agonizing, painful, and eventful months," Alexander Baugh has written of the "Mormon War" of the late summer and fall of 1838, "this disproportionate religious minority defended their rights, liberties, and property, against an overwhelming intolerant majority."[26]

On October 27, 1838, Governor Lilburn Boggs of Missouri, who had sent the state militia into northwest Missouri to fight the Mormons, issued his infamous "extermination order." Boggs stated that the "Mormons must be treated as enemies, and must be exterminated or driven from the State if necessary for the public peace—their outrages are beyond all description." Two days later, Livingston County militiamen killed seventeen Mormon settlers in what has become known to Mormons as the Haun's Mill Massacre. Surrounded and vastly outnumbered by the state militia at Far West, Smith surrendered on November 1. After hearing the news from Haun's Mill, Smith decided to surrender rather than risk death in a battle with the state militia. Smith was immediately threatened with execution and tried for treason. He eventually escaped to Illinois in April 1839. Although Missouri tried to extradite Smith numerous times, the attempts were never successful. Smith was later killed by a mob in Carthage, Illinois, in 1844. The Mormons would leave for Utah two years later.

The passage of time has certainly begun to heal the wounds caused by this conflict. Nearly 170 years later, on September 8 and 9, 2006, nearly six hundred people participated in a conference entitled "The Missouri Mormon Experience: From Conflict to Understanding." This conference was held in the Missouri capitol building in Jefferson City. Friday evening's events included a ceremony honoring Senator Kit Bond who, as governor of Missouri in 1974, had rescinded Governor Boggs's extermination order. After the ceremony, there was a dinner for the conference presenters at Lincoln University. Kenneth H. Winn, a scholar of Mormonism who was also Missouri State Archivist at the time, gave a talk about the place of the Mormon experience in Missouri history. On Saturday, the Missouri House of Representatives hosted the scholarly conference involving many historians, of Mormon and Missouri history. The point of the conference was to attempt to understand the troubles of the 1830s as well as to promote understanding between Mormons and non-Mormons in the state today.

This anthology is a product of that conference. The goal here is to provide the latest in scholarship about the Mormon experience in Missouri in a manner that is easily accessible to the public in both Missouri and Utah. The persecution of Mormons in Missouri greatly shaped Mormon faith and culture. It is a story that every Mormon is familiar with, and it sometimes makes them fearful of Missourians, even today. Let me tell just one story. I teach at Northwest Missouri State University. When I began to do work in the LDS archives in Salt Lake City in 2004, I placed a laptop bag that had the name of my university prominently displayed on the desk in the front of the reading room. Upon reading the logo, the archivist behind the desk (unconsciously, I think) took a noticeable step backward. I laughed and made some sort of (I hope) disarming joke. In contrast, the Mormon experience in Missouri during the 1830s has had little discernible impact on contemporary Missourians. It is a strange story that does not mean much to them although, as Ken Winn made clear in his keynote address the first night of the conference, that has not always been the case. As Winn contends in his essay in this volume, the

Mormon conflict gave antebellum Missourians a template to use for future vigilante action.

The ten essays here explore several crucial aspects of the Missouri Mormon experience. In his essay "The Missouri Context of Antebellum Mormonism," Winn argues that Mormons and Missourians viewed each other with suspicion and that the episode had a violent legacy for the state's history. According to Joseph Smith's revelations in the 1830s, western Missouri was to be the location of New Jerusalem, where his followers would be able to survive the fire and bloodshed of the end-times. The next two essays, "Reassessing Joseph Smith's 'Appointed Time for the Redemption of Zion'" by Ronald E. Romig and Michael S. Riggs and "Mormonism, Millenarianism, and Missouri" by Grant Underwood, explore the historical place of Missouri in the Mormon millennialist outlook. Both essays contend that Missouri had an important place in the theology of 1830s Mormonism.

One of Smith's revelations that has yet to be fulfilled was that Missouri was to see the building of the Latter-day Saints' greatest temple. In "The Great Temple of the New Jerusalem," Richard O. Cowan explains the development of this belief among LDS and LDS splinter groups that Missouri—in particular Independence, Missouri—would be the location of a grand temple. His essay examines the history of this belief and how it has evolved. However, Independence was not the only place that Mormon settlers tried to build a temple. Alexander L. Baugh's "The Mormon Temple Site at Far West, Caldwell County, Missouri" explores the attempt to build a temple in Caldwell County, Missouri. Baugh also gives the history of the temple site to the present. The Far West temple site remains a prominent tourist attraction in northwest Missouri today. Thousands of tourists—mostly Mormons—visit the site each summer.

In my essay, "'Was This Really Missouri Civilization?' The Haun's Mill Massacre in Missouri and Mormon History," I examine one of the seminal events of the Mormon War of 1838, the killing of seventeen Mormon settlers by the Livingston County Militia at Jacob Haun's mill on October 30, 1838. The Haun's Mill Massacre event and its aftermath have become a major part of Mormon history and culture. Scholars of Mormonism contend that the massacre convinced Joseph Smith to surrender at Far West two days later and agree that the Mormons would leave Missouri. Why did this massacre take place? What does it tell us about both the Mormons and the militiamen involved? How has it been portrayed in Mormon history? In Missouri history? In American history? While that undertaking necessarily involves recounting the events of the massacre and its aftermath, the focus here is on how the event has been viewed and interpreted by Mormons and Missourians since 1838.

In "But for the Kindness of Strangers: The Columbia, Missouri, Response to the Mormon Prisoners and the Jailbreak of July 4, 1839," Jean Pry and

Dale Whitman tell the little-known story of the escape of three Mormon church leaders from the Boone County jail in Columbia. Parley P. Pratt, Morris Phelps, and King Follett had been brought to Columbia from Ray County on a change of venue several weeks earlier. The description of events is taken primarily from two eyewitness accounts, those of Pratt and Laura Phelps, wife of Morris Phelps. In observing the generous treatment of the prisoners and of Laura Phelps herself while in Columbia, Pry and Whitman argue that central Missourians did not share the cultural political outlook of western Missourians and did not view the Mormons as negatively as western Missourians did. They raise a question that is little explored in much of the scholarship about the Missouri-Mormon conflict, that of regional differences within the state.

The Missouri experience had a major impact on the Mormon mind-set. In "Lessons Learned: The Nauvoo Legion and What the Mormons Learned Militarily in Missouri," Richard Bennett provides a history of Mormon militarism during the 1830s and 1840s. Bennett contends that their Missouri troubles convinced many Mormons that their security relied upon the development of a major military presence in the region. Bennett recounts the Mormon attempts at self-defense in northwest Missouri during the Mormon War, including the infamous Danite band. Bennett argues that, in the eyes of Mormon leaders, these earlier attempts were clearly inadequate. Bennett's contention is that the support for the impressive Nauvoo Legion—a military force that in 1844 was half the size of the U.S. Army—grew out of the Mormons' earlier experiences in Missouri.

Whether on their way to Nauvoo or Utah, Mormon migrants crossed into Missouri for much of the nineteenth century. What were their experiences like? Did they meet resistance from Missourians? In "Between the Borders: Mormon Transmigration through Missouri, 1838-1868," Fred E. Woods discovers that Mormon migrants had a relatively easy time in the state after the expulsion of 1838. Woods recounts some instances of the charity of Missourians towards Mormons, most notably the actions of the citizens of Lexington after the explosion of the steamboat *Saluday* on the Missouri River. Ultimately, Woods finds that, after the tumultuous 1830s, Missourians left alone the Mormon migrants passing through the state.

Even though many scholars of Mormon history have written about the Mormon-Missourian conflict, I would contend that little significant research has been undertaken to try and understand the point of view of other Missourians during the 1830s. Some historians have accepted the caricatures of contemporary Mormons that depicted the non-Mormons as loathsome, slavery-supporting, religiously bigoted, land-hungry barbarians. As a historian of Missouri history, I would like to learn why Missourians committed such indefensible acts to Mormon settlers during this period. I would contend that the Missouri-Mormon conflict of the 1830s is the result of a particularly noxious blend of cultural and social causes. I agree that the Missouri side of the conflict involved a defense of slavery, some religious bigotry, and land hunger. However, there is a fair amount of evidence that, as in other instances of vigilantism during the nineteenth century, Missourians also acted out of a tragically misguided sense of paternity as well as a desire for political control. One certainly should condemn the actions taken by Missourians against the Mormons during the 1830s, but a historian must also try to understand their motivations. Much more work regarding the motivations of those who took part in the howling mobs remains to be done. The Missouri-Mormon conflict teaches us a great deal about the true state of religious tolerance in the frontier United States during the 1830s. While some historians have argued that the American frontier during the nineteenth century was a haven for individualism and liberty, the Mormon experience in Missouri during the 1830s suggests otherwise.

Notes

1. Parley P. Pratt, *Autobiography of Parley Parker Pratt* (Salt Lake City: Deseret, 1950), 52; cited in Warren Abner Jennings, "Zion Is Fled: The Expulsion of the Mormons from Jackson County, Missouri" (PhD diss., University of Florida, 1962), 6.

2. Eleanor Atkinson, "The Winter of the Deep Snow," *Transactions of the Illinois State Historical Society* (1909): 49; cited in Jennings, "Zion Is Fled," 5.

3. Craig S. Campbell, *Images of the New Jerusalem: Latter-day Saint Faction Interpretations of Independence, Missouri* (Knoxville: University of Tennessee Press, 2004), 34–37.

4. Jennings, "Zion Is Fled," 7–8.

5. Prentiss Ingraham, ed., *Seventy Years on the Frontier: Alexander Majors' Memoirs of a Lifetime on the Border* (Chicago: Rand, McNally, 1893), 44; cited in Jennings, "Zion Is Fled," 62.

6. Jennings, "Zion Is Fled," 63, 77–80. The passage from Joseph Smith's letter to Phelps is quoted in *History of the Church of Jesus Christ of Latter-day Saints, Period 1: History of Joseph Smith, the Prophet, by Himself*, vol. 1 (Salt Lake City: Deseret, 1978), 316–17.

7. Jennings, "Zion Is Fled," 82–118.

8. Ronald E. Romig, *Early Jackson County, Missouri "Mormon" History Guide* (Missouri Mormon Frontier Foundation, 1996), 3.

9. Charles Brent Hancock, "Autobiography," LDS Church Archives, MS 5285.

10. *Evening and Morning Star* 2, no. 15 (December 1833), and no. 16 (January 1834).

11. Ibid., 119–24. The quotation is from the *Evening and Morning Star* 2, no. 13 (June 1833): 101.

12. Alexander Baugh, *A Call to Arms: The 1838 Mormon Defense of Northern Missouri* (Provo, Utah: BYU Studies, 2000), 6–7.

13. This passage is quoted in the *Evening and Morning Star* 2, no. 15 (December 1833): 114.

14. The text of the mob's proceedings was published in numerous newspapers such as the *Fayette Western Monitor* and *St. Louis Missouri Republican* of August 9, 1833, and also eventually in the *Columbia Missouri Intelligencer,* August 10, 1833, the *Jefferson City Jeffersonian,* August 17, 1833, the *National Intelligencer,* August 21, 1833, and *Niles' Weekly Register,* September 14, 1833.

15. Jennings, "Zion Is Fled," 142–52; Levi Jackman, "Diary, 1835 May–July 1844," LDS Church Archives, MS 8362. For more on Boggs's rumored role in the events, see *History of the Church, Period 1,* 391–92. To read William M. Boggs's denial that his father played a role in the events, see William M. Boggs's, "A Short Biographical Sketch of Lilburn W. Boggs, by His Son," *Missouri Historical Review* 4 (January 1910): 107.

16. *St. Louis Free Press,* August 15, 1933.

17. *St. Louis Missouri Republican,* August 9, 1833.

18. Jennings, "Zion Is Fled," 154–56.

19. *History of the Church, Period 1,* 410–15, 423–24.

20. Ibid., 424–25.

21. *Columbia Missouri Intelligencer,* November 16, 1833.

22. *St. Louis Missouri Republican,* November 15, 1833.

23. *History of the Church, Period 1,* 448–51, and 453–56.

24. Jennings, "Zion Is Fled," 208–41.

25. Ibid., 242–93. For more on Zion's Camp, see Roger D. Launius, *Zion's Camp: Expedition to Missouri, 1834* (Independence, Mo.: Herald Publishing House, 1984).

26. Baugh, *A Call to Arms,* 163.

1

The Missouri Context of Antebellum Mormonism and Its Legacy of Violence

Kenneth H. Winn

The Mormon Church's sojourn in northwestern Missouri in the 1830s is an interesting story but not a happy one. It reflects poorly at one point or another on virtually all of the actors involved.

Yet despite its troubles in Missouri, Mormonism has since become America's most successful indigenous religion. As of May 2007, the Utah-based Church of Jesus Christ of Latter-day Saints claimed nearly thirteen million adherents worldwide. Its smaller sibling, the Community of Christ, which has its headquarters in Independence, Missouri, claims an additional quarter of a million. Many thousands of these church members, of course, live peacefully in the very region their nineteenth-century forebears experienced such trouble.

It is a commonplace that history is written by the winners. The vanquished are described as deserving their fate, or their concerns or claims are marginalized or forgotten. Surely those who regarded Abraham Lincoln and Franklin Roosevelt as heroes have had a more influential voice than those who championed Jefferson Davis and Herbert Hoover.

But generally speaking, it is the losers in historic strife who have the longer memories, especially if they are "a people." Most Americans remember that the United States saved England and Europe's "bacon" in World War II, and then again, afterwards, with the Marshall Plan. Fewer Americans are aware that the United States sent troops to help overturn the Mexican Revolution in 1914 and the Russian Revolution between 1918 and 1920. Even fewer Americans remember that the CIA organized the coup that put the shah of Iran on the throne in 1953 or arranged for the democratically elected Guatemalan government to be overthrown in 1954. However, the Mexicans, the Russians, the Iranians, and the Guatemalans all remember. African-Americans still carry a consciousness and personal sense of injury about slavery that mystifies some whites, even as some prideful white southerners continue to uphold the "Lost Cause," calling the Confederate flag an emblem of heritage, not racism.

In this framework, the unhappy transit of the Church of Jesus Christ of Latter-day Saints is unusual. Mormon Church members unsurprisingly have the stronger knowledge of the history than do non-church members who live in Missouri. Every Mormon schoolchild of faithful parents knows the part the state played in the divine drama of the early church. It is hard to forget that the governor of a state ordered the banishment or extermination of your ancestors, or that the founder of your church was ordered shot by a Missouri firing squad, a sentence commuted at the last minute only to leave him to languish in jail without a trial. Dozens of church members, however, died in Missouri and nearly all lost their property.[1]

At the same time, the Mormons have proven the historical winners—both as a successful people and in the writing of this chapter in American history—at least mostly so. Initially church members interpreted what happened to them in Missouri as religious persecution, pure and simple. For some Mormons that remains the interpretation. But if bigotry is the answer, we need to understand why. Reducing the problem to evil's opposition to God's chosen people is not a satisfactory answer for historians. Beginning about forty years ago, many church scholars have attempted, often with great insight, to discuss these matters in a more sophisticated fashion. Since then a veritable army of historians have numbered the hairs on the prophet Joseph Smith's head and performed a study on his words during the 1830s, but few have looked at the church through the eyes of those who opposed its settlement in Missouri. Non-Mormon historians largely have not taken it up as an academic problem, nor is there a constituency of non-Mormon descendants clamoring for an explanation of the governor's "extermination order" or the massacre at the Mormon settlement known as Haun's Mill.[2]

If we really want to understand why Mormons and western Missourians hated each other in the 1830s and continued to fear and distrust each other into the twentieth century, we must reach deeper into the non-Mormon culture of the era and bring a more sophisticated understanding of Mormonism into that environment. Let me offer some ideas on approaching the task.

Here is Joseph Smith's classic observation about Missourians as the Mormons encountered them in 1831: The Mormons, he said, "coming from a highly cultivated society in the east" naturally observed "the degradations, leanness of intellect, ferocity, and jealousy of a people that were nearly a century behind the times," and "roamed about without the benefit of civilization, refinement and religion." The Saints found the Missourians' habits repugnant. Relatively abstemious in their own behavior, the Mormons recoiled from their neighbors' addictions to horse racing, gambling, drinking, and swearing. Another Mormon leader, W. W. Phelps, observed in an account he sent to a New York newspaper in late 1831 that the southerners who had settled the area held to "customs, manners, modes of living and a climate entirely different from the northerners, and they hate Yankees worse than snakes, because they cheated them or speculated on their credulity with so many Connecticut clocks and New England notions. The people are proverbially idle or lazy, and mostly ignorant; reckoning nobody their equal to themselves in many respects, and as it is a slave holding state, [and] Japheth will make Canaan serve him."[3]

Both Smith and Phelps were trying to explain and win sympathy for their troubles from non-Mormons back east, but they were not making things up. Here is how a nineteenth-century Clay County historian described the area's first state senator in 1826: "The successful candidate in 1826 was Martin Palmer . . . who lived on Fishing River . . . Palmer was a 'statesman' somewhat of the David Crockett species, uneducated, illiterate and uncultivated, but possessing natural good sense, a considerable amount of shrewdness, and an acquaintanceship with the ways of the world."[4]

"Uneducated," "illiterate," and "uncultivated": One man's degraded intellect, living a hundred years behind the time, was another's Davy Crockett, one of nature's noblemen. When the Mormons encountered them, these "old settlers," as they were called, had lived in the region less than ten years. Many of these immigrants had, in fact, come about the same time as the Saints. European and American settlement in what was to become Missouri in the eighteenth and early nineteenth century clung to the Mississippi River. But by the conclusion of the War of 1812, the Indian menace to interior migration had ended. The agriculturally rich Missouri River bottomland that stretched across central Missouri to the territory's western boundary proved a magnet for land-hungry settlers, culminating in the land rush of 1819. This settlement, which began in Howard, Saline, and Boone Counties, worked its way west, reaching the western counties in the 1820s: the legislature formed Lafayette County in 1820, Clay County in 1822, and Jackson County in 1826. By 1830, Lafayette had a population of 2,912; Clay had a population of 5,338; and Jackson 2,823. As small as these numbers seem to us today, the population was growing very fast.[5]

Most of the immigrants to the western Missouri River valley came from the Upper South—Virginia, North Carolina, Tennessee, and Kentucky. The endless parade of caravans flowing along the central-west ribbon across the state led the famed Baptist missionary, John Mason Peck, to declare, "Kentucky and Tennessee were breaking up and moving to the 'Far West,'" as the area was then known.[6]

Initially, living conditions on the western frontier were quite primitive.[7] Most settlers began as subsistence farmers, raising swine for cash and living in single-room log houses. Within a decade, however, the cabins had been replaced by white frame houses for most, brick homes for the wealthy. Latecomers to the region often took up tenant farming, which was recognized as a temporary condition in this economically mobile region and bore no social stigma.

These new immigrants, thus, were not hunters, trappers, or, except at the very beginning, mere subsistence farmers. They did not come as squatters to escape the growing civilization back east. Rather, they were enthralled by a single-minded pursuit of economic gain. By the early 1830s, many had made the switch from subsistence to commercial farming. As immigrants from the Upper South, they tried to duplicate the agriculture of their home states—sometimes successfully, sometimes not. Cotton growing, for example, was a notable failure, while tobacco and hemp growing proved successful. During the early years of settlement, the region's farmers shipped their produce to New Orleans for national and international distribution. As time passed, however, St. Louis became their end destination and the region's economic future in the years before the Civil War became firmly linked to that economically booming city.

Emulating the agriculture of the Upper South brought other consequences. Tobacco and hemp growing was hard, dirty, labor-intensive work that fueled the demand for slaves. When the Mormons met Missourians in the 1830s, few of the old settlers owned slaves but they aspired to, much as most Americans aspire today to owning their own home, a car, and other attributes of economic success. Slave ownership both served as such a symbol and promised greater wealth. The Missouri River counties stretching from Boone County to Jackson County (Columbia to Kansas City) at the state border would become the state's "Black Belt," with African American slaves making up about 24 percent of the population by 1850.

Yet as rooted as slavery became, it rarely approached the scale found on the large plantations of the Deep South; typically slaveowners held only a few slaves and they worked alongside them in the fields. By 1850, Jackson County's slave population had reached 21 percent; in Clay County it had reached 27 percent; in Lafayette County it had reached 34 percent, the highest of any Missouri county.

Eventually those from the Upper South who moved into the western Missouri River Valley proved economically successful, the region becoming the most prosperous agricultural area in the state. But when the Mormons started moving in the 1830s, they had just begun setting down the rudiments of political or social organization.

This essay began with the unflattering characterizations of Missourians by the Mormon prophet and William Phelps. The Missourians, for their part, had no higher respect for the Saints. In 1833, one anti-Mormon spokesman declared that "each successive autumn and spring pours forth its swarm of Mormons among us, with a gradual falling of the character of those who compose them." Samuel D. Lucas, a rabid Mormon-hater who would hound the church throughout the decade, was more rhetorically violent, terming the Saints a "mass of human corruption" and a "tribe of human locusts" who "from their pestilent hive in Ohio and New York" threatened to "scorch and wither a goodly portion of Missouri." One anti-Mormon manifesto claimed that if the Saints "had been respectable citizens in society and thus [religiously] deluded, they would have been entitled to our pity rather than to our contempt and hatred; but from their appearance, from their manners, and from their conduct since coming among us, we have every reason to fear that, with but very few exceptions, they were the very dregs of that society from which they came, lazy, idle, and vicious."[8] It has a familiar ring. Note that, like the Mormons, these writers have in mind an audience beyond their own community and are trying to explain their hostility to the church.

The basic outline of what happened when the Mormons settled in Missouri is well-known: the violent expulsion from Jackson County in 1833, the expulsion from Clay County in 1834, the creation of Caldwell County as an Indian-style reservation for Mormons in 1836, and finally the Mormon War, in which Governor Lilburn Boggs, a citizen of Jackson County, issued his famous extermination order expelling church members from the state in 1838.[9]

Historians have explored the effect of the church's violent transit across Missouri, from the psychological effect on the Saints to more practical matters, like the subsequent creation of the Nauvoo Legion in Illinois.[10] I would assert that the effect of the Mormon War cut two ways. Most historians of Missouri have treated the Mormon period in the state's history as a brief, if queer interlude, in which some peculiar-thinking northeasterners got chased out of the region. Then traditional patterns resumed and the Mormons left scarcely a ripple upon the pond of the state's history.

I do not believe this is true. Western Missouri was largely populated by young men in the 1830s. Governor Boggs was the old man of the group at forty-one when he first encountered the church as a merchant in Independence. Samuel Lucas was thirty-four when he took up active leadership against the church. When Alexander Doniphan and David Rice Atchison served as lawyers for the church after the Jackson County expulsion, they were twenty-five and twenty-six years old. When future governor Austin King presided over Joseph Smith's 1838 state "treason" hearing, he was thirty-six. These are the famous names, already the leaders in their communities. The rank and file who followed them were even younger.[11]

The Mormon War framed the thinking of an entire generation of young men in western Missouri, and helped frame it for violence. Governor Boggs's aggressive appetites apparently unsated by the Mormon conflict, he massed Missouri troops in 1839 to fight against the Iowa militia in the so-called Honey War, a state border dispute. More significantly, while Missourians supported the Mexican-American War in 1846, no part of the state furnished more troops and had a greater war spirit than western Missouri. Indeed, Alexander Doniphan became a national hero for his leadership of these soldiers.[12]

When "free-soilers" began flocking into Kansas territory in the 1850s, western Missourians described them as degraded New England fanatics. Missourians, of course, had no monopoly on denouncing antislavery men as insurrectionary scum, but the sectional strife prefigured in the Mormon War was reenacted as thousands of western Missourians, known as "border ruffians"—many of them Mexican War veterans—organized themselves into mobs, flocked into Kansas to cast pro-slavery votes, and physically intimidated northern settlers. Their leader was U.S. Senator David Rice Atchison. In 1854 he wrote Jefferson Davis, "We are organizing to meet their organization. We will be compelled to shoot, burn & hang, but the thing will soon be over. We intend to '*Mormanise*' the Abolitionists."[13]

The brutal violence born in western Missouri continued through the Civil War, most infamously manifesting itself in the massacre of two hundred unsuspecting men and boys in Lawrence, Kansas, in August 1863 during an attack by western Missourian guerrillas. The border troubles that afflicted Kansas and Missouri left an angry legacy, which, like the Mormon War, lasted well into the twentieth century.

The violent tradition continued into the early 1880s, symbolized best by Jesse James, a psychopathic thug originally romanticized as the Confederate guerilla who refused to surrender.[14] Through him and his lesser imitators, Missouri earned the unenviable national nickname of the "Robber State." Violence and political strife marked western Missouri for a full half century, with only occasional respite.

I am not arguing that persecuting the Mormons led to the Lawrence massacre or to Jesse James. There were many causes involved. Geography had a lot to do with it. Kansas is located on Missouri's western border, not Georgia's, to cite only one factor. But I am suggesting that the Missouri reaction to Mormonism worked as a poison pill, giving western Missourians a psychological framework, a language, and a behavior to deal with those whom they opposed. Were it not for the national events that led to the Mexican War or "Bleeding Kansas," these behaviors might have been muted or died out. Instead they strengthened the cultural violence found in the 1838 Mormon War. And violence once committed leaves a legacy not easily undone—a legacy often fraught with tragic consequences for generations to come.

Notes

1. There are no reliable figures for the number of Mormons who died in the Mormon War; estimates range from about thirty to one hundred (a surely exaggerated figure). Richard Lyman Bushman, *Joseph Smith: Rough Stone Rolling* (New York: Alfred A. Knopf, 2005), 633.

2. Thomas G. Alexander, "Historiography and the New Mormon History: A Historian's Perspective," *Dialogue: A Journal of Mormon Thought* 19 (1986): 25–49. In my own writing, I have made some attempt to see both sides of the Missouri conflict. Though I am not a church member, I still tended to see these events through Mormon sources and thus through Mormon eyes. Many non-church sources concerning the conflict have yet to be unearthed. See Kenneth H. Winn, *Exiles in a Land of Liberty: Mormons in America, 1830–1846* (Chapel Hill: University of North Carolina Press, 1989), 85–105, 129–51, and a subsequent essay on Mormon dissenter John Corrill, "'Such Republicanism as This': John Corrill's Rejection of Prophetic Rule," in Roger D. Launius and Linda Thatcher, eds., *Differing Visions: Dissenters in Mormon History* (Urbana: University of Illinois Press, 1994), 45–75.

3. Joseph Smith Jr., *History of the Church of Jesus Christ of Latter-day Saints,* ed. B. H. Roberts, 7 vols. (Salt Lake City: Deseret, 1978), 1: 189. The Mormon critique of their first neighbors in Missouri, as well as the "old settlers" critique of the Mormons that follows, is adapted in part from a broader discussion found in Winn, *Exiles,* 85–105, and *Evening and Morning Star,* January 1834.

4. *History of Clay and Platte Counties, Missouri, From the Most Authentic Official and Private Sources . . .* (St. Louis, 1885), 109.

5. *Abstract of the Returns of the Fifth Census* (1830).

6. John Mason Peck, *Forty Years of Pioneer Life* (Philadelphia, 1864), 146.

7. My social portrait of the central western region of Missouri is indebted to R. Douglas Hurt, *Agriculture and Slavery in Missouri's Little Dixie* (Columbia: University of Missouri Press, 1992).

8. Smith, *History of the Church,* 1: 396; Samuel Lucas, "Jackson County," in *Gazetteer of the State of Missouri,* comp. Alphonso Wetmore (St. Louis, 1837), 96, 9; Smith, *History of the Church,* 1: 375.

9. The best general account of the "Mormon War" in Missouri is Stephen C. LeSueur, *The 1838 Mormon War in Missouri* (Columbia: University of Missouri Press, 1987); for the concept of Caldwell County as an "Indian-style reservation" for the Saints, see Roger Launius, *Alexander William Doniphan: Portrait of a Missouri Moderate* (Columbia: University of Missouri Press, 1997), 40. Stephen Aron interestingly notes the similarity of Boggs's extermination order to the method in which "troublesome" Indians had been removed from the state—leave or face annihilation. Stephen Aron, *American Confluence: The Missouri Frontier from Borderland to Border State* (Bloomington: University of Indiana Press, 2006), 237; see also Winn, *Exiles,* 85–105, 129–51.

10. Winn, *Exiles,* 162.

11. Biographies of many of the major figures involved in the Mormon War—Lilburn Boggs, Alexander Doniphan, David Rice Atchison, and Austin King, among other figures—are profiled in Christensen et al., *The Dictionary of Missouri Biography* (Columbia: University of Missouri Press, 1999). Actually, the Mormon settlers were just as young. Joseph Smith himself was only twenty-six when he called for the gathering of a new Zion on the far western Missouri frontier. See Marvin S. Hill, "The Rise of Mormonism in the Burned-Over District: Another View," *New York History* 61 (1980): 426–27; Winn, *Exiles,* 46–47.

12. Launius, *Doniphan,* chapters 4–9.

13. For a discussion of the anxiety felt by western Missourians about free-soil immigrants to Kansas Territory (especially New Englanders) and the violence it subsequently provoked, see Nicole Ectheson, *Bleeding Kansas: Contested Liberty in the Civil War Era* (Lawrence: University of Kansas Press, 2004). See also Aron, *American Confluence,* 238. Historian Adam Arenson quotes William Walker, a Tennessee native, as telling David Rice Atchision in 1854 that "Virginia, Tennessee, and Kentucky ought to send their hardy sons out to claim their rights and maintain them too, [otherwise] the filth, scum, and offscourings of the East and Europe" would "pollute our fair land, to dictate to us a government, to preach Abolitionism and dig underground Rail Roads" (Adam Arenson, *The Cultural Civil War: St. Louis and the Failures of Manifest Destiny* [Cambridge, Mass.: Harvard University Press, forthcoming]). Atchison is quoted in William E. Parrish, *David Rice Atchison of Missouri: Border Politician* (Columbia: University of Missouri Press, 1961), 164.

14. Using Jesse James and his family as his foil, T. J. Stiles brilliantly traces Missouri's disordered antebellum culture through the Civil War and into the violent behavior for which James became famed. See T. J. Stiles, *Jesse James: Last Rebel of the Civil War* (New York: Alfred A. Knopf, 2002).

2

Reassessing Joseph Smith's "Appointed Time for the Redemption of Zion"

Ronald E. Romig and Michael S. Riggs

In the aftermath of the 1833 expulsion from Zion and for the remainder of the decade, it became Joseph Smith's prophetic preoccupation to restore his Missouri followers to their temporal properties and spiritual inheritance. Much attention has focused on Smith's first attempt called "Zion's Camp" to redeem properties he had prophetically designated as "promised lands" his followers were divinely entitled to inherit in Jackson County, Missouri. In 1834, Smith's prophecy was refuted, however, when the armed company he commanded was unable to fulfill their mission to restore to the Mormons their confiscated properties. According to one historian, this "failure seriously demoralized many of Smith's followers, thus contributing to a major apostasy crisis a few years later."[1]

It is logical to reason the manifest refutation resulting from the Zion's Camp failure to return Mormons to their legal and spiritual standing in Missouri would have resulted in mass disaffection among Smith's adherents. Joseph Smith's movement, however, not only survived the refutation of multiple prophecies during the 1830s relating to his quest to redeem the City of Zion or New Jerusalem, but the group actually grew during the period. Beyond the failure of Zion's Camp, this study is devoted to Joseph Smith's lesser-known second attempt to reestablish Zion, prophetically pronounced to have been accomplished before September 11, 1836.

Following the forcible removal of the saints from Jackson to Clay County in 1833, several Missouri state officials signaled there might be a remedy for Mormon losses. The state attorney general wrote to counsel for the LDS Church retained to seek legal remedy for loss of property in Jackson County that there "was no doubt the governor would send them military aid. He even suggested the Mormons might organize a force and receive arms from the State for their defense."[2] In May 1834, in response to this intelligence and by divine commandment, Joseph Smith Jr. piloted a band of eastern rescuers called Zion's Camp to upper Missouri, including some two hundred men and a few women and children.[3] With relief supplies in tow, the party was committed to assisting their dispossessed brethren to return to their homes in Jackson County.

When the mission failed, Smith explained his followers lacked obedience to the Lord's commands (as given by Smith), and as a result, supernatural support was withheld. Next, Smith moved to purge and consolidate power within his church's hierarchy. The mechanism used to restructure the local hierarchy was the establishment of the Missouri High Council. While a direct outgrowth of the Zion's Camp experience, the formation of this council also aligned Missouri LDS church governance with that in their Ohio headquarters town of Kirtland. Smith saw the council as the means to fulfill the expectations and obligations referred to in his earlier (Kirtland) Zion's Camp and Clay County Fishing River revelations.[4] Further, the creation of the High Council helped relieve the dissonance created among loyal membership by the unsuccessful attempt to take back lost landholdings in Jackson County.[5] Anthony B. van Fossen argues that generally, "to survive the failure of an important specific prophecy, a movement must become more hierarchical—demoting the unreliable and consigning nonbelievers to insignificance but, most importantly, elevating the prophet and his original and most trusted apostles and disciples."[6]

The Fishing River revelation conveys Smith's intention to mount a second armed attempt at retaking Zion. Apostle William E. McLellin reflected upon this predisposition in a letter to Joseph Smith III in 1872, indicating that the "spirit of war scattered and diffused in all the church in 1834, to go and gather up 'the strength of the Lord's house' to go up to Mo. to try to reinstate the church back upon their lands in Jackson Co."[7]

As the final phase of the Zion's Camp mission, in June 1834 the Mormon prophet established a local church government in exile called the "Missouri High Council." The conceptualized framework for this ecclesiastical body was derived in part by a recontextualization of a divine edict initially received following Joseph Smith's first trip to Jackson County in 1831. Smith's impressions from his 1831 visit to Missouri suggested it was strategically imprudent for his movement to gather exclusively in Jackson County as had been originally announced. A revelation on September 11, 1831, explained that key leaders should remain in Kirtland for the next five years and thereby allow God the opportunity to soften the hearts of "the wicked" Jackson County residents.[8] Following the 1833 forced removal to Clay County, the exegesis of the earlier 1831 revelation morphed into a retrospective spiritual rationalization to rally support for a second effort to reclaim Jackson County by September 11, 1836.

For this attempt, Smith planned to build his army in situ. In juxtaposition to the overtly public persona of Zion's Camp, he chose to employ a more gradual "gathering" process. W. W. Phelps fanned members' excitement about an early re-gathering to Zion in optimistic letters written back to Kirtland and printed in the official LDS newspaper, the *Messenger and Advocate.* Phelps provided enticing information about Fort Leavenworth, the anticipated Platte Purchase territory, Clay County, and western Missouri.[9] The intention was to instill in LDS members a desire to relocate to Missouri and be as close to Jackson County as possible.

Between 1833 and 1836, LDS missionaries also encouraged converts and existing adherents to gather in Clay County, Missouri, as a staging area for the projected second Jackson County campaign.[10] Smith understood the importance of setting his scattered Missouri church in order and preparing for a second military attempt to reoccupy Zion.

Back in Ohio, Smith described his intentions in an instructive letter to the Clay County high council. He told them to

> use every effort to prevail on the churches to gather to those regions and situate themselves to be in readiness to move into Jackson County, in two years from 11 Sep next [1834] which is the appointed time for the redemption of Zion. Verily I say unto you, if the Church, with one united effort, performs their duties if they do this, the work shall be complete. . . . Now my beloved brethren, you will learn by this we have a great work to do, and but little time to do it in; and if we do not exert ourselves to the utmost in gathering up the strength of the Lord's house, that this thing may be accomplished, behold there remaineth a scourge for the Church.[11]

After Zion's Camp, Joseph Smith continued to develop and share his vision for the redemption of Zion with followers. As prerequisites to the liberation of Jackson County, church members understood they must first build the House of the Lord (Temple) in Kirtland, Ohio. Then the Mormons were to receive a sacred ceremony known as the "endowment" in the Temple.[12] Only after the endowment was received would the way be opened for Zion's redemption.

Accomplishing Smith's goal would prove to be overly ambitious from the standpoint of cost and schedule. Missionaries recruited the necessary human and financial resources to accomplish the task. These missionaries were instructed to solicit their fellow members for funds while encouraging them to migrate to Missouri. They also commenced a political initiative. Traveling elders were to solicit signatures for a petition to the governor of Missouri, Daniel Dunklin. This is described by Mormon historian B. H. Roberts in *Missouri Persecutions:*

> The petitions the elders circulated throughout the States in their travels, asking the people to petition the governor of Missouri to reinstate the saints in their homes, met with a response that was considerable. I cannot learn how many names were attached to this petition, but when it was mailed on the ninth of December, 1835, the package was large, the postage amounting to five dollars. But all these efforts failed to move the State official of Missouri to make any effectual effort towards restoring the exiles to their own and protecting them in the quiet possession of their property and lives.[13]

Two great solicitations occurred in the spring of 1835. LDS high priest Jared Carter traveled to the eastern states to gather funds to complete the Temple. In addition, the newly instituted quorum of the Twelve Apostles' first mission was appointed for the purpose of visiting localities in the East to seek contributions for the redemption of Zion "by purchase."[14] Meeting minutes indicate that on May 10, 1835, the Westfield, New York, Conference appointed local "wise men" to solicit funds to "b[u]y land in order to [facilitate] their gathering."[15]

The June 1835 *Messenger and Advocate* announced Bishop Partridge and Isaac Morley were traveling east to collect funds for the benefit of those dispossessed of their homes.[16] Delays and frustrations reinforced the presumption among the LDS leadership that the use of force was increasingly justified to bring about the redemption of Zion. John Whitmer listed those appointed on September 24, 1835, at Joseph Smith's house to fill military leadership positions as the "Lord's host" to lead an army to Missouri.[17] Smith described the plans for the redemption of Zion in his 1835–1836 sketch book:

> September 24, 1835, This day the High Council met at my house to take into consid[e]ration the redeem[p]tion of Zion. It was the voice of the spirit of the Lord that we petition to the Governor [of Missouri]. That is those who have been driven out /should/ ~~to~~ do so to be set back on their Lands next spring. We [should] go next season to live or dy [*sic*] ~~to this~~

> ~~end so the dy is cast~~ in Jackson County. We truly had a good time and Covena[n]ted to strug[g]le for this thing u[n]till death shall desolve [*sic*] this union. And if one falls that the rest be not discouraged but pe[r]sue this object untill it is ac[c]omplished. Which may God grant u[n]to us in the name of Christ our Lord. This day drew up an Arti/c/le of inrollment for the redem[p]tion of Zion that we may obtain volunteers to go next spring /to Mo/. I ask God in the name of Jesus that we may obtain Eight hundred men /or one thousand/ well armed and that they may ac[c]omplish this great work. Even so. Amen.[18]

An expectation of imminent return is reflected in an October 29, 1835, Kirtland dinner conversation involving Joseph, Emma, Bishops Partridge and Whitney and others. Joseph wrote,

> While seated at the table we indulged in the free interchange of thought, and Bishop Whitney observed to Bishop Partridge that the thought had just occurred to his mind that perhaps in about one year from this time they might be seated together around a table in the land of Zion. My wife observed she hoped it might be the case that not only they, but the rest of the company present, might be seated around her table on that land of promise. . . . and my heart responded, Amen. God grant it, I ask in the name of Jesus Christ.[19]

Smith's followers were aware of the existence of a comprehensive strategy for the return to Jackson County and were seriously committed to its realization. A summary of the major elements of Smith's plan for the redemption of Zion follows:

* Church members residing in Clay County were to prepare and seek to become worthy
* Zion would be redeemed by a military effort aided by miraculous divine intervention
* Key leaders would gather to Kirtland, assist with the completion of the Temple, and receive an endowment to empower them in their redemptive roles in Jackson County
* Missionaries and even the Twelve Apostles were called to visit eastern jurisdictions to gather money for the redemption of Zion
* Jurisdictions were to designate "wise men" to gather money and buy lands in Missouri
* "Wise men" were also appointed as general church agents to buy Missouri property and prepare the Mormon organization "Army of Israel"
* Eastern members were counseled to gather in Missouri, preferably by spring 1836

* A committee composed of Smith, Hyrum, and Oliver were to receive loans from eastern members to generate funds to buy lands for gathering in Missouri
* Men and families were to inconspicuously gather in Clay County, Missouri, in order to build the Army of Israel in place
* Eight hundred or more additional young and middle-aged men were to be asked to volunteer for the Army of Israel, for a second Zion's Camp-like expedition in the spring of 1836
* Church presidents would locate in Missouri to preside over the culmination of the grand plan

Bringing the long planning for Zion's rescue into clearer focus, Joseph Smith convened a council in Kirtland on March 11, 1836.[20] Of this private meeting in the Temple, W. W. Phelps remembered that four men including himself as president of a committee were designated "wise men." These men were tasked to raise money and purchase "land in Jackson County and in the regions round a bout."[21] Securing property in Jackson County was intended to pave the way for Joseph Smith and other leaders in Kirtland to relocate to Missouri by the middle of 1836.

> Joseph also met with his trusted presidency and some of the Apostles, and counseled with them upon the subject of removing to Zion this spring. We conversed freely upon the importance of her redemption and the necessity of the Presidency removing to that place, and that their influence might be more effectually used in gathering the Saints to the country. We finally come to the resolution to emigrate on or before the 15th of May next if kind providence Smiles upon us and opens the way before us.[22]

The March 1836 ceremonial dedication (called an endowment) of the Kirtland Temple focused extensively on the redemption of Zion theme. On March 29, 1836, the Kirtland elites met to receive further revelation about "going to Zion."[23] The following day, the Kirtland endowment experience culminated with about three hundred official members gathering to prophesy, pronounce blessings, and enjoin curses upon their Jackson County enemies.[24]

By April 1836, plans for the redemption of Zion were proceeding on track. Smith became aware that one aspect of his strategy was actually working too well. In obedience to the council to "to build up the strength of mine house," eager enthusiasts were moving as families in large numbers to Clay County. There were rapidly becoming as many Mormons in Missouri as there were in the East. An LDS church committee composed of Joseph Smith, his brother Hyrum, and Oliver Cowdery were tasked with securing land in Missouri for those migrating west. Before leaving, adherents were asked to loan the committee money for this purpose.[25] Immigrants arriving in exiled Zion, however, found confusion. Little land was available in Clay County and Saints there were unprepared to ameliorate the impact of new arrivals. Concurrently, all possible routes to Jackson County remained blocked by the Missourians. Covert efforts to organize a "second Zion's Camp" had been compromised as an alarm was sounded by non-Mormons throughout Jackson and Clay counties. Early Clay County LDS member[26] Joseph Holbrook remembered that in the spring of 1836 "it appeared that war was even at our doors."[27]

Smith had to find a way to ease the tension building in Clay County. Up to that time, money designated for Missouri land purchases had been dedicated to buying out old settlers in Jackson County. In light of escalating difficulties, however, LDS leaders in Ohio realized land must first be obtained elsewhere. A refuge, even if temporary, was urgently needed. Clay County was not a solution as it would no longer accommodate the gathering Saints. Smith realized he could amass the Army of Israel in surrounding counties just as effectively.

In Ohio, the Kirtland and Missouri LDS Church leadership met again on April 2, 1836, to transact business "bearing upon the redemption of Zion." After this meeting, Smith and Cowdery devoted the rest of the day successfully raising funds to that end.[28] A few days later, on April 9, 1836, spiritually and financially endowed "wise men" left Kirtland for Missouri. Brothers Phelps, Partridge, Corrill, and Morley arrived in Clay County in early May.[29] Upon their arrival in Clay County, these leaders observed firsthand the urgent need to procure land wherever it was available to sustain those Mormons already there and those whom they expected shortly from the east.[30]

Word of a second attempt to return to Jackson County also was widely known among the non-Mormon community. Mormon apostle Parley P. Pratt noted that during the Mormon sojourn in Clay County, "the public journals of Upper Missouri in 1835 . . . printed charges and declarations against us."[31] However, even as they were being looked upon with fear and loathing by the Missourians, a fair amount of sympathy (especially in the early part of their stay in Clay County) had been extended to them as well. Lyman O. Littlefield remembered his father sending him to apprentice in Liberty at the *Missouri Enquirer* printing office along with one or two other Mormon boys. Littlefield recalled the newspaper editor and publisher Mr. Kelley (a Methodist preacher) was "friendly disposed towards our people and Mrs. Harriet Williams Kelley, (his wife) was a . . . kind hearted . . . friend and sympathizer."[32]

Clay County resident Joseph Thorp saw the Mormons "in the main" as "industrious, good workers . . . and could live on less than any people I ever knew."[33] Thorp had provided shelter to several migrating Mormon families and was curious enough to discuss their beliefs. Like the Kelleys, Thorp expressed compassion regarding the plight of the Mormons, but he viewed them as "poor, deluded mortals" recalling their practice in Jackson County of telling "the citizens of Clay the same old tale; that this country was theirs by gift of the Lord, and it was folly for them to improve their lands, they would not enjoy the fruits of their labor; that it would finally fall into the hands of the saints." What Thorp described as "insolence and impudent behavior" can more neutrally be articulated as expressing Mormonism's sense of supernatural entitlement.[34] An 1839 non-LDS account of the Mormon War reinforces the outsiders' perspective on the theological justifications of LDS supernatural entitlement.

> The misfortunes of these people [Mormons] seem to have arisen from practicing upon certain rules of action peculiar to themselves. The basis of these rules is the assumption that they are the "Saints of the Most High," to whom the Lord promised of old the inheritance of the earth; and that as such they have the right to take possession of whatever they may be inspired to desire. Any means are justifiable, in their belief to bring about the restoration to the "Children of God" or that which He has bequeathed to them.[35]

The Mormon believers who sincerely sought an 1836 pilgrimage to redeem Jackson County as their Zion personify what Mircea Eliade described as "Those who have chosen the Quest, the road that leads to the Center, must abandon any kind of family and social situation, and 'nest,' and devote themselves wholly to 'walking' toward the supreme truth."[36] In his study of "the Sacred and the Profane," however, Eliade fails to give voice to those designated as the profane "other."

By distinguishing between the sacred and profane both geographically and through religious affiliation, the Mormons alienated and insulted their nonbeliever neighbors. Clay resident Joseph Thorp resented it when an LDS church member asked him if he "didn't believe that they [the Mormons] would finally possess the land and yet build the temple in Independence." Was it not "the Lord's work, and they the chosen people of God to build the New Jerusalem?"[37]

During the exile, an attitudinal shift occurred among Clay's citizens towards their Mormon neighbors. Initial compassion for the saints faded, so that by the spring of 1836 most Missourians were becoming openly hostile. Historian Kenneth H. Winn argues this trend developed in the wake of Zion's Camp after which Missourians "no longer viewed the Saints as injured republicans, but as crazed fanatics."[38] This set the stage for increasing alienation and fearful mistrust of LDS intentions. In addition, by the spring of 1836, non-Mormons in western Missouri (and many other parts of the nation) were aware of Joseph Smith's plan for a near-term LDS reoccupation of Jackson County including his advocacy for using force if necessary. The disclosure of this information resulted in what had been to that point a general annoyance with the Mormons transforming into apprehension of violence at their hands. On May 3, 1836, a St. Louis newspaper published a warning of "ANOTHER MORMON INVASION."[39] News of a possible invasion was even published in a newspaper in Rochester, New York:

> ANOTHER WAR BREWING. — The Far West, published at Independence [Liberty], Missouri, says information has been received from Kirkland [sic], Ohio, through various channels of another movement among the Mormons to obtain possession of the "promised land," and to establish their Zion in Jackson County, the scene of their former disastrous defeat. They are said to be armed to the number of 1500 or 2000, and to be making way in parties to the "debatable ground." The Far West also states that the people of Jackson and their friends in the surrounding counties are taking affective [sic] measure for resistance.[40]

Such reports revealed a general knowledge of LDS leaders' plans to attempt a second restoration to Jackson County. In a repeat of what had happened before the departure of Zion's Camp, it was a resident in the Kirtland area who sent warning of a pending expedition. With lessons learned from his Zion's Camp experience, Smith attempted to mitigate this problem by encouraging members to restrain their tongues.

As can be seen by the May 12 letter below written by well-known Jackson County fur trader François Chouteau, however, the Missourians were also preparing themselves well in advance of September 11, 1836.

> Cher oncle . . . Apparently we are going to wage war here very soon with the Mormons. They have a force of 2000 men in Clay County who are organizing and making the arrangements necessary to attack us in Jackson County and we have to take measures in order to make serious resistance.
>
> It appears that they are disposed to retake possession of their land by force. We want to make the most advantageous propositions to them before taking up arms. And if they are unwilling to make any arrangements, it is certain that we will have to fight them. This situation is alarming and upsetting in our area. But, generally, we are determined to fight to the end rather than consent that the Mormons remain here, and really, if it were the case they would chase us from the country as they themselves were chased the first time. Consequently, I desire that Berenice not return here until the trouble be passed in one way or another.

> Recently, by all the boats that come up the Missouri, the Mormons are coming from their satellites and all are well armed. Jackson County is the Promised land where the New Jerusalem must be built.[41]

Chouteau along with his fellow non-Mormon residents' worst fears were validated by the number of Mormons encountered who were traveling to Clay County. Edmund Flagg, a western traveler, encountered a group of Mormons during the summer of 1836 who explained that "they were on their way to Mount Zion . . . the Saviour was about to descend in Jackson County, Missouri; the millennium was dawning, and that all who were not baptized . . . and forthwith repaired to Mount Zion . . . would assuredly be cut off, and that without remedy."[42]

In early 1836, people in Jackson County exhibited a heightened concern about a possible Mormon reinvasion. Recently transplanted Frenchman Louis Cortambert was aggressively interrogated by the old settlers, "Aren't you one of the Mormons?" At first, Cortambert did not understand the question, so "answered no, just at random" and added, "it was a good thing that I did not answer yes."[43] He soon learned much more about this religious sect who had been forced to "withdraw" to Clay County. Cortambert's final statement about the Mormons reflected the general view of his Jackson County neighbors: "they have not renounced New Jerusalem."[44]

Fear of a pending Mormon invasion and multiple other manifestations of general distaste for the Latter-day Saints progressed until violent acts were taken against them. On the night of June 28, 1836, "several outrages" were committed upon some of the Saints living in a settlement near Fishing River in eastern Clay County. An extralegal group of non-LDS men attacked the Mormons and "whipped one man nearly to death."[45]

Clay County citizens began a vigilant campaign of surveillance over the county roads, attempting to keep immigration of Saints into the county in check. When a non-Mormon named Jesse Clark and his cohorts turned away large groups of LDS members arriving from the east, militant Mormon leader Lyman Wight went on the offensive. Wight gathered a force of 250 to defend his brethren in the eastern part of the county and those still migrating to the area. The two armed bands never skirmished, however.[46]

Local resident Anderson Wilson indicated he, two brothers, and six other upset citizens agreed to defend one another to the death "should it be necessary, in order to drive away the Saints."[47] Wilson wrote:

> July 4th, 1836, Clay County, Missouri
>
> . . . They have been flocking in here faster than ever and making great talk of what they would do. A letter from Ohio shows plainly that they intend to

> Emigrate here til they outnumber us. Then they would rule the Contry [*sic*] at pleasure. Another letter shows that they are Borrowing all the money that [they] Can to procure land here & they Buy all on a credit that they Can get. . . . They have entered 1600 acres in Clinton Co. in the last few days Besides what they have entered in Clay & Ray co. They settle in towns as we Call them, one of which Contained 250 in our township, Besides another in Washington township nearly as large. . . . They are living on Rochhoalts panama, in the woods, in wagons in tents in Bark Houses in Cabins etc. This town is 4 miles long & so thick that you will not be out of Sight of a den the Whole route. . . . [They] will elect all their own officers from among the Brethren & even remove the postmaster by petition. . . . On 24 June we worked the road and nothing else was talked of They passed us in ever way and in Considerable numbers & we got very hot before night to think that we had to work a road for the invaders of our Cuntry [*sic*] to travel.[48]

Aware of growing resistance to their presence, Mormon leaders began to search for a location for resettlement as authorized by Smith in March 1836 at Kirtland.[49] By mid-May 1836, Missouri leaders dispatched survey parties to a nearly uninhabited northern portion of nearby Ray County to assess the alternatives.[50] John Corrill's history notes, "In May 1836 W. W. Phelps was exploring the outskirts of the county and reported to Kirtland . . . on Shoal Creek, Ray County; [there is] prairie, some timber on the streams, a large open country with a few settlers in the timber; bees abound and deer, turkeys and wild game in abundance. So we are preparing to leave our old neighbors."[51]

A second survey party was sent out to further explore what would soon become Caldwell County but was then the unorganized territory of northern Ray County. Partridge and Corrill entered land in the names of key LDS church leaders (primarily in the names of the Kirtland committee) on June 3 and 22, 1836. Historian Stephen LeSueur's "Missouri's Failed Compromise" emphasizes the importance of LDS land acquisitions in northern Ray territory having begun well before the June 29, 1838, Clay County public meeting in which established Clay County residents asserted that the Mormons must leave.[52] Relations between the saints and Missourians disintegrated rapidly, so much so that by mid-June Clay citizens organized a public meeting to discuss what should be done. With an ever greater awareness regarding a pending Mormon invasion, a heightened level of alarm resulted in more frequent sporadic acts of violence.

On June 29, 1836, Clay citizens publicly asked the Mormons to leave. Missouri-based LDS leaders willingly acceded to their recommendations. On July 1, 1836, LDS representatives agreed to leave voluntarily, "for the sake of friendship." Though the crescendo of tension between Mormons and their

Clay County neighbors did not peak until this time, the saints had already begun acquiring alternate land holdings in anticipation of the difficulties.[53]

The decision to remove from Clay County was conveyed to county citizens at a second public meeting held on July 2, 1836. Edward Partridge commented on this action in his journal: "They proposed us to stop the emigration to this Co. immediately to have the late emigrants leave soon . . . On the 30th Brs. Morley, Corrill, Marsh, E. Higby, myself and a few others, met the committee appointed at the Liberty meeting. We gave them to understand that we wanted peace and were willing to make sacrifices, to keep it. . . . to save the Co. from a civil war."[54]

In the midst of this dramatic turn against the Mormons, in July 1836, Alexander Doniphan and the church's other lawyers dealt another severe disappointment to church leaders. Ever since the Mormon expulsion from Jackson County in 1833, Doniphan had worked unsuccessfully to gain recompense for the LDS's losses during their expulsion from Zion. "While those efforts wound their way through the courts, many members of the sect had taken up residence in Clay County, where they had at first been welcomed."[55]

The lawsuits initiated by Mormon Church leaders against Jackson County residents centered on the destruction of the *Evening and the Morning Star* printing office. Since 1834, these actions had simply been "continued" from one court term to the next. Now, in 1836, rather than achieving the eagerly awaited and desperately needed victory in court over their Jackson County adversaries, the Mormons lost a key opportunity to establish their rights via court action. Rather than the victory in court, lawyers representing the Mormons settled the suits without the consent of their clients.[56]

Settlement of the lawsuits not only deflated the morale of the Mormons, it possibly deprived them of thousands of dollars of compensation intended to help fund their return to Jackson County.[57] Relinquishing their legal claims meant all means of negotiation with state officials were exhausted as well as any objective expectations for a positive outcome to redeem Zion. The Mormons began to physically and spiritually disengage from current homes in Clay County and their hoped-for return to Jackson County. These disappointments, however, ironically helped general LDS church members adapt quickly to the course correction that would lead them further north in Missouri. Reed Peck, one of Smith's adherents, suggested that the rank and file were not disappointed with the decision to relocate to the Ray territory.[58]

The Kirtland command structure was fully supportive when informed of the hasty decision made by local leaders to move their members from Clay County to the north. Smith concurred with the decision to depart and encouraged his followers to leave Clay County peacefully.

> Kirtland, Ohio, July 25, 1836.
> Dear Brethren:—Yours of the 1st inst. accompanying the proceedings of a public meeting held by the people of Clay, was duly received. We are sorry that this disturbance has broken out—we do not consider it our fault. You are better acquainted with circumstances than we are, and of course have been directed in wisdom in your moves relative to leaving the country. . . . We advise that you be not the first aggressors. Give no occasion, and if the people will let you dispose of your property, settle your affairs, and go in peace, go. . . . Be wise; let prudence dictate all your counsels; preserve peace with all men if possible; stand by the Constitution of your country; observe its principles, and above all show yourselves men of God, worthy citizens.[59]

This letter, addressed to W. W. Phelps, gave full sanction to the decision made by local LDS church leaders to agree to terms calling for their relocation out of Clay County to the north.

Local branches of the church selected independent committees on their own to search out new locations in northern Ray territory. Morris Charles Phelps remembered that

> To save expense, and keep down excitement; it was thought best and proper to send commites [*sic*] of three from every branch of the Church to view this new countery [*sic*] and look out good and convenient locations on the same. . . . For the branch located on the east Branch of Fishing River Clay Co. John Tailor Wheeler Baldwin and My self were chosen as a committee. . . By request of our Brethren we started the last of July we found a beautiful rich and fertile country though mostly prairie it lay high and was beautifully situated for farming, also with groves of timber . . . We made our location on long creek and bought out three of the Missourians the only setlers [*sic*] in that grove of timber. We returned and called a meeting and made our returns our Brethren expressed a general satisfaction.[60]

The Mormons adapted well to their situation and quickly exhibited a strong optimism about a future that offered security and safety.[61] Of the departure from Clay County, church member David Pettigrew observed,

> They came to the conclusion to give Caldwell County and that we Should live there by Ourselves, and thither we moved The land we had purchased we had to leave unsold, and we left behind us many graves of beloved fathers, mothers, brothers, sisters wives and husbands and children who had partly shared in our sufferings but now are gone to [their home where] there is neither strife, nor tribulation. Although some of the people believe that [we] were a persecuted people, that [we] were an innocent and

> offending Sect, yet, they dared not express their sentiments. After settling my business I followed the rest of the Mormons to Caldwell County.[62]

By June 1836, Smith had surreptitiously assembled the bulk of his immigrant army in upper Missouri. But the prophet's extensive plan had not succeeded in several critical respects. Designated leaders of the Army of Israel were still mostly in Ohio.[63] Also, public sentiment rapidly turned against the saints. And despite apocalyptic posturing, rank-and-file Missouri Mormons appeared willing to avoid further violence.

Smith had intended to come to Missouri to preside over the triumphant return to Jackson County. However, by the 1836 Kirtland Temple dedication, he had apparently realized his September 11, 1836, deadline was not likely to be achieved. By sending the "wise men" to buy land elsewhere, it freed Smith to focus on Kirtland issues, such as managing the debt accrued by temple construction. Smith's anticipated May 15, 1836, deadline for moving himself and family to Missouri quietly passed.[64] A massive infusion of cash might have resolved both church debt and funding the final stages of the church's Jackson County return. Smith's unsuccessful excursion to Salem, Massachusetts, in April 1836 to obtain secreted treasure was largely an effort to raise the capital necessary for the redemption of Zion. In the end, time ran out before Joseph Smith could muster either the required number of soldiers or finances.

That the Mormons were experiencing a severe cash flow problem was made clear at a council meeting of June 16, 1836, when President F. G. Williams said, "The case before us is an important one. The Church [is] poor, Zion [is] to be built and we have not means to do it unless the rich assist & because the rich have not assisted, the heads of the Church have to suffer and are now suffering under severe embarrassments and are much in debt."[65] John Corrill's *Brief History of the Church of Christ of Latter Day Saints* explained the church's 1836 financial situation further:

> After finishing the house of the Lord . . . the Church found itself something like fifteen or twenty thousand dollars in debt . . . Notwithstanding they were deeply in debt, they had so managed as to keep up their credit, so they concluded to try mercantile business. Accordingly, they ran in debt in New York, and elsewhere, some thirty thousand dollars, for goods, and shortly after some fifty or sixty thousand more. . . . They also spent some thousands of dollars in building a steam mill, which never profited them anything. They also bought many farms at extravagant prices, and made part payments, which they afterwards lost, by not being able to meet the remaining payments. They also got up a bank, for which they could get no charter . . . and, after struggling with it awhile, they broke down.[66]

LDS historian B. H. Roberts assigned blame for failing to redeem Zion in 1836 to the Mormons themselves: "events of a strange character were to occur that would prevent the carrying out of these resolutions. The saints did not comply with the conditions upon which Zion was to be redeemed. They did not with a united effort do their duty. They did not give of their means liberally, nor did their young men volunteer readily to go up to Zion. Hence, they were not entitled to the fulfillment of God's promise to redeem Zion."[67]

The severity of the LDS church's financial needs from March through July 1836 impelled the adoption of an interim course correction that redirected the Missouri Mormons to northern Ray territory. The decisions to buy land as a temporary gathering for saints from the East and to continue planning to redeem Zion by purchase remained as logical possibilities within Smith's readjusted longer-term goals. The move to the north kept alive the possibility in the minds of LDS members that Jackson County could yet serve as their ecclesial seat of government.

In the wake of the September 11, 1836, prophesy's failure to materialize, the Mormons began to redefine the boundaries of Zion and the meaning of its redemption.[68] Before the fall of 1836, the term "Zion," in Mormon theology, was reserved exclusively for Jackson County, Missouri. As the LDS church was reestablished in Ray County following the removal from Clay County, however, being "in" Zion gradually became less geographically tied to Jackson County. By 1840, Joseph Smith widened the geographic sphere of Zion even further to include their new domain in Illinois, and he eschewed firm end-time dating. In the minds of the Saints of the early 1840s, the Missouri years developed a dreamlike aura. Their image of the western Missouri setting became exaggerated and ultra-pastoral.[69] Soon after settling the town of Nauvoo in Illinois, an enlarged interpretation of New Jerusalem emerged. For example, Smith emphatically instructed Apostle Orson Hyde to encourage any Palestinian Jews who might be converted during his 1841 mission to Jerusalem to "gather" to Nauvoo and ironically not stay where they were to prepare for the return of Jesus.[70]

Most Mormons today identify Jackson County, Missouri, as the future site of the New Jerusalem and retain an eschatological expectation of gathering there in the future. What prevails in mountain LDS culture is a duality of thought that simultaneously affirms the appropriateness of longing for a Jackson County Zion while being content to dwell among the "pure in heart" within "the shadow of the everlasting hills."[71]

Not only had Joseph Smith's prophecies not produced an accurate prediction whereby the Mormons were to be first settled and then resettled in Jackson County, but each subsequent attempt to rally his followers placed them in a dangerous position. In 1833, disobedience of members rather than prophetic miscalculation was cited as the cause of the colony's expulsion from Jackson County. Yet the vast majority of believers continued with renewed faith that God, through Joseph Smith, would eventually redeem Zion.

In 1834, Zion's deliverance was retrospectively linked to an 1831 revelation and a date was set for September 11, 1836. But by the middle of 1836, the LDS Church's debilitating debts prompted Smith and his trusted lieutenants to initiate steps to acquire Missouri lands outside Clay and Jackson Counties. This was followed by the Mormons' voluntary relocation out of Clay County in 1836 in order to defuse a festering crisis. A consequence of this capitulation was a loss of cultural capital.[72] Although there were isolated violent clashes between the Mormons and their Clay County neighbors,[73] the relatively peaceful resolution of the crisis in 1836 may well have emboldened Missourians two years later as they moved to expel the Saints from the state altogether.[74]

During the Missouri period, Smith never gave up hopes of reclaiming Jackson County. Throughout 1836, Joseph strove to fulfill his prophecy to retake Jackson County by September 11. Upon their ultimate expulsion from Missouri in 1838, adherents were not condemned for disobedience or lack of faith. Having endured this great trial, the faithful were also freed from former expectations that they retain ownership titles to their confiscated Missouri holdings. Richard Bushman points out that early in the Nauvoo period, Joseph Smith realized he could turn "the Missouri experience into a usable past."[75] This recontextualization was vital to enable his movement to heal and move beyond his prophetic failures in Missouri.

Smith's September 11, 1836, prophecy can be viewed as a complete logistical failure. Insufficient funds combined with unprepared human resources doomed implementation of Smith's plan. Ironically, the Clay County non-Mormons staged their public meeting in order to preclude a Mormon attack. By the time the meeting was held, however, Joseph Smith had already decided to delay the initiative and was in the process of redirecting followers away from both Clay and Jackson counties. The 1836 LDS experience actually advanced the movement at a critical stage of its development. Joseph Smith's and his followers' recontextualization of these events was remarkably successful, so much so, in fact, that they have not been remembered as a series of inaccurate prophecies but rather as an epic saga of victimization that yet awaits an apocalyptic divine reckoning for their enemies.

Though the redemption of Zion did not occur as Joseph Smith prognosticated, the experience transformed Mormonism into an enduring movement. Tens of thousands of pilgrims visit Missouri annually, more than 170 years after their progenitors were expelled from the state in 1838. While most LDS tourists visit Independence in Jackson County, Missouri, some feel the need to trace the historical trail through Clay and Caldwell counties. Joseph Smith's legacy regarding the concept of Zion in the thoughts of many LDS people is a dual notion of a broader geographical boundary coupled with an equally strong expectation of a fixed center place in Jackson County, Missouri, where they will build their New Jerusalem. With the provocative October 2008 announcement by current LDS president Thomas S. Monson that a new temple will be built somewhere in the greater Kansas City area, Mormons will likely rekindle their efforts to establish their elusive city of Zion. Less predictable is the reaction of non-Mormon Missourians who, while more religious than their antebellum forefathers, are more constrained by civil society against using violence as a remedy against fellow Americans.

Notes

1. Kenneth H. Winn, *Exiles in a Land of Liberty: Mormons in America, 1830–1846* (Chapel Hill: University of North Carolina Press, 1989), 101.

2. "Walter B. Stevens on the Mormon War and After," *Journal of History* 9, no. 4 (October 1921): 391–92.

3. Community of Christ Doctrine and Covenants (CofC D&C), section 100.1a, 3a&b, 6c; LDS 103: 1, 11–13, 30.

4. CofC D&C, sections 100 and 102; LDS 103 and 105.

5. The pioneering work on the study of cognitive dissonance as it relates to unconfirmed prophecy events in millennial movements is Leon Festinger, Henry W. Riecken, and Stanley Schachter, *When Prophecy Fails: A Social and Psychological Study of a Modern Group that Predicted the Destruction of the World* (New York: Harper Torchbooks, 1956, 1964). This work has since been widely critiqued by scholars citing ethical problems in methodology they argue led to invalid conclusions. Our study found useful an edited work that compiles into one volume many of these articles: Jon R. Stone, ed., *Expecting Armageddon: Essential Readings in Failed Prophecy* (New York: Routledge, 2000).

6. Many rank-and-file Mormons were promoted after Zion's Camp. For their sacrifice, they were promised a spiritual endowment of power when they returned to Ohio. In addition, many who participated in the expedition later were elevated to a new priesthood office, becoming one of the missionary Seventy; Anthony B. van Fossen, "How Do Movements Survive Failures of Prophecy?" in Jon R. Stone, ed., *Expecting Armageddon: Essential Readings in Failed Prophecy* (New York: Routledge, 2000), 175. Also critical to this discussion is the distinction between "non-confirmation" and "disconfirmation" of a failed prophecy. Joseph Zygmunt emphasizes this concept: "The general problem confronting the group is to prevent non-confirmation from being interpreted as disconfirmation. This requires the social and ideological reinforcement of beliefs, a restructuring of expectations in a direction that makes them more easily 'confirmable' or 'renewable' by the group itself. In effect, this means the establishment and maintenance of a self-confirming symbolic-interactional system,

typically accomplished through the gradual institutionalization of the movement" ("When Prophecies Fail: The Theoretical Perspective on the Comparative Evidence," in *Expecting Armageddon,* 96).

7. McLellin to President Joseph Smith, Independence, Jackson County, Missouri, July 1872, P13.f213, Community of Christ Archives.

8. "I willeth not that my servant Frederick G. Williams should sell his farm, for I the Lord will to retain a strong hold in the land of Kirtland, for the space of five years, in the which I will not overthrow the wicked [in Jackson County, Missouri], that thereby I may save some; and after that day, I the Lord, will not hold any [adherents] guilty, that shall go, with an open heart, up to the land of Zion; for I, the Lord, requireth the hearts of the children of men. And it is not meet that my servants Newel K. Whitney and Sidney Gilbert should sell their store, and their possessions here, for this is not wisdom until the residue of the church, which remaineth in this place, shall go up unto the land of Zion." Doctrine and Covenants (D&C), section 21, 1835 edition, given September 11, 1831.

9. *Latter Day Saints' Messenger and Advocate* 1, no. 2 (November 1834) and 1, no. 3 (December 1834), letters no. 1 and no. 2, dated Liberty, Missouri, October 20 and November 6, 1834. Later, Phelps reveals this to be a continuing theme in a letter from Ohio to his wife Sally on October 27, 1835: "Zion and her redemption is our greatest desire and we pray and hope that the Saints who have been smitten and driven will be faithful and sanctify their hearts for the enjoyment of the blessings in store for them."

10. Parkin, "Latter-day Saint Conflict in Clay County," in Garr and Johnson, eds., *Regional Studies in Latter-day Saint Church History: Missouri* (Provo, Utah: Department of Church History and Doctrine, 1994, 253). According to Parkin, upon his return to Kirtland from the Zion's camp expedition, Joseph "developed plans for the 'little season' of preparation. He instructed Partridge and Phelps to take the initiative in the West in encouraging the eastern saints to gather to Clay County. The Prophet spoke of the two years which was provided for the 'little season' of preparation. The day he set for them to return to Jackson County was September 11, 1836—the appointed date for the 'redemption of Zion.'"

11. J. G. Stevenson, ed., "Autobiography of Edward Stevenson" (manuscript in the LDS archives, 1986). Stevenson's account is cited as Smith's original letter to leaders in Missouri is not extant.

12. *History of Joseph Smith, the Prophet, by Himself,* 7 vols. (Salt Lake City: Deseret, 1902–1932), 2: 329. Often cited as *LDS History of the Church,* hereafter cited as *HC.*

13. Roberts, *The Missouri Persecutions* (Salt Lake City: George Q. Cannon and Son, 1900), 167. For the significance of exercising the right of petitioning during this period of American history see Susan Zaeske, *Signature of Citizenship: Petitioning, Antislavery, and Women's Political Identity* (Chapel Hill: University of North Carolina Press, 2003). Also making effective use of analysis of petitions is John L. Brooke, *The Heart of the Commonwealth: Society and Political Culture in Worcester County Massachusetts, 1713–1861,* corrected ed. (Amherst: University of Massachusetts Press, 1989, 1992), 366–68.

14. See *HC,* 2: 222–26, 238. Purchasing lands in Jackson County had been the religious society's goal from the beginning. Even before the expulsion from Jackson County, church printer W. W. Phelps tried to quell Mormon boasting that the Saints might obtain Zion by force, observing in the *Evening and the Morning Star,* "But to suppose that we can come up here and take possession of this land by the shedding of blood would be setting at naught the law of the glorious gospel and also the word

of our great Redeemer. And to suppose that we can take possession of this country without making regular purchases of the same according to the laws of our Nation, would be reproaching this great Republic in which the most of us were born, and under whose auspices we all have protection" (*Evening and the Morning Star* 2, no. 14 [July 1833]: 110). After the expulsion, purchasing lands in Zion implied buying out non-Mormon landholders so the disciples could return to the county without opposition. Later buying lands in Zion came to mean acquiring any land in northwestern Missouri.

15. "A Record of the Transactions of the Twelve Apostles," 1835, Patriarchal Blessing Book, book 1.CR 500.2, LDS Church Historical Department, Archives, hereinafter cited LDS Church Archives; *The Evening and the Morning Star* defined a wise man as "choice of his heart, but the fool exposes his to the world, and is not the better for it," meaning a wise man keeps his intentions to himself (*EMS,* 2, no. 14 [July 1833]: 105).

16. *Messenger and Advocate,* 1: 139.

17. John Whitmer, manuscript history, chapter 17, September 24, 1835, 81; McKiernan and Launius, *An Early Latter-day Saint History: The Book of John Whitmer* (Independence, Mo.: Herald Publishing House), 151; afterwards cited as the *Book of John Whitmer.*

18. Scott H. Faulring, ed., *An American Prophet's Record: The Diaries and Journals of Joseph Smith* (Salt Lake City: Signature Books in association with Smith Research Associates, 1987), 34–35; see also Jessee, *Personal Writings of Joseph Smith,* 1: 99–100; and *HC,* 2: 281–82. While many were elevated following Zion's Camp, Lyman Wight was demoted despite having previously served as a key leader. Wight claimed to have been ordained to lead the army of Israel: "after being driven from Jackson county I went to Kirtland and in company with Joseph and Sidney I went to the state of N Y three hundred miles while at old Father Bosley's Joseph and I walked out in the sugrar [*sic*] orchard here Joseph ordained me to the office of Benamey [Baneemy] in the presence of an angel I shall never forget the conversation held between him and Br Joseph. Then I was ordained one of the twelve apostles and then one of the fifty went through two endowments then ordained to lead the armys of Israel to Zion as Mosses [*sic*] lead the children [of] Israel out of Egyt in this ordination I received a white stone in it a new name which no man knew or could know same him to whom it should be reveald this ordination I received from Joseph and a revelation to continue to preach for Zion as much as to say I never done any thing else for the last ten years of my preaching" (Wight, letter to *Northern Islander,* July 1855, P13.f79.21–26, Community of Christ Library-Archives).

19. Faulring, ed., *An American Prophet's Record: The Diaries and Journals of Joseph Smith* (Salt Lake City: Signature Books, 1989), October 29, 1835, 42–43; also *HC,* 2: 294.

20. McKiernan and Launius, eds., *An Early Latter Day Saint History: The Book of John Whitmer Kept by Commandment* (Independence, Mo.: Herald Publishing House, 1980), 154. A more probable date for this meeting, per Smith's journal, is March 13, 1836. Smith makes no mention of such a meeting on March 11, 1836. However, of the 13th Smith wrote, "Met with the presidency & some of the 12, and counseled with them upon the subject of removing to Zion this spring. We conversed freely upon the importance of her redemption and the necessity of the Presidency removing to that place, and that their influence might be more effectually used in gathering the saints to the country. We finally come to the resolution to emigrate on or before the 15th of May next if kind providence Smiles upon us and opens the way before us" (Jessee, ed.,

The Papers of Joseph Smith [Salt Lake City: Deseret, 1992], 2: 188).

21. "A Short History of W. W. Phelps' Stay in Missouri," Salt Lake City, Utah, April 21, 1864, LDS Church Archives, Ms d 6019.fd 7. Parkin, *LDS in Clay County*, 266.

22. Faulring, *An American Prophet's Record*, March 13, 1836, 140–41.

23. Dean C. Jessee, *The Papers of Joseph Smith* (Salt Lake City: Deseret, 1992), 2: 203.

24. The regimen ended with a common covenant, "that if any more of our brethren are slain or driven from their lands in Missouri by the mob that we will give ourselves no rest until we are avenged of our enemies to the uttermost" (Jessee, *Papers of Joseph Smith*, 2: 206).

25. Reed Peck provided an alternative view of the process of land acquisition: "While the Society were making arrangements to remove from Clay county, Joseph Smith H. Smith and O. Cowdery borrowed some thousands of dollars of the church in Ohio giving the lenders orders on their agents in Missouri for land in payment" (*Reed Peck Manuscript*, Tanner edition [Salt Lake City: Modern Microfilm, n.d.], 4).

26. In this paper, "LDS church" (small c) refers to Joseph Smith's movement during the Clay County period, "Church of the Latter Day Saints." In May 1834, Smith changed the official name of his movement, known to that point as the "Church of Christ," formally adopting the name "Church of the Latter Day Saints." In April 1838 Smith further adjusted the name to the familiar "Church of Jesus Christ of Latter Day Saints." The use of "LDS church" in this paper is in reference to the 1834–1838 "Church of the Latter Day Saints" and not the modern entity known as the "Church of Jesus Christ of Latter-day Saints"; see "Communicated," *Evening and the Morning Star* 2, no. 20 (May 1834): 160. The exception is the use of "LDS" in reference to the modern publication of movement scripture in the Doctrine and Covenants. Reference is made to early editions where possible, but in some instances, the scripture in question was not included into the canon until later editions were published by the modern entities the Church of Jesus Christ of Latter-day Saints and Community of Christ/RLDS.

27. *The Life of Joseph Holbrook* (http://www.sedgwickresearch.com/holbrook/jh_history.htm).

28. Jessee, *Papers of Joseph Smith*, 2: 208–9.

29. The date of Partridge, Phelps, Corrill, and Morley's departure from Kirtland to Missouri was April 9, 1836 (Shipps and Welsh, *Journals of William E. McClellin* [Urbana: University of Illinois Press, 1994], 214); date of return to Upper Missouri, Edward Partridge wrote, "Friday the 6th—arrived at Clay Co. Liberty landing about 3 P.M. Arrived at my family about 5 P.M. and found them well" (Edward Partridge journal, LDS Church Archives); see also *The Book of John Whitmer*, 156.

30. They knew more members were on the road to Missouri and must have places to live. They also found that the Mormon reoccupation plan was no longer a secret.

31. Parley Parker Pratt, *The Autobiography of Parley Parker Pratt, one of the Twelve Apostles of the Church of Jesus Christ of Latter-day Saints, Embracing his Life, Ministry and Travels, with Extracts, in Prose and Verse, from his Miscellaneous Writings, edited by his son, Parley P. Pratt [Jr.]* (New York: Russell Brothers, 1874; repr. 1980), 105.

32. Lyman Omer Littlefield, *Reminiscences of Latter-day Saints: Giving an Account of Much Individual Suffering Endured for Religious Conscience* (Logan, Utah: *Utah Journal*, 1888), 32.

33. Judge Joseph Thorp, *Early Days in the West: Along the Missouri One Hundred Years Ago* (Liberty, Mo.: Liberty Tribune, 1924), 76.

34. Ibid., 77–79.

35. Thomas J. Farnham, *An 1839 Wagon Train Journal: Travels in the Great Western*

Prairies, the Anahuac and Rocky Mountains and in the Oregon Territory (New York: Greeley and McElrath Tribune Buildings, 1843; repr. Northwest Interpretive Association, 1983), 4. From the LDS perspective, Clay County citizens initially benefited from the influx of refugees from Jackson County. Church members became more of a threat as they became established and began to prosper economically. In later years, Mormon leader George A. Smith provided a succinct description of the Saints' condition during the Clay County period: "most of them remained there about three years, during which time they performed a great amount of labor for the people of Clay county, for the inhabitants were mostly new settlers who possessed nothing seemingly in the way of property save Indian corn, hogs and cattle. They hired the saints to labor, who made brick, built fine houses, and enlarged their farms, erected mills, and, in fact, acquired considerable property by industry in laboring for the people in Clay county" (George A. Smith, "Historical Discourse by President George A. Smith," June 20, 1869, *Journal of Discourses* 13 [Liverpool: Horace S. Eldredge, 1871]: 79).

36. Mircea Eliade, *The Sacred and the Profane: The Nature of Religion,* translated from French by Willard R. Trask (San Diego: Harcourt Brace, 1959, 1987), originally published as *Das Heilige und das Profane* (Verlag, GmbH: Rowohlt Tashenbuch, 1957), 184. For a comment on Jonathan Z. Smith's challenge to Eliade's position, see Michael S. Riggs, "The Cutlerite Migration to Minnesota: An Epic Perilous Journey into Diaspora," in Newell G. Bringhurst and John C. Hamer, eds., *Scattering of the Saints: Schism within Mormonism* (Independence, Mo.: John Whitmer Books, 2007), 177n3.

37. Thorp, *Early Days in the West,* 79.

38. Historian Kenneth H. Winn argues this trend developed in the wake of Zion's Camp after which Missourians "no longer viewed the Saints as injured republicans, but as crazed fanatics." Kenneth H. Winn, *Exiles in a Land of Liberty: Mormons in America, 1830–1846* (Chapel Hill: University of North Carolina Press, 1989), 101.

39. "Mr. Editor: Letters from Kirtland, Ohio have been received here by the last mail from persons of undoubted veracity, giving information, that the Mormons in that place and its vicinity, to the number of 1500 or 2000, are arming and coming on to the upper Missouri. The letters state that they will not come in a body, but in small detached parties." *Daily Missouri Republican,* St. Louis, 15, no. 953 (May 17, 1836).

40. *The World as It Is, and General Advertiser,* Rochester, N.Y., 1, no. 47 (July 16, 1836).

41. Francois Choteau to Monsieur Pierre Menard Sr., Kaskaskia, State of Illinois, May 21, 1836, quoted in Dorothy Brandt Marra and David Boutros, ed., *Chere Oncle, Cher Papa: The Letters of Francois and Berenice Chouteau* (Kansas City: Western Historical Manuscript Collection–Kansas City, 2001), 154.

42. Edmund Flagg, *The Far West; or, A Tour Beyond the Mountains,* 2 vols. (New York: Harper and Brothers, 1838), 2: 111.

43. Louis Cortambert, "Journey to the Land of the Osages, 1835–1836," trans. Mrs. Max W. Myer, *Bulletin—Missouri Historical Society* 19, no. 3 (1963): 207. Interestingly, Cortambert provides an important economic interpretation of the reasons for the conflict between the Jackson County settlers and the Mormons: "several articles of their doctrine, notably the abolition of slavery, tended to turn the settlers against them. But the finishing touch to irritating the almost completely mercantile population of Independence was this: the Mormons, wishing to devote themselves to commerce and at the same time to agriculture, had brought in a considerable quantity of merchandise; since they were in need of country produce for their subsistence, they offered the neighboring farmers their merchandise in exchange, in place of money. The farmers, finding the merchandise of good quality and cheap, turned to the Mormons, and the other shops

were neglected. Hence a general market town insurrection against the new sectarians. A political coloration was given to the affair, and the Jacksonians, or Democrats, who are in the great majority in Jackson County—organized a regular persecution of the Mormons."

44. Cortambert, "Journey to the Land of the Osages," 208.

45. Parkin, "Latter-day Saint Conflict in Clay County," 256, citing Drucilla Hendricks, "Historical Sketch," 10, LDS Church Archives.

46. Parkin, "Latter-day Saint Conflict in Clay County," 256.

47. Durward T. Stokes, ed., "The Wilson Letters, 1835–1849," *Missouri Historical Review* 60 (July 1966): 507. Originals in Southern Historical Collection, University of North Carolina, Chapel Hill.

48. Stokes, ed., "The Wilson Letters," 495–517. Lloyd Rockhold owned eighty acres, SW Qtr. S24, TS 53, R30, Clay County, Annette Curtis, ed., *1836 Clay County, MO, State Tax List* (Independence, Mo.: Missouri Mormon Frontier Foundation, 2003), 82.

49. Smith apparently realized his September 11, 1836, deadline for the redemption of Zion was going to pass unrealized.

50. Eliza, Bishop Partridge's daughter, recalled that after her father's "return he with others went to look for a location for the saints as the people with whom we resided began to be somewhat uneasy about us." Eliza Partridge Lyman Smith Young, Ms f 873.item 3, LDS Church Archives.

51. Joseph Grant Stevenson, *Stevenson Family History,* vol. 1 (Stevenson's Genealogical Center, 1986), 16.

52. LeSueur, "Missouri's Failed Compromise," *Journal of Mormon History* 32, no. 3 (2006): 120.

53. Ibid.

54. Edward Partridge journal, 1818, 1835–36, MS 536, box 5, folder 8, LDS Church Archives.

55. Launius, *Alexander William Doniphan: Portrait of a Missouri Moderate* (Columbia: University of Missouri Press, 1997), 37.

56. "A History, of the Persecution, of the Church of Jesus Christ, of Latter Day Saints in Missouri," *Times and Seasons* 1, no. 4 (February 1840): 50–51, cited in Smith, *The History of the Reorganized Church of Jesus Christ of Latter Day Saints,* 2: 54.

57. There is probably greater linkage between the failure of the suits and Doniphan's enthusiasm for the creation of a county for the Mormons than has been generally understood.

58. "To remove from Clay County was in accordance with their feelings, having for some time contemplated a settlement in some new and uninhabited place that they could enjoy their constitutional privileges as other societies." *Reed Peck Manuscript,* 3.

59. Rigdon, Joseph Smith, Cowdery, Williams, and Hyrum Smith to W. W. Phelps and others, Kirtland, Ohio, July 25, 1836, *Messenger and Advocate* 2, no. 10 (July 1836): 359. See also Rigdon, Joseph Smith, Cowdery, Williams, and Hyrum Smith to Thornton, Rogers, Robertson, Thompson, Wood, Moss, Hughes, Atchison, and Doniphan, Kirtland, Ohio, July 25, 1836, ibid., 355–59.

60. Morris Charles Phelps, MS 271, LDS Church Archives.

61. "In August, 1836, the saints commenced settling upon their new location, in great numbers, and made preparations for the coming winter, by constructing comfortable dwellings for themselves and gathering as much food for their cattle, horses, etc., as their straitened circumstances would permit. Here they settled with the fond anticipation of being permitted to dwell in quietness and peace upon their posses-

sions without molestation; consequently large entries of the public lands were made by individuals of the society, and extensive farms were soon opened." Smith, *The History of the Reorganized Church of Jesus Christ of Latter Day Saints,* 2: 73.

62. David Pettigrew papers, MS 2282, LDS Church Archives.

63. A survey of John Whitmer's listing of leaders of the war department shows that, with the exception of John Whitmer and W. W. Phelps, other designated leaders were yet in Kirtland. John Whitmer, manuscript history, 81; *Book of John Whitmer,* 151.

64. Faulring, *An American Prophet's Record,* March 13, 1836, 140–41.

65. Collier and Hartwell, *Kirtland Council Minute Book,* June 16, 1836 (Salt Lake City: Collier, 1996), 178.

66. John Corrill, *A Brief History of the Church of Christ of Latter Day Saints* (St. Louis: n.p., 1839), 26–27. A look at Joseph Smith's indebtedness through the lens of Marvin Hill, C. Keith Rooker, and Larry T. Wimmer, *The Kirtland Economy Revisited: A Market Place Critique of Sectarian Economics* (Provo, Utah: Brigham Young University Press, 1977), suggests the LDS president was probably not overleveraged. However, sources cited in this study suggest that at least one significant aspect of Smith's debt problem was not considered for the purposes of their book. Contemporary sources strongly suggest Joseph Smith's multilayered plan for the redemption of Zion seriously overextended the resources of the young movement. Smith, try though he did, could not extract enough funds from his followers to accomplish his entire prophetic agenda. Something had to be sacrificed and the only priority that did not require immediate attention (would not result in a lawsuit) was his plan for a military operation to retake Jackson County.

67. Roberts, *The Missouri Persecutions,* 167.

68. See Craig S. Campbell, "Zion Generalized," in *Images of the New Jerusalem: Latter Day Saint Faction Interpretations of Independence, Missouri* (Knoxville: University of Tennessee Press, 2004), 89.

69. Ibid., 83.

70. Joseph continued, "If Elder Hydes & Pages [*sic*] testimony to the Jews at Jerusalem should be received then they may know 'that the set time hath come': I will write more particular instructions to them afterwards." Dean C. Jessee, ed., *Personal Writings of Joseph Smith,* rev. ed. (Salt Lake City: Deseret, 1984, 2002), 521–22. Hyde was a Missouri-era dissenter who had been recently reinstated to his rank as apostle in the LDS hierarchy.

71. This could be contrasted on another spectrum of Mormonism by the experience of coauthor Michael S. Riggs, who was approached at a John Whitmer Historical Association annual meeting and asked by a Community of Christ member what he knew about "Adam-ya dah-ya dah."

72. See, for example, Pierre Bourdieu and Richard Nice, trans., *Outline of a Theory of Practice* (Cambridge, UK: Cambridge University Press, 1977, 1987), 183–84.

73. See, for example, Drucilla Hendricks, MS 2050, box 4.f9, item 2, LDS Church Archives.

74. LeSueur broadly argues the Missourians on an individual level both knew about and were frightened by the existence of the Danites, but this only seems to have encouraged collective actions taken against the Saints during the 1838 Mormon War. Stephen C. LeSueur, "A Scarter Man Than One of Them Was I Never Saw: Attitudes and Perceptions of Missourians during the 1838 Mormon War," *Mormon Papers,* no. 1 (Sandy, Utah: Mormon Miscellaneous, May 1986).

75. Richard Lyman Bushman, *Joseph Smith: Rough Stone Rolling* (New York: Alfred A. Knopf, 2005), 404.

3

Mormonism, Millenarianism, and Missouri

Grant Underwood

Christian beliefs about the millennium, its nature, how it will be introduced, or how near it is, have varied considerably over the centuries. Originally, millennialism as an eschatology (a term derived from Greek, meaning, literally, doctrine of the "last things" or "end times"), was an outgrowth of Jewish apocalypticism. Its novelty was the expectation of a future "golden age" on earth before the final, apocalyptic transformation at the end of time. Various versions of the millennial dream developed. Some retained the vivid and dramatic spirit of Jewish apocalypticism, lashing out against contemporary society and promising imminent vindication for besieged believers who, these Christians added, would experience the millennium on a physically renovated earth personally ruled by Jesus Christ. Others adopted a more accommodationist approach to the world around them and interpreted the prophecies figuratively.[1] "The millennial hope is a paradoxical one," explains historian James Moorhead, "and one can extrapolate a dismal or optimistic view of history, encompassing temporal disaster or progress, or both. . . . Efforts to seize the Kingdom by violence, passive withdrawal from corruption to await the Second Coming, or melioristic reform efforts—all these and other responses have been adduced from eschatological symbols."[2]

A more metaphorical understanding of the millennium was the dominant eschatological orientation of 1830s America. Flush with the success of the "Second Great Awakening" and the activities of the "Benevolent Empire," the prevailing view was that the religious revivals of the day would Christianize the world and usher in a millennium of religious harmony and piety.[3] Mormons, however, were among a minority of American Christians who did not share this optimism. Their view was that Christendom was spiritually bankrupt and the world firmly in the grip of sin. While they hoped that through the preaching of the gospel restored by Joseph Smith a righteous remnant would be gathered out of "spiritual Babylon" before the end, the Saints' apocalyptic version of millennialism proclaimed that only an outpouring of divine judgment, culminating in Christ's personal return to earth, could comprehensively and permanently eliminate wickedness and establish the millennium.[4]

Apocalyptic millenarianism is the dream of the "great reversal." It promises that the first will be last and the last first. Millenarian prophets like Joseph Smith were, according to historian Susan Juster, "filled with holy indignation over what they saw [as] the unredeemable corruption of the [American] political and economic order, an order that consigned the mass of ordinary [farmers] and laborers to poverty, political invisibility, and social humiliation. . . . To be a prophet was, ipso facto, to be ignored and despised by the high and mighty. Living in a state of righteous alienation, prophets from apostolic days to [Joseph Smith's time] felt emboldened to attack the very foundations of church and state."[5]

In 1833 Smith published in the *American Revivalist, and Rochester Observer* an open letter to the American public discussing what he considered the apostate nature of contemporary Christianity and the beginning of God's judgment on a world gone awry. "Distruction," he wrote, "to the eye of the spiritual beholder seemes to be writen by the finger of an invisable hand in Large capitals upon almost evry thing we behold." Therefore, "I will proceed to tell you what the Lord requires of all people . . . [to] escape the Judgments of God which are almost ready to burst upon the nations of the earth—Repent of all your sins and be baptized in water for the remission of them." As if to underline what he had already proclaimed, he added, "I am prepared to say by the authority of Jesus Christ, that not many years shall pass away before the United States shall present such a scene of *bloodshed* as has not a parallel in the hystory of our nation . . . Therefore I declare unto you the warning which the Lord has commanded me to declare unto this generation . . . Repent ye Repent, ye and imbrace the everlasting Covenant and flee to Zion before the overflowing scourge overtake you."[6] As an 1831 revelation to Joseph Smith urged, "let the wicked take heed & let the rebellious fear & tremble & let the unbelieving hold their lips for the day of wrath shall come upon them as a whirlwind & all flesh shall know that I am God."[7]

Though the dramatic conclusion to human history envisioned by apocalyptic millennialism promised devastating outcomes for unbelievers, such consequences could be a source of reassurance to the faithful. On one occasion Joseph Smith wrote to followers in Colesville, New York, who eventually moved as a body to Jackson County, Missouri: "The judgements of the Lord are already abroad in the earth and the cold hand of death will soon pass through your neighborhood, and sweep away some of your most bitter enemies, for . . . the earth will soon be reaped,—that is, the wicked must soon be destroyed from off the face of the earth, for the Lord hath spoken it . . . Then shall come to pass that the lion shall lie down with the lamb &c."[8] In a follow-up letter several months later, he added, "Lift-up your heads and rejoice for your redemption draweth nigh . . . the sword, famines and destruction will soon overtake them [the wicked] in their wild career, for God will avenge." Therefore, "be faithful in witnessing unto a crooked and a perverse generation, that the day of the coming of our Lord and Savior is at hand."[9]

Bearing faithful witness of impending apocalyptic judgment was a major rationale for Mormon proselytizing. "I the Lord am angry with the wicked," declared one revelation, "and will come down . . . and consume the wicked with unquenchable fire. And behold this is not yet, but by and by: Wherefore seeing that I the Lord have decreed all these things upon the face of the earth . . . every man should . . . lift a warning voice unto the inhabitants of the earth; And declare both by word and by flight, that desolation shall come upon the wicked."[10]

The Saints' "flight" was to be to a special gathering place in Jackson County, Missouri, the Mormons called Zion. There believers were to gather "against the day when tribulation and desolation are sent forth upon the wicked: For the hour is nigh, and the day soon at hand."[11] In a world spiraling downward toward its cataclysmic conclusion, Zion would be the one safe haven, "a land of peace, a city of refuge, a place of safety."[12]

From 1831 to 1833, a sporadic stream of Mormons made their way to Jackson County in hopes of realizing their dream of creating an earthly New Jerusalem. By summer 1833, over a thousand Latter-day Saints had settled in several western Jackson County townships, including Independence, and constituted a significant minority of the population there. As their numbers grew, so did tensions with the non-Mormon settlers. Economic rivalry, political competition, even cultural differences (most Mormons had roots in New England, while many Missourians had migrated from the Carolina Piedmont or upper South) helped produce a "them-us" mentality on both sides. So did the Mormon religion, with its exclusionary understanding of salvation and its claim to replicate the visions, revelations, and other extraordinary spiritual gifts mentioned in the Bible. Such a faith was viewed as dangerously outside the denominational consensus of the day.[13]

So tense was the situation by summer 1833 that a single remark in the July issue of the church's periodical the *Evening and the Morning Star,* taken out of context, was sufficient to trigger a riot. The offending comment was an observation about contemporary national affairs that "much is doing towards abolishing slavery and colonizing the blacks in Africa." By itself it could be (and was) read as an antislavery remark. Yet the observation was immediately prefaced by a clarification that the church had "nothing to say" regarding slavery. Moreover, after reprinting Missouri laws regarding the proper admittance of "free people of color" into the state, the paper conservatively warned that "great care should be taken on this point. The saints must shun every appearance of evil."[14]

The article was the proverbial straw that broke the camel's back. Several hundred non-Mormon settlers met and issued an ultimatum to the Saints demanding that they leave the county, "peaceably if they will or forcibly if they must." When church leaders hesitated, the crowd turned violent, attacking the Mormon printing establishment, vandalizing the Mormon store several blocks away, tarring and feathering presiding church officer Edward Partridge, and threatening other leading elders. Such bullying tactics achieved their objective, and three days later church leaders signed an agreement to leave the county.

Days after the July disturbance, John Whitmer, a Mormon leader in Missouri, wrote to his colleagues in Ohio: "Although the enemy has accomplished his design ~~of~~ in demolishing the Printing establishment they cannot demolist [*sic*] the design of our God, for his decrees will stand & his purposes must be accomplished notwithstanding the great rage of Satan, which we can behold in his followers."[15] To describe the violence as a manifestation of the "great rage of Satan" and to see its perpetrators as Satan's "followers" reflects a worldview that is both biblical and apocalyptic. Apocalypticism anticipates just such an end-time showdown between the forces of good and evil. Moreover, the social reductionism inherent in such classifications as "the wicked" or "the enemy" is central to an apocalyptic worldview. As one scholar has noted, in apocalyptic millenarianism a "rhetoric of polarization" takes the complicated moral judgments often required in life and resolves them "into a series of binary oppositions: . . . good-evil, pious-hypocrite, elect-damned. And a final reckoning [is] proclaimed for the near future."[16] Another study points out that millenarian movements take the disquieting and "unmanageable manyness" of society and reorder it into "sharply contrasted contraries."[17]

Not surprisingly then, for millenarian Mormons the lines between good and evil, between saintly and satanic, were clearly drawn. From an apocalyptic perspective, "it is natural," writes one religious historian, "for the adherents of the Kingdom to perceive a coherent, sinister intelligence animating the various problems they encounter."[18] As the Saints saw it, the Jackson County disturbance had little to do with competing economic, social, or political concerns. Rather, it was round one in the final war between the Lord and Lucifer that would end in a complete rout of the wicked and the salvation of the Saints.

After receiving word in August 1833 of what he called the "Calamity in Zion," Joseph wrote a long and sympathetic letter to his traumatized associates in Missouri. "O Lord what more dost thou require at their hands before thou wilt come and save them[?]" he asked rhetorically. "May I not say thou wilt[?] Yea I will, . . . we have had the word of the Lord that you shall [be] deliverd from you[r] dainger and <shall> again flurish in spite of hell." Before sending the letter, he revised an earlier sentence to read more emphatically: "~~let~~ thine anger <is> ~~be~~ enkindled against them ~~and~~ <~~let~~> ~~them~~ <and they shall> be consumed before thy face and be far removed from Zion."[19] In December 1833, after hearing of the Saints' expulsion from Jackson County, Joseph wrote to church leaders in Missouri: "we have nothing to fear if we are faithful: [if] God will strike through kings in the day of his wrath [cf. Psalms 110:5] . . . what do you suppose he could do with a few *mobbers* in Jackson County, where, ere long, he will set his feet when earth & heaven shall tremble."[20] When a people feel the weight of the oppressor's heel, it is understandable that of all the facets of the eschatological drama the one they emphasize is the destruction of the "wicked."

Some of the Saints, however, seem to have felt the imminence of divine vindication a little too keenly. In November 1833, Edward Partridge reported that an overenthusiastic church elder, Parley Pratt, "prophesied that we shall be enabled to return to our houses by the first of next Jany & enjoy the fruit of our labor & none to molest or make afraid, he says he was constrained to prophesy & if he ever spoke by the spirit of God he then did & if it does not come to pass we may call him a false prophet."[21]

Throughout the Mormon experience in Missouri, as persecution intensified, yearning for apocalyptic judgment increased. As Michael Barkun says, "Men cleave to hopes of imminent worldly salvation when the hammerblows of disaster destroy the world they have known."[22] Counseled Joseph Smith, "We must . . . call on [God] with out ceaseing to make bare his arm for our defence for naught but the arm of the almighty can save us." His prayer was, "O god send forth Judgement unto victory O come . . . and cause the mou[n]tains to flow down at thy presence."[23]

Yet Smith's millennial vision was not one of passive or pacificist withdrawal to await the day of deliverance. "In the mean time," he noted, "god will send Embasadors to the authorities of the government and sue for protection and redress that [Missouri antagonists] may be left with out excuse that a ritious Judgment might be upon them."[24] This, of course, did not sit well with the

Saints' opponents. When they learned in fall 1833 that the Saints were attempting to mount a legal defense, they moved to drive the Mormons from the county in early November. Days later, in his letter to the Prophet, Edward Partridge fell back on a millenarian assessment of the situation: "If we are delivered & permitted to return to our homes it must be by the interposition of God, for we can see no prospect of help from government & it appears to me that nought but the judgements of God will open the way for our return . . . my mind is to have the disciples all leave the land & see if God will not pour out his judgments in some way ~~or an other~~ upon that wicked people."[25] Concurred W. W. Phelps in his own letter to the Prophet, "I am sensible that we shall not be able to live again in Zion, till God, or the president rules out the mob."[26]

Joseph Smith held out hope for the latter. Press forward seeking legal redress, he advised. If the local courts prove antipathetic, petition the governor. If he refuses to help, then we shall take our case to the president of the United States. "And if the president heed [us] not," apocalyptic judgment will take over. In the words of a December 1833 revelation, "then will the Lord arise and come forth out of his hiding place, and in his fury vex the nation."[27] "He will not fail to exicute Judgment upon your enemies and to avenge his own elect," assured the Prophet. Christ "will come with ten thousand of his saints and all his advisaries shall be distroyed by the breath of his lips!"[28]

If Smith blended his apocalypticism with faith in the American constitutional system of petitions and appeals, that faith had limits. To be sure, revelation told the Saints to "renounce war and proclaim peace," and Smith reminded them that "if our kingdom was of this world then we would fight but our weapons are not carnal."[29] Still, in the face of repeated enemy aggression and rejection of Mormon peace proposals, revelation promised that God would eventually "justify them in going out to battle."[30]

In 1836, after repeated efforts to restore the Zion refugees to their Jackson County homes, Joseph declared at a meeting of church leaders in Ohio, "I want to enter into the following covenant, that if any more of our brethren are slain or driven from their lands in Missouri by the mob that we will give ourselves no rest until we are avenged of our enimies to the uttermost, this covenant was sealed unanimously by a hosanna and Amen."[31] That same year the Missouri legislature created two new counties in the sparsely settled northwest part of the state. By a "gentlemen's agreement," one of the counties—Caldwell—was understood to be the place where the Mormons could settle without fear of molestation. The Zion refugees began to move there, and two years later Joseph Smith himself emigrated to Far West, Caldwell's county seat, encouraging his fellow Ohio Saints to do the same.

By summer 1838, the Mormon population in Caldwell and surrounding counties had swollen to nearly five thousand, and the Saints intended to stay. At an Independence Day celebration that year in Far West, Smith's lieutenant Sidney Rigdon read a Mormon "declaration of independence" from persecution and "mobocracy" that ended with these emphatic words: "We this day then proclaim ourselves free, with a purpose and a determination, that never can be broken, 'no never! *no never*!! NO NEVER!!!'"[32] Several weeks later, Joseph Smith, who was then editor of the church's newspaper, the *Elders' Journal*, printed this endorsement of Rigdon's speech:

> We would recommend to all the saints to get [the published *Oration*], to be had in their families, as it contains an outline of the suffering and persecutions of the Church from its rise. As also the fixed determinations of the saints, in relation to the persecutors, who are and have been, continually, not only threatening us with mobs, but actually have been putting their threats into execution; with which we are absolutely determined no longer to bear, come life or come death, for to be mobbed any more without taking vengeance, we will not.[33]

Not surprisingly, conflict soon erupted. Homes were burned and property pillaged on both sides by marauding bands of Mormons and Missourians. State militia units were called up to help restore order, but the escalation of tensions and the prospect of widening, armed conflict soon led Governor Lilburn Boggs to issue Executive Order No. 44, the infamous "extermination order," directing that the Mormons either be expelled from the state or killed. Fortunately, pragmatism prevailed over posturing, and the Saints surrendered before too much blood had been shed.[34]

Once again, apocalyptic millennialism provided the Saint with hope in a world turned upside down. A hymn composed near this time is typical:

> How long, O Lord, wilt thou forsake
> The Saints who tremble at Thy word?
> Awake, O Arm, O God! Awake
> And teach the nations Thou art God.
> Descend with all Thy holy throng,
> The year of Thy redeemed bring near,
> Haste, haste the day of vengeance on,
> Bid Zion's children dry their tear.[35]

The detailed account kept by one Mormon and sent to his family in Massachusetts provides a good example of how rank-and-file Saints made sense of what was happening. "Be not shaken at what I wrote in my last" letter, encouraged Albert Rockwood. "The scenes which we have passed thro of late is a bright evidence that the work in which we have enlisted is of the Lord, for these things must all be before the comeing of Christ[—]Pestilence, Sword, Blood, Famine, & Fire."[36] Ultimately, God would issue his own extermination order against the Saints' oppressors: "The testimony of Judgements," wrote Rockwood, "have now commenced & like a whirlpool will sweep [the] inhabitants off the U. States." To bolster his point, he cited the remarks of Joseph Smith's father: "The Patriarch observed last fast day that the time would soon come when a man should be considered of more value than a talent of gold [Isa 13:12] for God would assuredly make the earth empty & waste by Judgements & but very few would be left [Isa 24:6]."[37]

Ironically, such comments were intended to be comforting. The trials and tribulations of the last days "were part of an immutable guarantee that no matter how much the wicked seemed to triumph in the present age, God would supernaturally set the scales of Justice aright at the Day of Judgment."[38] Indeed, philosophically and eschatologically, the Saints read their persecutions as a kind of backhanded assurance that all was proceeding according to divine plan, that everything was in place for the "great reversal" soon to be effected by Christ.

The Saints' millenarianism taught them that not just wicked oppressors and turncoat traitors would suffer God's wrath. They also realized that part of the purpose for eschatological tribulation was to purify the faithful, to be a "refiner's fire." An 1837 revelation, which was read to the Saints in the midst of the 1838 conflict, warned that while "vengeance cometh speedily upon the inhabitants of the earth, a day of wrath, a day of burning, a day of desolation, of weeping, of mourning, and of lamentation . . . upon my house shall it begin."[39] In light of these words, Rockwood reminded his relatives to "not let the Scourges of Zion weaken your faith. These things will all work out for the purifying of the church from dross & the ultimate Glory of God."[40]

Similar sentiments had been expressed during the difficulties of 1833. "My daily prayer," wrote John Whitmer at the time, "is that the Lord will cleanse Zion of all the remaining wickedness that is on this *Holy Land*."[41] For holy it was to be. "This is Zion, the pure in heart," explained a revelation, and church leaders had regularly reminded the Saints that holiness resided in the soul, not the soil.[42] "It was necessary that these things should come upon us," declared Oliver Cowdery; "there was no other way to cleanse the Church."[43] The much-awaited December 1833 revelation offering a providential explanation of the expulsion from Jackson County began, "I the Lord have suffered the affliction to come upon them . . . in consequence of their transgressions . . . Therefore, they must needs be chastened, and tried."[44] "Until they learn obedience," declared a subsequent revelation, "if it must needs be by the things which they suffer."[45] "This one thing is sure," wrote Joseph Smith to followers in Missouri, "that they who will live Godly in Christ Jesus shall suffer persecution and before their robes are mad[e] white in the blood of the Lamb it is to be expected they will pass through great tribulation according to John the Revelator."[46]

Though the Saints' tribulations could be seen as a refiner's fire, they also foreshadowed the expected imminent vindication of the beleaguered faithful by apocalyptic judgment. From his "crucible of adversity" in a Liberty, Missouri, jail in 1839, Joseph Smith prayed that the Lord would avenge the Saints of their wrongs, expressing at the same time abiding faith that "the time soon shall come when the son of man shall descend in the clouds of <heaven>" and shall "have our oppressors in derision" and "<will laugh> at their calamity and mock them when their fear comith."[47]

Ultimately, however, Smith decided that God's timetable both for settling accounts with the wicked and for establishing a New Jerusalem in Missouri was far in the future. An 1841 Nauvoo, Illinois, revelation announced that God had "accepted the offerings of those whom I commanded to build up a city and a house unto my name, in Jackson county, Missouri, and were hindered by their enemies." Therefore, "it behoveth me to require that work no more at the hands of those sons of men."[48] For the time being, the effort to build a Missouri Zion was put on hold.

To be sure, apocalyptic millenarianism continued to serve as a potent psychological and emotional resource for Mormons throughout the remainder of the nineteenth century and into the twentieth, especially when they perceived themselves as suffering severe persecution. This was less true of the smaller churches who also laid claim to the heritage of Joseph Smith because most did not practice polygamy (or for very long) and, therefore, experienced less aggressive persecution. However, in the years following 1890, when the LDS church announced the cessation of further plural marriages, Mormons in Utah joined their spiritual cousins in making a sustained effort to fit into the larger social, economic, and political environment of the United States. Along the way, their apocalyptic rhetoric of polarization "diminished dramatically."[49]

The social trajectory throughout the twentieth century and into the twenty-first for all religious bodies tracing their roots back to the Missouri Mormon experience, whether based in Salt Lake City, Utah, Independence, Missouri, or any other locale, has been one of increasing compatibility. Joseph Smith's heirs have earned a reputation for being respectful neighbors and model citizens, and though they still talk about the end-times, for many these doctrines have a detached and textbookish quality. The polarizing social ramifications of their eschatology are rarely if ever discussed today. The term "wicked," for instance, no longer refers to all unbelievers. Today, it is applied only to the morally corrupt, and the good and honorable of all religions are expected to live to enjoy the millennium. As people make their peace with the world, the apocalyptic dream of the "great reversal" recedes.

For more than a century now, the more abrasive features of early Mormon millenarianism, which met the needs of Joseph Smith and his first-generation followers, have been quietly, perhaps unwittingly, though not unwisely, laid aside by their spiritual heirs. Whatever role those heirs might play in Missouri's future, it will likely reflect their now well-established reputation for neighborliness and civic responsibility. As a result, they can be expected to reciprocate the same spirit of mutual understanding and appreciation that motivated Governor Christopher Bond when in 1976 he rescinded Executive Order No. 44. Thus, the modern descendants of 1830s Mormons and Missourians alike have gone far toward creating a harmonious community not dramatically dissimilar from the millennial Zion for which the early Saints so anxiously yearned.

Notes

1. The literature on millennialism is voluminous. Happily, three of its leading scholars combined to produce the *Encyclopedia of Apocalypticism*, 3 vols. (New York: Continuum, 1998), a definite, if not definitive, starting place for the study of the subject.

2. James H. Moorhead, *American Apocalypse: Yankee Protestants and Civil War, 1860–1869* (New Haven, Conn.: Yale University Press, 1978), 8.

3. James H. Moorhead, "Between Progress and Apocalypse: A Reassessment of Millennialism in American Religious Thought, 1800–1880," *Journal of American History* 71 (December 1984): 524–42.

4. Grant Underwood, *The Millenarian World of Early Mormonism* (Urbana: University of Illinois Press, 1993).

5. Susan Juster, *Doomsayers: Anglo-American Prophecy in the Age of Revolution* (Philadelphia: University of Pennsylvania Press, 2003), 7, 15.

6. Joseph Smith to N. C. Saxton, editor of the *American Revivalist, and Rochester Observer*, January 4, 1833, Joseph Smith letterbook 1, Joseph Smith Collection, LDS Church Archives. Reproduced in Dean C. Jessee, *Personal Writings of Joseph Smith*, rev. ed. (Salt Lake City: Deseret, 2002), 294–98.

7. Revelation, Kirtland, Ohio, August 30, 1831, MS, 3 pp., Newel K. Whitney Collection, Harold B. Lee Library, Brigham Young University, Provo, Utah. This revelation was first published in the Missouri Mormon publication *Evening and the Morning Star* 1 (February 1833): [70–71], and eventually in *A Book of Commandments* (Zion [Independence, Mo.]: W. W. Phelps, 1833), 150–57, and *Doctrine and Covenants of the Church of the Latter Day Saints* (Kirtland, Ohio: F. G. Williams, 1835), 141–45.

Hereafter, unless a revelation's wording differed significantly in extant earlier manuscripts, the *Book of Commandments* version will be cited (or *Doctrine and Covenants,* if the revelation was first published there).

8. Joseph Smith and John Whitmer to Beloved in the Lord, August 20, 1830, copied in Newel Knight Autobiography, 132–33, original in possession of Robert Allen, Salem, Utah.

9. Ibid., December 2, 1830, copied in Newel Knight Autobiography, 201–4, original in possession of Robert Allen, Salem, Utah.

10. "A Revelation given in Kirtland, Ohio, August, 1831," in *Book of Commandments,* section 64, verses 33, 36–40 (p. 153).

11. "A Revelation to the church of Christ, given in the presence of six elders, in Fayette, New-York, September 1830," in *Book of Commandments,* section 29, verses 9–10 (pp. 61–62).

12. "A Revelation to the church, given in Kirtland, Ohio, March 1831," in *Book of Commandments,* section 48, verse 59 (p. 110).

13. For a detailed discussion of these tensions and for an expanded history of events summarized in the following paragraphs, see Richard L. Bushman, "Mormon Persecutions in Missouri, 1833," *BYU Studies* 3 (Autumn 1960): 11–20; and Warren A. Jennings, "Factors in the Destruction of the Mormon Press in Missouri, 1833," *Utah Historical Quarterly* 35 (Winter 1967): 57–76. An insightful extended analysis of Mormon/non-Mormon misunderstandings is Kenneth H. Winn, *Exiles in a Land of Liberty: Mormons in America, 1830–1846* (Chapel Hill: University of North Carolina Press, 1989).

14. *Evening and the Morning Star* 2 (July 1833): 111, 109.

15. John Whitmer to Joseph Smith and Oliver Cowdery, July 29, 1833, LDS Church Archives.

16. John G. Gager, *Kingdom and Community: The Social World of Early Christianity* (Englewood Cliffs, N.J.: Prentice Hall, 1975), 25.

17. Kenelm Burridge, *New Heaven, New Earth: A Study of Millenarian Activities* (New York: Schocken Books, 1969), 147.

18. Moorhead, *American Apocalypse,* 7.

19. Joseph Smith to Brother William [Phelps], John [Whitmer], Edward [Partridge], Isaac [Morley], John [Corrill], and Sidney [Gilbert], August 18, 1833, in Jessee, *Personal Writings of Joseph Smith,* 307–8. The words in angle brackets were inserted above the original line.

20. Joseph Smith to Edward [Partridge], William [Phelps], and others of the firm, March 30, 1834, in Jessee, *Personal Writings of Joseph Smith,* 338.

21. Edward Partridge to Joseph Smith, November 19, 1833, LDS Church Archives.

22. Michael Barkun, *Disaster and the Millennium* (New Haven, Conn.: Yale University Press, 1974), 1.

23. Smith to Phelps et al., August 18, 1833, in Jessee, *Personal Writings of Joseph Smith,* 309, 11.

24. Ibid., 310.

25. Partridge to Smith, November 19, 1833.

26. W. W. Phelps to "Dear Brethren," December 15, 1833, in *Evening and the Morning Star* 2 (February 1834): 128.

27. "Revelation given December, 1833," in *Doctrine and Covenants,* section 97, paragraph 12 (p. 239).

28. Joseph Smith to Beloved brethren, December 10, 1833, in Jessee, *Personal Writings of Joseph Smith,* 331.

29. The first quote is from a revelation received on August 6, 1833, communicated by Joseph Smith, Sidney Rigdon, Frederick G. Williams to Beloved Breatheren, August 6, 1833, LDS Church Archives. See also *Doctrine and Covenants,* section 85, paragraph 3 (p. 217). The second quote is from an August 18, 1833, letter from Joseph Smith to church leaders in Missouri. See Jessee, *Personal Writings of Joseph Smith,* 310.

30. See Joseph Smith et al., to Beloved Breatheren, August 6, 1833; and *Doctrine and Covenants,* Section 85, paragraph 6 (p. 218).

31. Joseph Smith, "Sketch Book," March 30, 1836, in Jessee, *Personal Writings of Joseph Smith,* 215–16.

32. Rigdon's speech was published as *Oration Delivered by Mr. S. Rigdon on the 4th of July, 1838* (Far West, Mo.: [Elders'] Journal Office, 1838). The quote is from p. 12.

33. *Elders' Journal* 1 (August 1838): 54. Around this time, Smith was heard to say that the sword had been "unsheathed" and he would not again sheath it until the Saints could live "in safety and in peace" wherever they would. See Dean C. Jessee and David J. Whittaker, "The Last Months of Mormonism in Missouri: The Albert Perry Rockwood Journal," *BYU Studies* 28 (Winter 1988): 25; and *Correspondence, Orders, &c,* 135.

34. See Stephen C. LeSueur, *The 1838 Mormon War in Missouri* (Columbia: University of Missouri Press, 1987). A balanced, recent summary of the Mormons' final days in Missouri is Richard Lyman Bushman, *Joseph Smith: Rough Stone Rolling* (New York: Knopf, 2005), 342–72.

35. Samuel Russell, ed. and comp., *The Millennial Hymns of Parley Parker Pratt* (Cambridge, UK: Cambridge University Press, 1913), 19.

36. Jessee and Whittaker, "Last Months of Mormonism in Missouri," 30.

37. Ibid., 31.

38. James Davidson, *The Logic of Millennial Thought* (New Haven, Conn.: Yale University Press, 1977), 83.

39. "The word of the Lord, given unto Thomas B. Marsh, at Kirtland July 23, 1837," in *Doctrine and Covenants* (1844 ed.), section 104, paragraphs 9–10 (pp. 416–17).

40. Jessee and Whittaker, "Last Months of Mormonism in Missouri," 31.

41. Whitmer to Smith and Cowdery, July 29, 1833.

42. "Revelation given August, 1833," in *Doctrine and Covenants,* section 81, paragraph 5 (p. 210).

43. Cowdery to Phelps et al., August 10, 1833.

44. *Doctrine and Covenants,* section 97, paragraph 12 (p. 235).

45. "Revelation given on Fishing River, Missouri, June 22, 1834," in *Doctrine and Covenants* (1844 ed.), section 102, paragraph 2 (p. 390).

46. Joseph Smith to Edward Partridge, December 5, 1833, RC, in Joseph Smith letterbook 1: 67, LDS Church Archives.

47. Joseph Smith to the Church of the Latter-day Saints, March 20, 1839, in Jessee, *Personal Writings of Joseph Smith,* 432.

48. "Revelation given to Joseph Smith, January 19, 1841," in *Doctrine and Covenants* (1844 ed.), section 103, paragraph 15 (p. 401).

49. See Thomas G. Alexander, *Mormonism in Transition: A History of the Latter-day Saints, 1890–1930* (Urbana: University of Illinois Press, 1986); and Gordon Shepherd and Gary Shepherd, *A Kingdom Transformed: Themes in the Development of Mormonism* (Salt Lake City: University of Utah Press, 1984). The quotation is from Shepherd and Shepherd, *A Kingdom Transformed,* 196.

4

The Great Temple of the New Jerusalem

Richard O. Cowan

The book of Ezekiel ends with the prophet's description of the latter-day inheritances of the twelve tribes of Israel in the Holy Land. He indicates that there would be a holy city, forty-five hundred cubits (approximately one and one-third miles) square in which the Lord would be present.[1] In the Apocalypse, John similarly spoke of latter-day events, including the final judgment and millennium. He declared that he had seen a new heaven and a new earth and "the holy city," the dwelling place of God known as the "New Jerusalem," descending down from heaven to the earth.[2]

Since their beginning, Latter-day Saints have been fired with the vision of this holy city, or Zion, on earth. The Book of Mormon, published in March 1830, declared that New Jerusalem would be built upon "this land," meaning the American continent.[3] In December of that year, when Joseph Smith published the writings of the ancient prophet Enoch, Latter-day Saints were not only thrilled with descriptions of the power and glory of the ancient city of Zion, but also learned that in a future era of righteousness the elect would be gathered into a similar "Holy City" to be known as Zion or the New Jerusalem.[4] Two months later, Joseph Smith revealed that there would be a temple in the New Jerusalem. As he unveiled the "law of consecration," he indicated that, among other things, the consecrated funds would be used for the "building up of the New Jerusalem" where the faithful would gather at the time Christ would come to His temple.[5] Another revelation the following month intensified the Saints' anticipation of establishing this latter-day Zion: "And it shall be . . . a land of peace, a city of refuge, a place of safety for the saints of the Most High God; And the glory of the Lord shall be there."[6]

Location of the "Center Place"

Information concerning the location of the latter-day Zion and the specific nature and design of the great temple to be built there was not stated all at once but was received piecemeal. Mormon leaders unfolded their plans for building a temple over a period of years, delivering a series of revelations and pronouncements that gradually revealed the temple's location and size. Similarly, church leaders have focused on different aspects of building the future temple; their emphases can often be related to the circumstances of the Saints to whom they were speaking at a particular time.

In September 1830, Hiram Page announced revelations through a "certain stone" in his possession concerning "the upbuilding of Zion" and other subjects.[7] A revelation through the prophet to Oliver Cowdery declared that "no man knoweth where the city of Zion shall be built." Nevertheless, Oliver was called to "go unto the Lamanites" (D&C 28:8) and was told that Zion would be "on the borders by the Lamanites" (verse 9).

When the Mormons began to gather in Ohio, some supposed that Kirtland might be the "place of the New Jerusalem spoken of in the Book of Mormon."[8] A few months later, the elders in Ohio were told to convene their next conference in Missouri, upon the land God would "consecrate" to his people.[9] In July 1831, they arrived there with heightened feelings of anticipation. Newel Knight wrote,

> Our feelings can be better imagined than described when we found ourselves upon the Western frontiers. The country itself presented a pleasant aspect with its rich forests bordering its beautiful streams, and its deep rolling prairies spreading far and wide, inviting the hand of industry to establish for itself homes upon its broad bosom. And this was the place where the Lord had promised to reveal unto us where . . . the New Jerusalem [or] Zion should be and our hearts went forth unto the Lord desiring the fulfillment, that we might know where to bestow our labors profitably.[10]

Joseph Smith was likewise moved to exclaim, "When will Zion be built up in her glory, and where will Thy temple stand, unto which all nations shall come in the last days?"[11] The new arrivals did not have to wait long for the answer. On July 20, their leader specified that Independence was to be the "center place" and that the temple should be built not far west of the courthouse.[12]

On August 3, 1831, Joseph Smith and a small group of elders went to a knoll about a half-mile west of the Independence courthouse, turned south from the old road (now Lexington Avenue), and made their way about two hundred feet through the thick forest. The prophet indicated the specific spot where the temple was to stand and placed a stone to mark the northeast corner of the future structure. Relevant scriptures were read and a dedicatory prayer was offered, in accordance with previous instructions.[13] "The scene was solemn and impressive."[14] In December of that year, Bishop Edward Partridge purchased in behalf of the church some 63.27 acres that included the spot dedicated for the temple.

For the next two years, Independence, Jackson County, was a focal point of Mormon activity. Interest grew when, in June 1833, Joseph Smith released his plan for the city of Zion. At the center of the mile-square city, he envisioned two large blocks containing twenty-four sacred "temples." These would be assigned to specific priesthoods and were to serve a variety of functions. He anticipated that the city would have a population of fifteen to twenty thousand, so these twenty-four buildings would be needed as "houses of worship, schools, etc."[15] Because all inhabitants of the city should be living on a "celestial" level, all these structures could properly be regarded as "temples"—places of communication between heaven and earth.[16]

Joseph Smith prepared his plat for the city of Zion when he was also in the midst of planning Kirtland and its temple. In May, a revelation called for three sacred structures at the center of Kirtland.[17] A communication given June 1 gave more details concerning the design and functions of the temple itself: "You should build a house, in the which house I design to endow those whom I have chosen with power from on high. Let the house be built, not after the manner of the world, for I give not unto you that ye shall live after the manner of the world; Therefore, let it be built after the manner which I shall show."[18] The plat for Zion (drawn up the same month as this latter revelation) therefore represented an expansion in the number of sacred buildings from three to twenty-four.

Joseph specified that "none of these temples are to be smaller than . . . the house of the Lord for the Presidency," which would measure 87 by 61 feet.[19] At least three sets of plans for this temple are extant. The first two sets, sketched freehand, follow the dimensions specified by Smith, so they were undoubtedly linked with his June 1833 plat for the city of Zion. The third set, drafted more precisely, extended the length of the building by ten feet. Only fragments of the first set have survived. All three sketches described a building with many of the features that would characterize the slightly smaller Kirtland Temple—the unique system of veils, box pews with reversible seating, and a series of pulpits at each end of the main halls.[20] These buildings were suited to the needs of the Saints in the 1830s and to construction methods common at the time. (That Latter-day Saints did not consider these the last word concerning the appearance of the ultimate New Jerusalem Temple became evident in later years.)

But the temple in Zion was not to be built at that time. Anti-Mormon violence flared in Jackson County, and the Saints' press at Independence was destroyed on July 20, less than one month after the prophet had drawn up his plat for the city of Zion. By late fall, the Mormons had to sell their homes in the chosen land. During the years following their expulsion, they empathized with the ancient Israelites who sat down by the rivers of Babylon and "wept when [they] remembered Zion."[21] In 1838, Joseph Holbrook, a Latter-day Saint then living in northern Missouri, returned to Jackson County on business: "At Independence I saw the temple lot that had been dedicated and consecrated to the Lord of hosts by the Prophet Joseph Smith, Jr. as the capital of Zion in the last days and now the Saints are driven from Jackson County and their inheritance laid waste and no Mormon is safe in this county, if known. . . . When shall we build the temple [?]" Holbrook mused. "The Lord must truly work a work upon this land before this can be fulfilled so Lord, let it be."[22]

Interest Continues Following the Mormons' Trek West

Even after Brigham Young, Joseph Smith's successor, led the Mormon pioneers to Utah in 1847, their hope to build the "center place" and its glorious temple remained bright. While walking through the Temple Block in Salt Lake City, Young recalled Jackson County. He described what he thought the great temple might look like: Each building would have its own tower, and in the center of the "temple complex" there would be a "high tower" and a square beautified by "hanging gardens" where the people could meet.[23] "When Zion is established in her beauty and honor and glory," declared Apostle John Taylor in 1858, "the kings and princes of the earth will come, in order that they may get information and teach the same to their people."[24]

The following year, Charles W. Penrose, president of the London Conference (or district), explained that at the Second Coming, the Savior would first appear at New Jerusalem. "He will come to the temple prepared for him, and his faithful people will behold his face, hear his voice, and gaze upon his glory. From his own lips, they will receive further instructions for the development and beautifying of Zion."[25]

The importance of the Saints' preparation was emphasized early. "When will Zion be redeemed?" asked Brigham Young in 1861; only "as soon as the Latter-day Saints are ready and prepared," he insisted.[26] His stressing the need for hard work reflected the immediate demands on the pioneers: "Where is the man that knows how to lay the first rock for the wall that is to surround the New Jerusalem?" God will not do the work that we should do for ourselves, President Young emphasized, unless we "let him work by, through, and with us, . . . we shall fall short and shall never have the honor of building up Zion on the earth."[27]

The Saints in Utah were naturally interested in the prospects of returning to Jackson County, many assuming that the time of the return was not distant. In 1862, Brigham Young declared that he wanted to push construction of the Salt Lake Temple as far as possible before returning to Jackson County. "The way things are going," he believed, "the way will soon be clear." In fact, President Young hoped that it would be his privilege to see the temple in Jackson County finished before any other temple.[28] Other events, however, would alter the Saints' timetable.

During the Civil War, the Mormons felt secure in the relative isolation of their Rocky Mountain stronghold. They viewed the destruction that the North and South were heaping on one another as just recompense for the nation's earlier mistreatment of the Latter-day Saints and supposed that this desolation would open the way for their return to Jackson County. When this failed to materialize, the Saints looked to a later return.

Orson Pratt, one of the original twelve apostles of the church, exhibited this shift in feeling. In 1872, he quoted Joseph Smith's 1832 pronouncement that the "temple shall be reared in this generation."[29] Noting that most who were living when that revelation was given had passed away, Elder Pratt concluded that "the time must be pretty near when we shall begin that work."[30] Just three years later he referred to the same prophecy, but this time he emphasized that he believed that God was not "limited to any definite period."[31]

During the 1870s, a number of Latter-day Saints in Utah engaged in a variety of cooperative ventures known as "united orders." They recalled an 1834 affirmation given by Joseph Smith at Fishing River, Missouri, that specified that the people must be united and impart to the poor according to a celestial law before Zion could be established.[32] Mormon leaders emphasized the need to live this "higher law" before New Jerusalem and its temple could be built. "We are not yet prepared to go and establish the Center Stake of Zion," President Young emphasized. The Lord gathered the Saints to the place where New Jerusalem would be built and gave them laws concerning the establishment of Zion, "but the people could not abide them, and the Church was scattered."[33]

Speaking in 1874, Orson Pratt recalled the "Fishing River revelation" of forty years before and declared that if the Saints in their prevailing way of life were to attempt to build the temple on the consecrated spot, "we should be cast out again," because "the Lord would not acknowledge us as his people." Elder Pratt continued, "If we would go back then, we must comply with the celestial law, the law of consecration, the law of oneness."[34] "When we go back to Jackson County, we are to go back with power," he declared on another occasion. "Do you suppose that God will reveal his power among an unsanctified people who have no regard nor respect for his laws?"[35]

Brigham Young likewise cautioned, "If we are not very careful, the earth will be cleansed from wickedness before we are prepared to take possession of it. We must be pure to be prepared to build up Zion."[36] Apostle George Q. Cannon insisted that before Jesus would come to his latter-day temple, "The organization of society that exists in the heavens must exist on the earth; the same condition of society, so far as it is applicable to mortal beings, must exist here."[37]

Likewise Wilford Woodruff, another of the apostles, reminded the people of Enoch's example and stressed that New Jerusalem will have to be built "by the united Order of Zion and according to the celestial law."[38] A portion of the property consecrated to the Lord's storehouse, explained Orson Pratt, "will be used for the building of temples."[39]

The opening of the St. George Temple, the first Mormon temple in Utah, in 1877 sparked a revival of interest in temples and temple ceremonies. This, in turn, heightened interest in the anticipated temple of New Jerusalem. During the next two or three years, Orson Pratt spoke repeatedly on the function and design of this magnificent future structure. Citing an 1833 revelation directing that no unclean thing should be allowed to enter and defile the temple,[40] he emphasized that "there are certain places appointed, and certain provisions to be complied with" in order for the fullness of the priesthood "ordinances" to be made known by which families are united for eternity. "This is the object of Temples," he declared.[41]

Elder Pratt then reviewed how the pattern of temple design had unfolded: there had been no provisions for sacred ordinances at Kirtland, but a font was added at Nauvoo. Likewise, the New Jerusalem temple would not be built "according to the pattern of our present Temples." But "there will be, according to the progress of this people, and the knowledge they receive," many features not found in present temples.[42] Speaking in the recently dedicated tabernacle in Salt Lake City, Orson Pratt shared his idea of what the temple would look like. It would be "much larger, very much larger" than any existing Latter-day Saint building. "The Lord our God will command his servants to build that Temple in the most perfect order," Elder Pratt testified. "When we build a Temple that is never to be destroyed, it will be constructed after the most perfect order of the celestial worlds." For this purpose, he concluded, we must have prophets in our midst who can receive "the whole pattern thereof given by revelation."[43]

Wilford Woodruff saw in a dream that the glorious latter-day temple would be built with the help of heavenly beings:

> I saw a short distance from the Missouri River, where I stood, twelve men . . . [whose] hands were uplifted while they were consecrating the ground; and later they laid the corner-stones of the house of God. I saw myriads of angels hovering over them, and above their heads there was a pillar-like cloud. I heard the most beautiful singing in the words: "Now is established the Kingdom of our God and His Christ, and He shall reign forever and forever, and the Kingdom shall never be thrown down, for the Saints have overcome." I saw people coming from the river and from distant places to help build the Temple. It seemed as though there were hosts of angels helping to bring material for the construction of that building.[44]

Orson Pratt was also interested in the visible manifestation of God's glory at the future temple: "A cloud of glory [will] rest upon that temple by day, the same as the cloud rested upon the tabernacle of Moses. . . . Not only that, but a flaming fire will rest upon the temple by night." He continued, "You will have no need of any artificial light, for the Lord God will be the light thereof, and his glory will be there, and you will see it and you will hear his voice."[45] This conspicuous display of God's glory would have "quite a tendency to strike terror to all the nations of the earth." Elder Pratt expected that its fame would become known worldwide and that people would travel from around the earth to see it.[46]

Developments at the "Center Place"

During the later nineteenth century, even though the Mormons in Utah gave up the idea of an immediate return to Missouri and anticipated a more distant fulfillment of prophecies concerning New Jerusalem and its temple, activities in the appointed "center place" did not cease. In 1867, a small group of former Mormons who were now followers of Granville Hedrick returned to Independence and began the process of quietly purchasing two and a half acres including the spot where Joseph Smith had placed the temple cornerstone more than three decades earlier. This group would form the "Church of Christ (Temple Lot)." During the 1870s and 1880s, the Reorganized Church of Jesus Christ of Latter-Day Saints, followers of Joseph Smith III (and more recently known as the Community of Christ) also returned and eventually established their headquarters at Independence.

During these years, the Utah Latter-day Saints lived in relative isolation, but this situation changed with the 1890 "Manifesto" announcing the end of plural marriage. During the decade of goodwill that followed, LDS missions in places such as Missouri that had lain dormant for several decades now began to revive. This led these Saints to become more aware of contemporary developments affecting the temple site. In the early 1890s, for example, Utah newspapers covered the major features of the "Temple Lot Case" between the Church of Christ (or Hedrickites) and the Reorganized Church. Interest was particularly high during March 1892, when attorneys from both sides came to Salt Lake City to interview witnesses during a series of formal hearings.[47]

Utah interest in Missouri was reawakened in 1904 when the Church of Jesus Christ of Latter-day Saints began to purchase 20 of the 63 acres originally acquired by Bishop Edward Partridge for the temple and other uses in Independence. In 1907 the Church located headquarters of the Central States mission there, and also established a press, Zion's Printing and Publishing Co., from which millions of missionary tracts as well as copies of the Book of Mormon and the *Liahona* magazine were issued.

Latter-day Saints noted the activities of other groups interested in building a temple at the appointed site. As early as 1914, Utah papers reported that the Church of Christ (not to be confused with the large Protestant denomination) was actively considering temple construction. James A. Hedrick, a descendant of that church's founder, believed that Joseph Smith's 1832 declaration that the temple would be built "in this generation"[48] meant the work would need to be completed within 100 years of that date.[49] As the deadline drew closer, a Hedrick apostle, Otto Fetting, announced a series of revelations commanding that the work proceed, and on April 6, 1929, the Church of Christ "broke the sod" for the temple. An excavation was made for the 90-by-180-foot structure.

Speaking at the October 1929 LDS general conference in Salt Lake City, Anthony W. Ivins of the First Presidency referred to appeals for funds and to invitations from the Church of Christ for the Utah church to join them in building the temple. "With all good feelings toward these people," however, he observed, "you will readily understand the impossibility of such a coalition."[50] LDS apostle Joseph Fielding Smith affirmed that God had not released the Saints from their responsibility to establish Zion and to build the temple on the designated spot. He insisted that the temple would have to be built by those possessing proper priestly authority and a knowledge of the purposes of temples and temple ordinances.[51] An editorial in the *Liahona* declared that "all premature, unauthorized movements" to build the temple must inevitably "come to naught."[52]

When Fetting's apostasy in 1930 drew away about one-third of the Church of Christ's four thousand members, progress on the temple project halted. In 1946, the Hedrickites had the excavation filled in, the ground leveled, and the lot seeded in grass. They now view themselves as guardians of this sacred property awaiting the time when all of the followers of Joseph Smith who are "pure in heart" will unite to build the temple.

A More Cautious Interest

Even though Mormon church leaders spoke of the New Jerusalem temple publicly less often during the twentieth century than previously, their occasional statements reflect a continuing interest. For example, speaking at the dedication of the impressive Alberta Temple (at Cardston in western Canada) in 1923, Apostle Rudger Clawson anticipated that "the time will come when we shall have much finer temples. That which is to be built in the Center Stake of Zion, in Jackson County, will be far more magnificent than any yet erected."[53]

During the 1960s, Alvin R. Dyer, who had been a mission president at Independence, said he envisioned "a temple complex such as has never been known." At its center would be the great temple of the New Jerusalem in which the Lord would make his appearance, and from which he will govern all the earth.[54]

LDS apostle Bruce R. McConkie also emphasized the importance of the temple. He insisted that New Jerusalem could not be "built up" as "a holy city, a city of Zion," until a temple is erected there. "The Lord will not reign in or send forth his law from a city in which he has no house of his own." Nevertheless, Elder McConkie did not believe that this temple needed to be built immediately: "Because the Saints were 'hindered by the hands of their enemies, and by oppression,' the Lord withdrew the time limitation (D&C 124:49-54), and the command now in force is 'Zion shall be redeemed in mine own due time'" (D&C 136:18).[55]

During the 1970s, the Utah Saints' attention again turned to Missouri. In 1971, the LDS Church dedicated a visitors' center designed to highlight the significance of Independence, both in the past and in the future. However, the Mormons' belief in prophesied events has sometimes led them to attach undue significance to present-day developments in Missouri. In 1978, for example, when the Church of Jesus Christ of Latter-day Saints purchased more than four thousand acres of land across the river in Clay County, many Mormons concluded that this was a sign of the temple's immediate construction. Church leaders stressed that the purchase was for investment purposes only.[56]

Rather than placing emphasis on moving to Missouri, Mormon leaders have continued to urge the Saints to develop the qualities that must characterize those who build Zion. Apostle Harold B. Lee cautioned, "The Lord has placed the responsibility for directing the work of gathering in the hands of the leaders of the Church." He emphasized that the Saints would do well, therefore, to look to the First Presidency for instructions as to when and where they should gather.[57]

Consistent with this more cautious emphasis, developments in Missouri received relatively little public attention during the later twentieth century. Even though Utah newspapers covered the sensational story of the arson-caused fire that destroyed the Hedrickites' headquarters on New Year's Day 1990, they gave little or no attention to a more significant story—the Reorganized Church's beginning construction of their temple across the street during that same year. The new structure featured a three-hundred-foot spiral tower, regarded as a "divinely inspired plan that would speak in a universal language to all persons throughout the world."[58]

The "Center Place" as Viewed by a Worldwide Church

The Latter-day Saints' feelings about the land of Missouri have necessarily been affected by the growing emphasis on the church's broader worldwide mission. Throughout the twentieth century, LDS leaders have urged the Saints to remain in their own lands, strengthen the church there, and establish "stakes of Zion." For example, at the 1972 Mexico City area conference, Elder Bruce R. McConkie again stressed the need to build up the Church in many lands: "The place of gathering of the Mexican Saints is in Mexico; the place of gathering for the Guatemalan Saints is in Guatemala; the place of gathering for the Brazilian Saints is in Brazil; and so it goes throughout the length and breadth of the whole earth. Japan is for the Japanese; Korea is for the Koreans; Australia is for the Australians; every nation is the gathering place for its own people."[59]

As part of its broadened focus, the LDS Church has increasingly erected temples in many lands. Latter-day Saints believe these developments pave the way for fulfilling prophecies that temple activity would accelerate even faster during the millennium. "When the Savior comes," foresaw Elder Wilford Woodruff, "a thousand years will be devoted to this work of redemption; and Temples will appear all over this land of Joseph—North and South America—and also in Europe and elsewhere."[60]

"To accomplish this work," President Brigham Young explained as early as 1856, "there will have to be not only one temple but thousands of them, and thousands and tens of thousands of men and women will go into those temples and officiate for people who have lived as far back as the Lord shall reveal."[61]

Likewise in 1975, LDS president Spencer W. Kimball looked forward to the time "when the temples will be used around the clock and throughout the year."[62]

In an era of international growth and temple building worldwide, what were the Latter-day Saints to think about Missouri? "Let Israel gather to the stakes of Zion in all nations," exclaimed Elder McConkie. "Let temples arise wherein the fullness of the ordinances of the Lord's house may be administered. But still there is a center place, a place where the chief temple shall stand, a place to which the Lord shall come, . . . and that center place is what men now call Independence in Jackson County, Missouri."[63] Hence, despite the Mormon Church's broader view of the gathering and of temple building, the Saints have continued to show a keen interest in the land of Missouri, the center place, and the future temple to be built there.

Notes

1. Ezekiel 48:30–35.
2. Revelation 21:1–4.
3. Book of Mormon, Esther 13:2–3.
4. Pearl of Great Price, Moses 7:13–19, 62.
5. The Doctrine and Covenants (hereafter cited as D&C), 42: 35–36; cf. 36: 8 and 133: 1–2.
6. D&C, 45: 66–67.
7. Joseph Smith, *History of the Church of Jesus Christ of Latter-day Saints,* ed. B. H. Roberts, 7 vols. (Salt Lake City: Deseret, 1980), 1: 109–10.
8. John Whitmer, *An Early Latter Day Saint History: The Book of John Whitmer Kept by Commandment,* eds. F. Mark McKiernan and Roger D. Launius (Independence, Mo.: Herald Publishing House, 1980), 54.
9. D&C, 52: 2.
10. Newell Knight's journal, "Scraps of Biography," in *Classic Experiences and Adventures* (Salt Lake City: Bookcraft, 1969), 71.
11. Smith, *History of the Church,* 1: 189.
12. D&C, 57: 3.
13. Ibid., 58: 57.
14. Smith, *History of the Church,* 1: 199; Richard and Pamela Price, *The Temple of the Lord* (Independence, Mo.: Richard and Pamela Price, 1982), 20–25.
15. Ibid., 1: 358–59.
16. D&C, 105: 5.
17. Ibid., 94.
18. Ibid., 95: 8, 13–14.
19. Smith, *History of the Church,* 1: 358–59.
20. Richard O. Cowan, "The House of the Lord in Kirtland: A 'Preliminary' Temple," in *Regional Studies in Latter-day Saint Church History: Ohio* (Provo, Utah: Brigham Young University, Department of Church History and Doctrine, 1990), 107–10.
21. Psalms 137:1.
22. Joseph Holbrook, "The Life of Joseph Holbrook," t.s., L. Tom Perry Special Collections, Harold B. Lee Library, Brigham Young University, Provo, Utah, 17.
23. Wilford Woodruff, historian's private journal, July 7, 1863, Ms F 348, no. 4, Church Archives, Church of Jesus Christ of Latter-day Saints, Salt Lake City.

24. John Taylor, in *Journal of Discourses* (Salt Lake City: Church of Jesus Christ of Latter-day Saints, 1966), 6: 169.
25. Charles W. Penrose, "The Second Advent," *The Latter-day Saints Millennial Star,* September 10, 1859, 582–83.
26. Brigham Young, in *Journal of Discourses,* 9: 137.
27. Ibid., 13: 313.
28. Woodruff, Historian's Private Journal, August 22, 1862.
29. D&C, 84:4.
30. Orson Pratt, in *Journal of Discourses,* 17: 111.
31. Ibid., 19: 215.
32. D&C, 105: 3–5.
33. Brigham Young, in *Journal of Discourses,* 11: 324.
34. Orson Pratt, in *Journal of Discourses,* 17: 112.
35. Ibid., 15: 362.
36. Young, in *Journal of Discourses,* 9: 137.
37. George Q. Cannon, in *Journal of Discourses,* 13: 99.
38. Wilford Woodruff, in *Journal of Discourses,* 17: 250.
39. Pratt, in *Journal of Discourses,* 21: 153.
40. D&C, 97: 15–17.
41. Pratt, in *Journal of Discourses,* 19: 18.
42. Ibid., 19: 19.
43. Ibid., 21: 153.
44. Matthias F. Cowley, *Wilford Woodruff: History of His Life and Labors as Recorded in His Daily Journals* (Salt Lake City: Deseret News, 1909), 505.
45. Pratt, in *Journal of Discourses,* 21: 330–31.
46. Ibid., 24: 29.
47. *Deseret Evening News,* March 24, 1892.
48. D&C, 84: 4.
49. *Journal History of the Church* (September 17, 1914), ms., Church Archives, 6.
50. Anthony W. Ivins, in *One Hundredth Semi-Annual Conference of the Church of Jesus Christ of Latter-day Saints,* October 1929 (Salt Lake City: Church of Jesus Christ of Latter-day Saints, n.d.), 96–97.
51. Joseph Fielding Smith, "The New Jerusalem and Its Temple," *Improvement Era* (May 1930): 469.
52. Orson F. Whitney, "Zion and Her Stakes," *Liahona: The Elders' Journal* (July 1930): 31.
53. Susa Young Gates Papers, Utah Historical Society.
54. Alvin R. Dyer, "The Center Place of Zion," *Speeches of the Year,* February 7, 1967 (Provo, Utah: Brigham Young University, 1966), 8.
55. Bruce R. McConkie, *The Millennial Messiah: The Second Coming of the Son of Man* (Salt Lake City: Deseret, 1982), 280–81.
56. "Church Buys 4250 Acres for Investment in Missouri," *Deseret News, Church News,* Salt Lake City, December 16, 1978, 12.
57. Harold B. Lee, in *The 118th Annual Conference of the Church of Jesus Christ of Latter-day Saints,* April 1948 (Salt Lake City: Church of Jesus Christ of Latter-day Saints, n.d.), 55.
58. Wallace B. Smith, *Preparing for the Temple* (Independence, Mo.: Herald Publishing House, 1989), 45.
59. Bruce R. McConkie, in *Official Report of the First Mexico and Central America Area General Conference of the Church of Jesus Christ of Latter-day Saints,* August 1972

(Salt Lake City: Church of Jesus Christ of Latter-day Saints, 1972), 45.

60. Wilford Woodruff, in *Journal of Discourses,* 19: 230.

61. Brigham Young, in *Journal of Discourses,* 3: 372.

62. Spencer W. Kimball, "Greater Need Brings Temple's Renovation," *Church News* (April 19, 1975), 3.

63. Bruce R. McConkie, *A New Witness for the Articles of Faith* (Salt Lake City: Deseret, 1985), 595.

5

The Mormon Temple Site at Far West, Caldwell County, Missouri

Alexander L. Baugh

Located in Mirabile Township in Caldwell County, Far West, Missouri, was a relatively short-lived Latter-day Saint community, existing from 1836 to 1839. Before this community was established, Jackson County served as the main gathering place from 1831 to 1833. However, in late 1833, violence erupted between Jackson's citizenry and the Mormons, resulting in their expulsion from the county.[1] At the time of their removal, most Church members relocated north to Clay County, where the citizens were considerably more open and fair-minded than Jackson's earlier settlers. However, Clay's citizens never expected the Saints to remain in the county permanently; by the early summer of 1836, continued immigration into the region led to increased tensions and threats of renewed hostilities. On June 29, a committee of citizen leaders drafted a lengthy petition requesting that the Latter-day Saints relocate, promising assistance in removing peaceably. To avoid conflict and for the sake of friendship, Church leaders agreed to look elsewhere.[2]

As early as 1834, Mormon families had begun moving north and east from Clay into the more sparsely populated areas in Ray County. Still later, in March 1836, Missouri Church leaders began searching out possible sites for permanent settlement in the more uninhabited regions of that county. After making extensive explorations, on August 8, 1836, William W. Phelps and John Whitmer, two members of the Missouri presidency acting as agents in behalf of the Church, purchased a one-mile-square plat (640 acres) near Shoal Creek as the main gathering place in Missouri. The site was subsequently named Far West.[3]

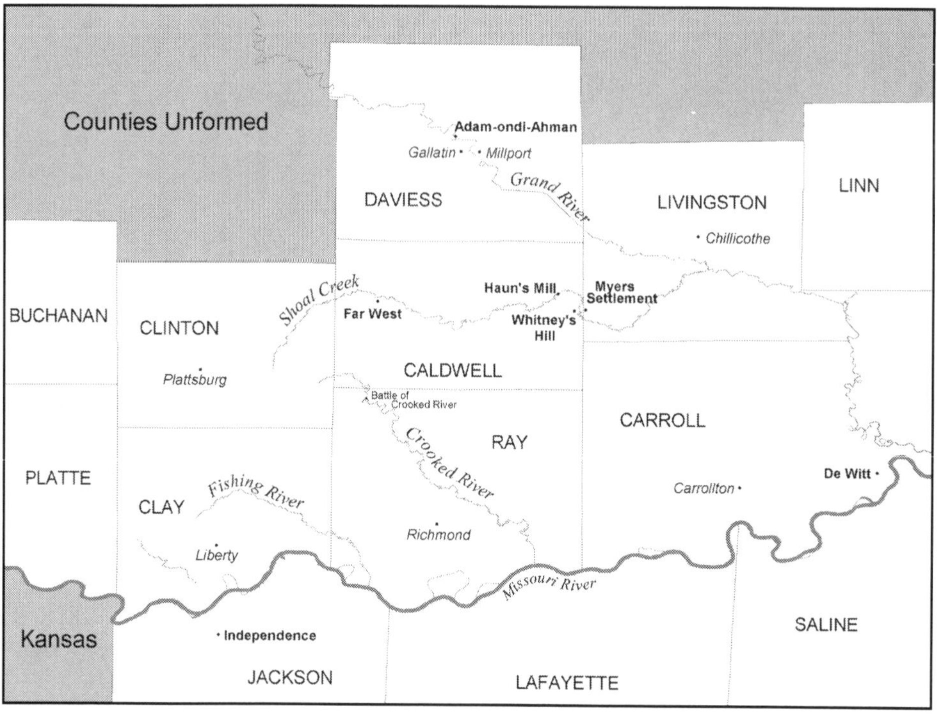

The counties of northwestern Missouri, 1838. Map courtesy of Alexander L. Baugh.

As Latter-day Saints began moving into Far West and the surrounding region, Missourians thought the Mormon problem might be solved if a separate county were created exclusively for them. Alexander W. Doniphan, Clay County's representative to the state legislature and a Mormon sympathizer, spearheaded the bill. Passage of the measure came on December 29, 1836. The new county was named Caldwell in honor of Matthew Caldwell of Kentucky, a friend, Indian scout, and soldier who had served with Joseph Doniphan, father of Alexander W. Doniphan.[4]

For nearly three years, from 1836 to until 1839, Far West was the center of the religious and political activities of the Latter-day Saints in northern Missouri. By late 1838 it had become the largest settlement north of the Missouri River.[5] With the creation of Caldwell County in December 1836, Far West was designated as the county seat.[6] For a period of exactly eleven months (March 14, 1838, to February 14, 1839), Far West was the official headquarters of The Church of Jesus Christ of Latter-day Saints.[7]

Plans to Build a Mormon Temple at Far West

Just a few months after the initial establishment of Far West, Missouri Church leaders began to discuss building a temple in the new Mormon center. At a meeting of the Missouri presidency, high council, and bishopric held at Far West on April 7, 1837, Jacob Whitmer, Elisha H. Groves, and George M. Hinkle were designated as the "building committee of the house of the Lord in this city," after which the body appointed the Missouri presidency, consisting of David Whitmer, John Whitmer, and William W. Phelps, "to superintend the building of the house of the Lord in . . . Far West."[8] Shortly thereafter, they decided to construct the temple in the geographic center of the community on the northeast quarter section of the public square. July 3, 1837, was selected as the day for the official groundbreaking. W. W. Phelps reported some of the events of the day in a letter to Joseph Smith and other Mormon leaders in Ohio: "Monday, the 3rd of July, was a great and glorious day in Far West, more than fifteen hundred Saints assembled at this place and at half-past eight in the morning, after prayer, singing, and an address, they proceeded to break ground for the Lord's House. The day was beautiful; the Spirit of the Lord was with us. An excavation for this great edifice, one hundred and ten feet long by eighty feet broad was nearly finished."[9]

One interesting aspect of Phelps's letter is that he provides the projected dimensions of the building—110 by 80 feet. In comparison, the temple completed in Kirtland, Ohio, in 1836 was 79 by 59 feet while the temple constructed in Nauvoo, Illinois, in the 1840s measured 128 by 88 feet; the Far West Temple was to be considerably larger than the Kirtland Temple but only slightly smaller than the Nauvoo Temple. It appears the Far West Temple was to be similar to the Kirtland Temple in design and function. According to John Wycliff Rigdon, a son of church leader Sidney Rigdon, the building was to include a lower hall or auditorium for congregational worship and an upper hall to be used primarily as a schoolroom, both of which were characteristics of the temple in Kirtland.[10]

As noted, W. W. Phelps's July 7, 1837, letter to Joseph Smith in Ohio informed the Mormon leader that plans for building the temple were under way and that the foundation for the structure had already been dug. At least initially Smith had no objections to the decision made by Missouri Church leaders to build the temple. However, in late September 1837, Joseph Smith and Sidney Rigdon left Kirtland and traveled to Far West, arriving around the first of November. Their stay was not long—about ten days—during which time they presided over a conference and held other instructive meetings with the

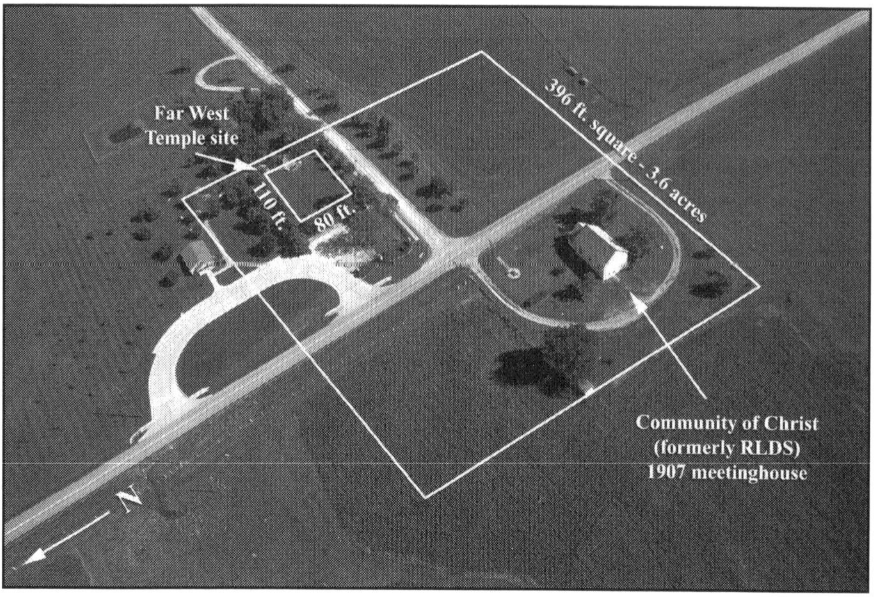

Aerial photograph showing a general outline of the public square of Far West, including the location of the temple site, 2000. Photograph courtesy of Intellectual Reserve.

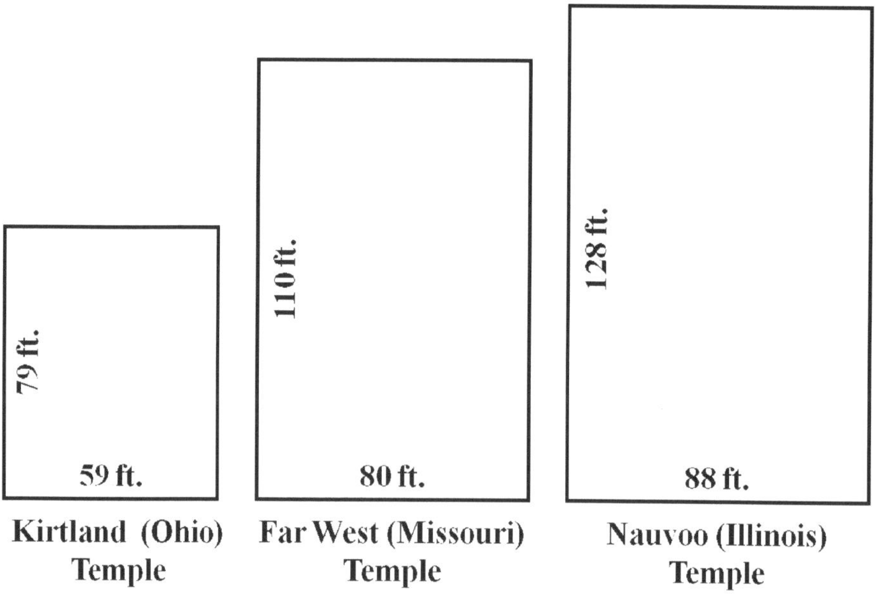

Outline showing the projected size of the Far West Temple in comparison to the Kirtland (Ohio) Temple and the Nauvoo (Illinois) Temple. Image courtesy of Alexander L. Baugh.

leading elders. A council meeting on November 6 proposed "that the building of the House of the Lord be postponed until the Lord shall reveal it to be His will to have it commenced."[11] In other words, construction on the Far West Temple was not to proceed until Joseph Smith received a revelation instructing builders to move forward.

Following his November visit to Far West, Joseph Smith returned to Ohio. However, his stay there was short as well. For months, internal dissension within the Church had been mounting. At the core of the dissent was the failure of the Kirtland Safety Society Anti-Banking Company, organized and established by Smith and other Church leaders in early 1837. Believing that support in the Ohio region was crumbling, on January 12, 1838, the Mormon leader made the decision to abandon Kirtland and relocate to Missouri. Following a two-month journey, Smith's arrival at Far West on March 14 marked Far West as the new Mormon center and the official headquarters of the Church.[12]

On April 26, six weeks after his arrival in Far West, Joseph Smith received the anticipated temple revelation. The revelation, addressed to the Church's First Presidency (Joseph Smith, Sidney Rigdon, and Hyrum Smith), not only gave divine sanction to build the sacred structure, it also provided instructions regarding the timetable for its construction. The revelation read as follows:

> Let the City Far West, be a holy and consecrated land unto me, and it shall be called most holy for the ground upon which thou Standest is holy. Therefore I command you to build an house unto me for the gathering together~~ing~~ of my Saints that they may worship me, and let there be a begin[n]ing of this work; and a foundation and a preparatory work, this following Summer; and let the begin[n]ing be made on the 4th day of July next; and from that time forth let my people labour diligently to build an house, unto my name, and in one year from this day, let them recommence laying the foundation of my house; thus let them from that time forth laibour diligently untill it Shall be finished, from the Corner Stone thereof unto the top thereof, untill there Shall not any thing remain that is not finished.
>
> Verrily [*sic*] I say unto you let not my Servant Joseph neither my Servant Sidn[e]y, neither my Servant Hyrum, get in debt any more for the building of an house unto my name. But let my house be built unto my name according to the pattern which I will Shew unto them, and if my people build it not according to the pattern which I Shall Shew unto their presidency, I will not accept it at their hands. But if my people do build it according to the pattern which I Shall Shew unto their presidency, even my Servant Joseph and his Councilors; then I will accept it at the hands of my people.[13]

These instructions called for the Latter-day Saints to dedicate the foundation of the temple on July 4, 1838, and then to make additional preparations, such as securing rock, lumber, and other building materials, so that actual construction could begin "in one year from this day," namely April 26, 1839.

Temple Site Dedication

The July 4, 1838, temple site dedication was conducted in grand style. Owen H. McGee, a non-Mormon, escorted two young Mormon women to the all-day affair and estimated some five thousand Latter-day Saints were in attendance.[14] The festivities commenced at 10 a.m. with a grand parade consisting of military infantry, Church leaders, "ladies and gentlemen," and cavalry. The entire procession marched to the public square to the music of a brass band led by Dimick B. Huntington. After assembling at the temple site, the entire company formed a circle around the excavation with the ladies in front. Joseph Smith, president of the Church, offered the opening prayer.[15]

Early Mormon temple site dedications were characterized by the placement of a large cornerstone, cut and roughly shaped beforehand, at each of the corners of the excavated foundation, after which a prayer of dedication was offered. The cornerstones were cut by Elisha Averett (chief mason), Dimick B. Huntington, and Cornelius Lott.[16] Each stone was approximately seven feet long, four feet wide, and two feet thick.[17] The cornerstones were dedicated in order by the following leaders, each of whom was assisted by twelve men: (1) southeast (Missouri stake presidency), (2) southwest (presidents of the elders), (3) northwest (the bishop), and (4) northeast (president of the teachers). After each stone was laid, the band struck up a song.[18]

The day before the July 4 dedication and festivities, Joseph Smith asked Levi Hancock to compose a song for the ceremonies. "He worked on it much in the night, and had it ready for the occasion," wrote Levi's son, Mosiah Hancock. The song, titled "Song of Freedom," was lengthy, consisting of twelve stanzas. The first verse is as follows:

> Come lover of freedom, to gather,
> And hear what we now have to say.
> For surely we ought to remember
> The cause that produced this great day.
> Oh, may we remember while singing
> The pains and distresses once borne
> By those who have fought for our freedom
> And often for friends called to mourn.[19]

Original southeast cornerstone of the Far West Temple, 1991. Photograph courtesy of Alexander L. Baugh.

At the conclusion of the cornerstone ceremonies, Church leaders and dignitaries took their places on a stand constructed for the occasion. Sidney Rigdon, first counselor in the First Presidency, gave the oration. Rigdon used the occasion to recount eloquently the principles of freedom by which the founders established the U.S. government and the rights that religious societies are entitled under its provisions. Speaking in general terms, he also spoke of the false reports circulated about Mormonism as well as the persecution and suffering experienced by the Church from its earliest beginnings. But in his closing statements, the speech took on a different tone. Buoyed by the relative peace that had existed in northern Missouri since 1836, and secure in the notion that continued immigration would result in a steady increase in their population, Rigdon announced that the Latter-day Saints would no longer suffer abuse at the hands of their enemies. His final words were words of warning: "That mob that comes on us to disturb us; it shall be between us and them a war of extermination, for we will follow them, till the last drop of their blood is spilled, or else they will have to exterminate us; for we will carry the seat of war to their own houses, and their own families, and one party or the other shall be destroyed." In the end, Rigdon's expressions proved to be partly prophetic.[20]

Following Rigdon's speech, those assembled participated in the "hosanna shout," a sacred vocal expression in which the Saints exclaim in unison, "Hosanna, Hosanna, Hosanna, to God and the Lamb. Amen, Amen, and Amen," repeated three times.[21] With the ceremonies completed, Church leaders left the stand and took a position on the south side of the temple excavation. Here the military officers and troops paraded and passed in review before the Church leaders, after which the entire procession was dismissed.[22]

The 1839 Mission of the Twelve to Great Britain

As discussed, Smith's April 26, 1838, revelation instructed the Saints to dedicate the temple site on July 4, 1838, but to suspend actual construction until April 26, 1839.[23] On July 8, 1838, four days after the dedication ceremonies of the temple site, Joseph Smith received another revelation, part of which pertained to the temple property. The revelation instructed the Twelve Apostles that they were to fill a mission to Great Britain the following spring and that they were to assemble at the Far West temple site on April 26, 1839, the same day the construction on the temple was to commence. The revelation reads in part, "And next spring let them depart to go over the great waters, and there promulg[at]e my gospel in the fullness thereof, and to bear record of my name[.] Let them take l[e]ave of my Saints in the City Far West, on the Twenty sixth day of April next, on the building spot of mine house saith the Lord."[24] However, later that summer, hostilities broke out between the Missourians and the Mormons, culminating in Governor Lilburn W. Boggs issuing the extermination order in late October 1838. The result was the imprisonment of Joseph Smith and several other leading Mormon officials, and the forced expulsion and evacuation of the leadership of the Church and the main body of Latter-day Saints to Quincy, Illinois, during the early winter months of 1839.

On March 17, 1839, Brigham Young, recently elevated to a senior member of the Twelve, presided over a council meeting in Quincy, Illinois, in which it was decided that the Twelve would return to Far West to fulfill the instructions called for in the two revelations—to "recommence" laying the temple cornerstones and to take leave of their appointed mission to Great Britain. Accordingly, during the third week of April, five of the ordained apostles—Brigham Young, Heber C. Kimball, Orson Pratt, John Taylor, and John E. Page—with Wilford Woodruff and George A. Smith, who had been appointed to fill vacancies in the Quorum of the Twelve, made their way back to Far West. There, during the early morning hours of April 26, the apostles and a small number of Latter-day Saints assembled at the temple site. Wilford Woodruff recorded the proceedings of the private meeting:

> At a Council held at Far West by the Twleve [*sic*], High Priests, Elders, & Priests on the twenty Sixth of April 1839 The following resolutions were adopted:
>
> Resolved that the following persons should be no more fellowshiped [*sic*] in the Church of Jesus Christ of Latter Day Saints but excommunicated from the Same. . . . [Woodruff lists the names of thirty men and women who had apostatized from the Church and were cut off by the Twelve].
>
> The Council then proceded [*sic*] to the building spot of the Lords house when the following business was transacted: Part of a Hymn was sung on the mission of the Twelve. Elder [Alpheus] Cutler the Master workman of the house then recommenced laying the foundation of the LORD'S house agreeable to revelation by rooling [rolling] up a large stone near the South east corner.
>
> The following of the Twelve were present: Brigham Young, Heber C. Kimble [*sic*], Orson Pratt, John E. Page, & John Taylor, who proceded [*sic*] to ordain (on the chief corner stone of the building) Willford [*sic*] Woodruff & George A. Smith, (who had been previously nominated by the first Presidency, accepted by the Twelve, & acknowledged by the Church,) to the office of the Twelve to fill the place of those who had fallen. Darwin Chase & Norman Shearer (who had Just been liberated from Richmond prison whare [*sic*] they had been confined for the cause of Jesus Christ) were then Ordained to the office of the Seventies.
>
> The Twelve then offered up vocal Prayer in the following order: Brigham Young, Heber C Kimble, Orson Pratt, John E. Page, John Taylor, Willford Woodruff & George A. Smith, after which we Sung Adamondi ahmon [Adam-ondi-Ahman] & then the Twelve took (the parting hand) their leave of the following Saints agreeable to revelation. . . . [Woodruff lists the names of eighteen other Latter-day Saints who were present along present along with the seven members of the Twelve.]
>
> Elder Alpheus Cutler then placed the stone before alluded to in its regular position after which in consequence of the peculiar situation of the Saints he thought it wisdom to adjourn untill [*sic*] some future time when the Lord should open the way expressing his determination then to procede [*sic*] with the building.[25]

The meeting over, the Twelve and other Latter-day Saints made a hasty departure out of the state, most arriving back at Quincy the first part of May.

John and Jacob D. Whitmer, Caretakers of the Temple Property

Following the departure of the Latter-day Saints from northern Missouri, new settlers were eager to occupy the farms and property vacated by the Mormons in Caldwell County. However, one former Latter-day Saint chose to return to the Far West area—John Whitmer. Whitmer had been formally excommunicated by the Missouri high council in March 1838. The following month, David and Jacob Whitmer were excommunicated, as was Oliver Cowdery, a brother-in-law. In June, the entire Whitmer clan (including parents, brothers, sisters, in-laws, and their families) left Far West and relocated in Ray County.

As mentioned earlier, W. W. Phelps and John Whitmer arranged for the original 640-acre purchase of the Far West plat by the Church in 1836. So when the Mormons abandoned Far West and left Missouri under Boggs's removal order, Whitmer must have felt it was partially his right to stake his claim to the vacated land. By May 1839, Whitmer had moved his family back to Far West, establishing their family residence one-half mile east of the center section of Far West. He later purchased several hundred acres of land in the area, including the northeast quadrant of the public square, which included the temple excavation.[26] Whitmer lived the rest of his life—nearly forty years—on his Far West property. He must have considered the temple site sacred ground, for he never plowed or cultivated the site but left it as fallow pasture, and he never removed the four cornerstones.[27] Eventually, due to the effects of grazing, erosion, and plant growth, the excavation became nothing more than a large sunken depression.

Wilford Woodruff (age eighty-five), Sainsbury and Johnson Photograph Studio, 1892. Woodruff was ordained a Mormon apostle on the southeast cornerstone of the Far West Temple on April 26, 1839. He became president of The Church of Jesus Christ of Latter-day Saints in 1887. Photograph courtesy of the LDS Church History Library.

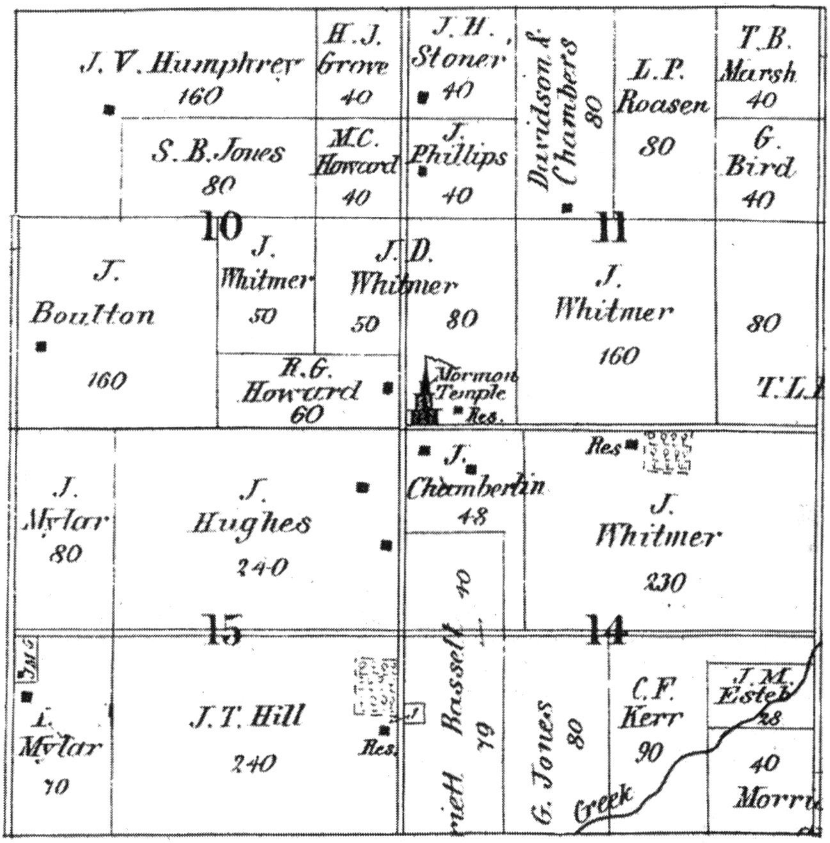

A portion of the Mirabile Township plat map, from *An Illustrated Historical Atlas of Caldwell County* (1876), 37. Note the drawing of the figure identified as the "Mormon Temple" in the southwest corner of section 11.

John Whitmer retained ownership of the temple site property until October 29, 1874, when he sold approximately 130 acres to his son Jacob D. Whitmer for one thousand dollars, included the temple site property.[28] *An Illustrated Historical Atlas of Caldwell County,* printed in 1876, shows Jacob's property holdings, including the section with the temple site. It also includes a small drawing that depicts a church structure, labeled "Mormon Temple," despite the fact that the edifice was never built.[29]

During the nineteenth and early twentieth centuries, LDS Church leaders, members, and missionaries crisscrossing the country often made an effort to visit Mormon-related sites in New England, New York, Pennsylvania, Ohio,

Missouri, Illinois, and elsewhere. This was especially the case with Missouri, primarily because of its central geographic position in the United States and because it was a main transportation thoroughfare. For example, on September 9, 1878, two LDS apostles from Salt Lake City—Orson Pratt and Joseph F. Smith—visited Far West. The two Mormon leaders, on a short-term mission to the East, had just come from Independence, Missouri, where they had visited William E. McLellin, a former apostle, and Richmond, where they interviewed David Whitmer, one of the three witnesses to the Book of Mormon. Had they come to Far West two months earlier, they could have met with John Whitmer, who had passed away in July. During the 1830s, John Whitmer was the Church historian, and at the time of this visit, Orson Pratt was the current LDS Church historian. It appears that one of Pratt and Smith's purposes in coming to Far West was to see if they might be able to secure any historical documents from the Whitmer family.

It had been thirty-nine years since the aging Pratt (nearly sixty-seven) had left Far West in April 1839 with the other members of the Twelve to commence their mission to Great Britain. The younger Joseph F. Smith (age thirty-nine) was born in Far West on November 13, 1838, two weeks after his father, Hyrum Smith, had been taken into custody by the Missouri authorities. He was particularly interested to see the place where he was born. When Pratt and Smith arrived at Far West, they went to Jacob D. Whitmer's home, where they received a cool reception. When they asked Jacob if he would take them around the old town to point out some of the early Mormon places of interest, he refused. And when asked if the family had any important documents, he told them his father had sent them to Richmond years earlier. However, before making their departure from the community, Elders Pratt and Smith viewed the Far West temple lot, where they saw the cornerstones still in place.[30]

In September 1888, ten years after Pratt and Smith's visit, Jacob D. Whitmer was visited by another set of LDS representatives from Salt Lake City—assistant church historian Andrew Jenson, Joseph S. Black, and Edward Stevenson—who were in the Midwest on a fact-finding mission for the Church. On this occasion, Whitmer treated the visitors more hospitably and provided them with lunch. In the course of their conversation, he offered to sell his Far West property to the Utah Church for fifty dollars per acre. Although Jenson, Black, and Stevenson were in no position to negotiate in behalf of the LDS First Presidency, it is significant that Whitmer was willing to make an offer. Significantly, twenty years later, the Church and Whitmer would strike a deal.[31]

Before leaving, the three men went to the temple site, where they observed that the lot was enclosed with a wire fence and that a fifty-foot tree had grown out of the excavation. They proceeded to the southeast cornerstone, knelt down, and entered into the following agreement:

> Temple Grounds, Far West, Caldwell County, Mo.
> Sept. 15, 1888.
> We agree that we will not cease our exertions until the work of the Lord is commenced that has been predicted by the Prophet Joseph Smith to take in this land in the latter days.
> Signed on the S. E. Cornerstone of the contemplated Temple, Far West, Caldwell County, Missouri.[32]

Finally, the visit by Springville, Utah, photographer George Edward Anderson to Far West is worth recounting. In 1907, while en route from Utah to England on a mission, Anderson visited scores of early Mormon historic sites, taking photographs and notes of each locality. Anderson spent part of three days, May 15-17, in Far West, where, like previous Mormon visitors, he was entertained by Jacob D. Whitmer. Anderson used the occasion to take two photographs of the temple site—one a view from the southest looking to the northwest, and the other a view from the northwest looking to the southeast. In these excellent images, one can clearly see the outline of the excavation, which as mentioned appears as a bowl-like depression. In one view, the southeast cornerstone is visible. A third photograph is believed to be Joseph and Emma Smith's Far West home site. The view is from the southwest looking to the northeast, and the temple site appears several hundred yards away in the background. The photographs provide a significant visual record of the property near the turn of the century.[33]

Reacquisition of the Temple Site by the LDS Church

During the first decade of the nineteenth century, the LDS Church purchased five properties of significant historical interest: (1) the Carthage Jail in Carthage, Illinois, where Joseph Smith and his brother Hyrum were killed (1903); (2) twenty-six acres in Independence, Missouri, part of which included the original 1831 temple site property (1904); (3) the Solomon Mack farm in Sharon/Royalton, Vermont, where Joseph Smith was born (1905); (4) the original Joseph Smith Sr. farm in Manchester, New York (1907); and (5) an eighty-acre parcel in Far West that included the original 1837 temple excavation (1909). Joseph F. Smith, sixth president of the Church, played the key role in the acquisition of these sites and properties.

What motivated President Smith to purchase the Far West temple property, particularly since the site could hardly have served any practical purpose

Photograph of the Far West temple site by Utah photographer George Edward Anderson, May 16, 1907. Photograph courtesy of the LDS Church History Library.

to the Church given its isolated location? First, as noted, Smith was born in Far West, so he would have had some personal interest in the community. Perhaps his visit to Far West in 1878 profoundly affected him and generated strong feelings of attachment and belonging. Second, he deeply revered his uncle Joseph Smith and his father, Hyrum, and believed these historical sites, including Far West, to be sacred to their lives and memory. Third, and perhaps most important, President Smith believed that the Far West temple site was still of vital interest to the Church and that acquiring it was part of the larger objective of reestablishing the Church in Missouri. From 1900 to 1907 several significant developments showed that the Church intended to establish a greater physical presence in the area. These included (1) moving the Southwestern States Mission headquarters from St. Johns, Kansas, to Kansas City, Missouri (1900); (2) purchasing part of the original Independence temple site property and renaming the mission the Central States Mission (1904); and (3) purchasing eighty-two acres from Jacob and Celia Whitmer, a parcel that included the Far West temple site.[34] (Later land records show that the actual property consisted of 76.7 acres.)[35] Samuel O. Bennion, president of the Central States Mission, likely acted as the agent in behalf of the Church. Because the land was essentially an uncultivated field, it required little effort to maintain it in any kind of a stable condition. Any upkeep or maintenance was done by missionaries or local members. It is noteworthy that although the property was considered sacred to the Church, for the next sixty years no measures were taken to physically enhance the site.

Temple Site Development

The Far West temple site remained unimproved until the mid-1960s, when the first steps were undertaken to convert the property into an official Church historical site. This occurred in large part thanks to Alvin R. Dyer, who served as president of the Central States Mission from 1954 to 1958. During his time as mission president, he became intensely interested in understanding and researching the early history of the Church in Missouri.[36] A few months after his release from his mission, he was called as an Assistant to the Quorum of the Twelve (and later called as an additional counselor in the First Presidency). As an LDS general authority, he exercised his influence for approval to develop three Church-owned historic properties in Missouri—the Liberty Jail LDS Visitors' Center (1963), the Far West temple site (1968), and the Independence LDS Visitors' Center (1971).

To gain the support needed to develop the Far West temple property, Dyer personally escorted the two leading LDS Church officials to Missouri—ninety-two-year-old Church president David O. McKay, and eighty-nine-year-old

Jacob D. (J. D.) Whitmer, son of John Whitmer, ca. 1895. Whitmer sold the original Far West temple site property to the Church of Jesus Christ of Latter-day Saints in 1909. Photograph courtesy of Lorene E. Pollard.

Joseph Fielding Smith, president of the Quorum of the Twelve. During their two-day visit (June 1-2, 1966), McKay, Smith, and Dyer visited Independence, Liberty Jail, Adam-ondi-Ahman (the site of an early Mormon settlement in Daviess County, Missouri), and Far West. At Far West, Dyer recounted some of the history associated with the community and the temple site and some of the significant events that transpired there, hopeful that President McKay would recognize the need to improve the property. Dyer's efforts paid off. Immediately following the visit, President McKay approved the appropriation of Church funds to improve the Far West temple site property.[37]

Emil B. Fetzer, LDS Church architect, designed the changes and improvements. On-site construction was not extensive. The ground was contoured and leveled, which unfortunately necessitated the removal of the four cornerstones. In resetting them, the stones were cast in concrete to be permanently fixed, but proper attention was not taken to ensure that they were placed back in precisely the original positions. Today, the distance between the stones is 118 feet by 81 feet, not 110 feet by 80 feet, the dimensions of the original building. Near each cornerstone is a plaque containing a description of the Melchizedek or Aaronic priesthood office (or offices) each cornerstone represents. The most prominent feature is a three-panel monument bearing inscriptions that describe the significance of the Far West in LDS Church history. Trees, shrubs, and grass were planted, a parking lot was constructed, and an attractive iron fence was installed to enclose the entire site (including the parking area). Professional contractors were hired to do much of the work, but missionaries and local members contributed time and labor to the project.

A significant contingent of LDS Church authorities and their wives traveled from Salt Lake City to be present at the August 3, 1968, dedication of the redesigned and landscaped Far West temple site property. Church dignitaries included Joseph Fielding Smith (president of the Quorum of the Twelve and an additional counselor in the First Presidency), Alvin R. Dyer (additional counselor in the First Presidency), Harold B. Lee and Mark E. Petersen (members of the Quorum of the Twelve), James A. Cullimore (Assistant to the Quorum of the Twelve), and Victor L. Brown (counselor in the Presiding Bishopric). President Dyer conducted the services and offered the dedicatory prayer. Approximately six hundred Latter-day Saints were in attendance.[38]

To further secure its Far West temple property, in 1974, 1975, and 1978, the LDS Church made additional land purchases to the southwest, west, and southeast of the temple site, bringing the total amount of acreage owned by the Church to just over 582 acres.[39] It is likely that the Church will make additional purchases in the future if land becomes available.

The Far West temple site before the LDS Church made improvements to the property, ca. 1965. Photograph courtesy of LaMar C. Berrett.

Since 1968, very few changes have been made to the temple site enclosure. However, a few physical facilities have been made to the property. Restroom facilities have been built, picnic areas created, and some additional signage placed to accommodate visitors. A concrete turnabout was added so that tour buses could more easily turn around. Finally, to guard against vandalism, tempered glass casings were placed over the four cornerstones and lighting added.

Conclusion

Latter-day Saints have a deep sense of connection with their historical past, particularly the era associated with Mormonism's founder, Joseph Smith (1805–1844). This sense stems from the fact that so much of the doctrine and faith tradition of the Church is also associated with its history. This is certainly the case with Far West. Although little remains of the original community, Far West will always remain an important place in the minds and hearts of the Latter-day Saints.

LDS General Authorities at the dedication of the Far West temple site property, August 3, 1968. Seated, l-r: Jessie Evans Smith (wife of Joseph Fielding Smith), Joseph Fielding Smith (president of the Quorum of the Twelve and an additional counselor in the First Presidency), May Dyer (wife of Alvin R. Dyer), Alvin R. Dyer (additional counselor in the First Presidency), and Harold B. Lee (Quorum of the Twelve). Seated behind Dyer is James A. Cullimore (Assistant to the Twelve). Seated behind Harold B. Lee is Mark E. Petersen (Quorum of the Twelve). Photograph courtesy of John R. Garvin.

In the motion picture *Field of Dreams,* the most famous phrase is "If we built it, they will come." The same could be said of the LDS Far West temple site. Although it is situated in a relatively isolated location, since 1968 thousands upon thousands have come to the site. And over the years the numbers have increased. The LDS Church has shown no indication that an actual temple will be built at Far West, neither in the near or distant future, although the possibility has not been ruled out. In the meantime, the Far West temple site will probably remain very much the same as it is today, a visible physical reminder of the Missouri period of Mormonism.

LDS Monument at the Far West, Missouri, LDS temple site, 2000. Photograph courtesy of Alexander L. Baugh.

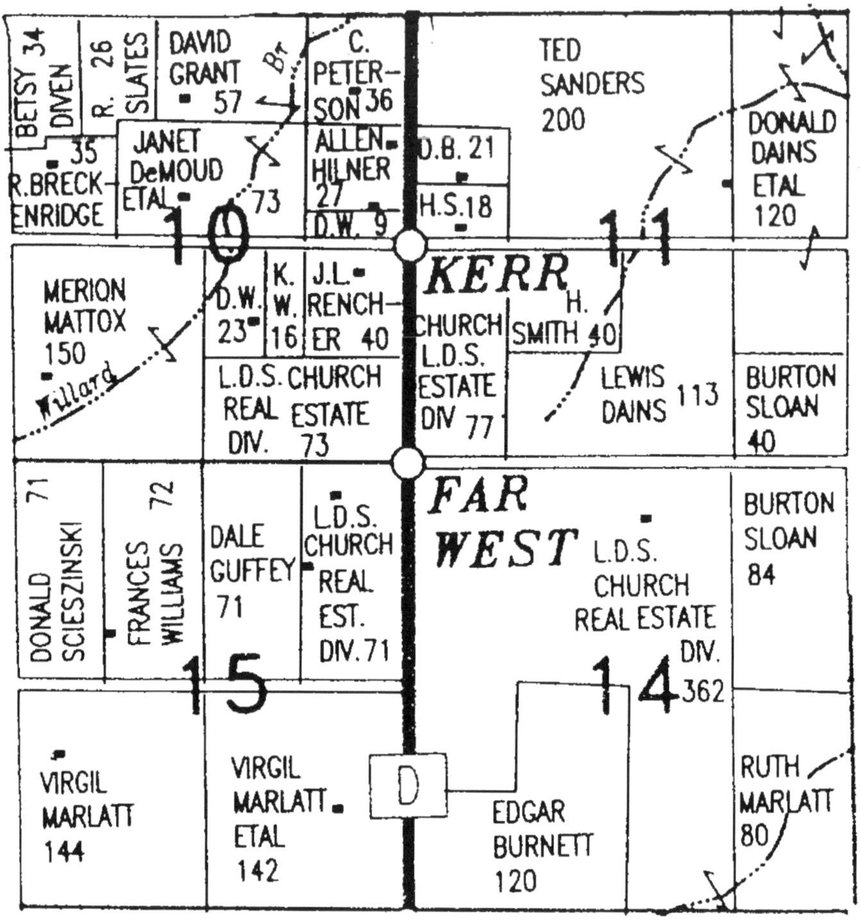

Portion of a 1995 plat map of Mirabile Township showing the property holdings of the Church of Jesus Christ Latter-day Saints around Far West. The original temple site is located in the southwest corner of section 11. The LDS Church owns all of the property surrounding the temple site, with the exception of a small parcel in the northeast corner of section 15 owned by the Community of Christ (formerly RLDS).

Notes

1. The most complete examination of the Mormon experience in Jackson County, Missouri, from 1831 to 1833 is Warren Abner Jennings, "Zion Is Fled: The Expulsion of the Mormons from Jackson County, Missouri" (PhD diss., University of Florida, 1962); see also Jennings, "The Expulsion of the Mormons from Jackson County," *Missouri Historical Review* 64 (October 1969): 41–63.

2. See "Minutes of a Public Meeting at Liberty," in Joseph Smith Jr., *History of The Church of Jesus Christ of Latter-day Saints,* ed. B. H. Roberts, 2nd rev. ed., 7 vols. (Salt Lake City: Deseret, 1971), 2: 481 (hereafter cited as *History of the Church*). See also Max H. Parkin, "Latter-day Saint Conflict in Clay County," in Arnold K. Garr and Clark V. Johnson, eds., *Regional Studies in Latter-day Saint Church History: Missouri* (Provo, Utah: Department of Church History and Doctrine, Brigham Young University, 1994), 254–58.

3. *History of Caldwell and Livingston Counties, Missouri* (St. Louis: National Historical Company, 1886), 120. For a historical overview of the Far West settlement, see Clark V. Johnson, "Let Far West Be Holy and Consecrated," in Larry C. Porter and Susan Easton Black, eds., *The Prophet Joseph: Essays on the Life and Mission of Joseph Smith* (Salt Lake City: Deseret, 1988), 226–45.

4. *History of Caldwell and Livingston Counties, Missouri,* 103–5; see also *Laws of the State of Missouri, 1st Session, 9th General Assembly, 1836–1837* (Jefferson City, Mo.: Jeffersonian Office, 1837), 46–47, 155, 188, 204.

5. An early published history of the county states, "At the time of the Mormon War [1838] the population of Far West was about 2,500, and it was the largest town in the state, north of the Missouri River" (*An Illustrated Historical Atlas of Caldwell County, Missouri* [Philadelphia: Edwards Brothers of Missouri, 1876], 5). At the same time, the total population of Caldwell County was estimated to be around five thousand. See *History of Caldwell and Livingston Counties, Missouri,* 118.

6. According to the *History of Caldwell and Livingston Counties, Missouri,* a schoolhouse was constructed by the Mormons in the southwest quarter of the town that was later moved to the public square in the town center and served as a school, church, town hall, and the county's first courthouse (121). However, there is some evidence to suggest that the schoolhouse situated in the southwest part of town was not moved, and that a frame schoolhouse was constructed on the public square. Significantly, even after the Mormon exodus in 1839, Far West remained the county seat. "Far West continued to be the County Seat until 1842. But Far West was within a few miles of the western boundary of the County, which rendered it less accessible to the citizens of the eastern part than was desirable. So a law was passed in 1842, directing a change of [the] County Seat to a more central point. . . . The commissioners then selected the site of Kingston, which was so named after Austin A. King, then judge of our circuit court. In 1843, all the public offices and records were transferred from Far West to the new town" (*An Illustrated Historical Atlas of Caldwell County, Missouri,* 7, 9).

7. Joseph Smith left Kirtland, Ohio, on January 12, 1838, and arrived at Far West on March 14, where he took up permanent residence, thereby marking Far West as the Church's new headquarters. See *History of the Church,* 3:1, 8–9. Joseph Smith's arrest and incarceration in Liberty Jail during the winter of 1838–1839 left the leadership responsibilities of the Church upon Brigham Young and the Quorum of the Twelve Apostles. Young's departure from Far West for Quincy, Illinois, on February 14, 1839, brought an end to Far West as the Mormon "capital." See *History of the Church,* 3:261.

8. See Donald Q. Cannon and Lyndon W. Cook, *Far West Record: Minutes of the Church of Jesus Christ of Latter-day Saints, 1830–1844* (Salt Lake City: Deseret Book, 1983), 103–4; see also *History of the Church,* 2: 481. In 1838, Thomas B. Marsh accused the Missouri presidency (David Whitmer, W. W. Phelps, and John Whitmer) of impropriety because they "selected the place for the city of Far West, and appointed the spot for the house of the Lord to be build on, drew the plan of said house, and appointed and ordained a committee to build the same, without asking or seeking counsel at the hand of either [the] Bishop, High Council, or first Presidency; when it was well understood that these authorities were appointed for the purpose of counseling on all important matters pertaining to the Saints of God" (Thomas B. Marsh to Wilford Woodruff, *Elders' Journal* 1, no. 3 [July 1838]: 37). It appears they did fail to seek authorization, at least initially. At a *Far West Record* meeting of the Missouri high council on April 3, these accusations were brought against W. W. Phelps and John Whitmer (David Whitmer's name was not mentioned). See Cannon and Cook, *Far West Record,* 107–8. However, as noted, during a meeting held four days later on April 7, the Missouri presidency did indeed receive authorization from the bishopric and high council to move ahead with plans for the temple.

9. William W. Phelps letter, July 7, 1837, in *Latter Day Saints' Messenger and Advocate* 3, no. 10 (July 1837): 529; also in *History of the Church,* 2: 496. According to William F. Switzler, a nineteenth-century Missouri historian, five hundred Mormon men and boys dug the four- to five-foot foundation in less than a day. See William F. Switzler, *Switzler's Illustrated History of Missouri* (St. Louis: C. R. Barns, 1879), 243.

10. See John Wyckliffe Rigdon, "The Life and Testimony of Sidney Rigdon," in Karl Keller, ed., "'I Never Knew a Time When I Did Not Know Joseph Smith': A Son's Record of the Life and Testimony of Sidney Rigdon," *Dialogue: A Journal of Mormon Thought* 1 (Winter 1966): 31.

11. *History of the Church,* 2: 521.

12. Ibid., 3: 8–9.

13. Joseph Smith, Journal (Scriptory Book), April 26, 1838, 33–34, LDS Church History Library, Family and Church History Department, The Church of Jesus Christ of Latter-day Saints, Salt Lake City, Utah; also in Dean C. Jessee, ed., *The Papers of Joseph Smith,* 2 vols. (Salt Lake City: Deseret, 1989–1992), 2: 232–33. The passage is now canonized as Doctrine and Covenants, 115: 7–16.

14. Joseph H. McGee, "History of Daviess County: Incidents and Reminiscences in its Early Settlement, Etc., &c," *North Missourian* (Gallatin, Mo.), March 4, 1888, n.p. Owen's estimate is probably too high, but it indicates that hundreds, perhaps even a few thousand, were present and that even non-Latter-day Saints were in attendance.

15. "Celebration of the 4th of July," *Elders' Journal* 1, no. 4 (August 1838): 60; see also *History of the Church,* 3: 41–42.

16. Elijah Averett wrote, "Elisha Averett, my brother, Demick [*sic*] Huntington and Cornelius Lot[t] quarried the rock for the temple, Elisha being the chief mason laying the foundation that day" (Elijah Averett, A History of Elijah Averett, typescript, 1, L. Tom Perry Special Collections, Harold B. Lee Library, Brigham Young University, Provo, Utah; hereafter cited as Perry Special Collections).

17. Joseph Holbrook, Autobiography of Joseph Holbrook, 39, Perry Special Collections. Holbrook helped haul the cornerstones from the quarry to the temple excavation.

18. "Celebration of the 4th of July," 60. Some of the leaders involved in the cornerstone dedications can be identified. As indicated, the southeast cornerstone was dedicated by the "Presidents of the stake," or who would have been the Missouri pres-

idency. At the time of the July 4 activities, the Missouri stake presidency consisted of Thomas B. Marsh, David W. Patten, and Brigham Young, the three senior members of the Twelve. On April 6, 1838, Marsh, Patten, and Young replaced David Whitmer, W. W. Phelps, and John Whitmer as the presidency of the Missouri stake. See Cannon and Cook, *Far West Record,* 158. The northwest cornerstone would have been dedicated by Edward Partridge, the bishop in Missouri. The "presidents of the elders [quorums]" and the "president of the teachers [quorum]" who dedicated the southwest and northeast cornerstones could not be precisely identified.

19. See Mosiah L. Hancock, Autobiography, typescript, 5–8, Perry Special Collections. In his autobiography, Mosiah recalls that his father Levi Hancock sang the song, and that his uncle Solomon Hancock "helped father sing the song." However, the *Elders' Journal* newspaper report of the dedication published in August, just a month after the event, clearly states that Solomon sang a solo. See "Celebration of the 4th of July," 60. Mosiah was only fourteen at the time and probably confused the facts.

20. Sidney Rigdon, *Oration Delivered by Mr. S. Rigdon, on the 4th of July, 1838, at Far West, Caldwell County, Missouri* (Far West, Mo.: Journal Office, 1838), 12. The entire document has subsequently been published in Peter Crawley, "Two Rare Missouri Documents," *BYU Studies* 14, no. 4 (Summer 1974): 517–27.

21. It is not known if this was the exact phrase used on the occasion, but it would have been something similar. In more recent times when the shout was performed, the congregation exclaimed, "Hosanna, Hosanna, Hosanna, to God and the Lamb," repeated three times, followed by "Amen, Amen, and Amen," at the same time waving white handkerchiefs in the air. It does not appear at the time of the dedication at Far West that the Mormons waved handkerchiefs. For an explanation of the history of the hosanna shout in LDS Church history, see Jacob W. Olmstead, "From Pentecost to Administration: A Reappraisal of the History of the Hosanna Shout," *Mormon Historical Studies* 2, no. 2 (Fall 2001): 7–37. Parley P. Pratt briefly mentions the hosanna shout being performed at the dedication of the Far West temple cornerstone. See Parley P. Pratt, *Autobiography of Parley P. Pratt* (Salt Lake City: Deseret Book, 1985), 149–50.

22. "Celebration of the 4th of July," *Elders' Journal* 1, no. 4 (August 1838): 60; also *History of the Church,* 3: 42. One other activity was done in conjunction with the Far West temple site dedication, namely the erection of a liberty pole, or flag pole, adjacent to the excavation. This was not done as part of the official dedicatory services, however. Luman Shurtliff was one of several individuals who participated and recorded the following:

"On the 3rd of July [1838], I, with several others of my company, went into the timber of Goose Creek, got the largest tree we could and made a liberty pole, and on the 4th of July, 1838, the brethren and their families assembled in Far West to celebrate the day and to lay the cornerstone of our temple in the city of Far West.

"Early in the morning we raised the pole, raised the Stars and Stripes and then laid the cornerstone of our temple. We then assembled under the flag of our nation and had an oration delivered by Sidney Rigdon. This orator became quite excited and proclaimed loudly our freedom and liberty in Missouri. Although Sidney was a great orator and one of the leading brethren, his oration brought sorrow and gloom over my mind, and spoiled my further enjoyment of the day.

"After the services, the multitude dispersed. This was on Saturday. On Sunday a cloud came over Far West, charged with electricity, and lightning fell upon our liberty pole and shivered it to the ground. When the news reached me, I involuntarily proclaimed, 'Farewell to our liberty in Missouri.'" Luman A. Shurtliff, Biographical Sketch of the Life of Luman Andros Shurtliff, typescript, 33, Perry Special Collections.

23. Smith, Journal (Scriptory Book), April 26, 1838; also in Jessee, *Papers of Joseph Smith,* 2: 232; and *History of the Church,* 3: 45. The passage is now canonized as Doctrine and Covenants 115: 8–11.

24. Smith, Journal (Scriptory Book), July 8, 1838, also in Jessee, *Papers of Joseph Smith,* 2: 257; and *History of the Church,* 3: 46–47. The passage is now canonized as Doctrine and Covenants 118: 4–5.

25. Wilford Woodruff, *Wilford Woodruff's Journal, 1833–1898, Typescript,* ed. Scott G. Kenney, ed., 9 vols. (Midvale, Utah: Signature Books, 1983–1984), 1: 326–27.

26. Former Missouri presidency member William W. Phelps was excommunicated from the Church and remained for a time in Far West after the Mormons evacuated. On May 1, 1839, he wrote a letter from Far West to his wife, Sally, who was in St. Louis, probably making preparations to move to Dayton, Ohio, where her immediate family resided. In the letter, William mentions John Whitmer's return to Far West: "John Whitmer is enlarging his buildings—has bought and removed Henry Woods house just before his south door, for a kitchen. He seems to be preparing to stick in Far West a while" (William W. Phelps to Sally W. Phelps, May 1, 1839, LDS Church History Library). For an explanation and historical analysis of the letter, see Alexander L. Baugh, "A Community Abandoned: W. W. Phelps' 1839 Letter to Sally Waterman Phelps from Far West, Missouri," *Nauvoo Journal* 10, no. 2 (Fall 1998): 19–32.

27. J. M. Terry, "A Glimpse of Far West," *Zion's Ensign* 8, no. 42 (October 14, 1897): 3; also published in the *Missouri Mormon Frontier Foundation Newsletter,* no. 12 (Winter 1997): 3.

28. Caldwell County, Missouri, property records, book 49, 131, Kingston, Missouri. Jacob David Jefferson Whitmer (May 26, 1844–December 21, 1921) lived his entire life in Far West. A short biography of him appeared in the *History of Caldwell and Livingston Counties, Missouri* (St. Louis: National Historical Company, 1886), 340.

29. See plat drawing of Mirable Township in *An Illustrated Historical Atlas of Caldwell County, Missouri,* 37. The atlas shows Jacob D. Whitmer owning a total of 180 acres. It is interesting to note that later atlases also include a depiction of the "unconstructed" Mormon Temple on the Mirable Township plats. See William P. Bullock, *Atlas of Caldwell County, Missouri* (St. Joseph, Mo.: Press of Lon. Hardman, 1897), 12; and W. H. Sheridan McGlumphy, *Atlas of Caldwell County, Missouri* (Hamilton, Mo.: Filson Publishing, 1907), 15.

30. "Report of Elders Orson Pratt and Joseph F. Smith," *Latter-day Saints' Millennial Star* 50, no. 40 (December 16, 1878): 785–86. See also Joseph Fielding Smith, *The Life of Joseph F. Smith, Sixth President of the Church of Jesus Christ of Latter-day Saints* (Salt Lake City: Deseret News Press, 1938), 259–50; and Breck England, *The Life and Thought of Orson Pratt* (Salt Lake City: University of Utah Press, 1985), 270.

31. Andrew Jenson, *Autobiography of Andrew Jenson, Assistant Historian of the Church of Jesus Christ of Latter-day Saints* (Salt Lake City: Deseret News Press, 1938), 158–59.

32. Joseph Smith Black, "The Journal of Joseph Smith Black," in Kate B. Carter, comp., *Our Pioneer Heritage,* 20 vols. (Salt Lake City: Daughters of the Utah Pioneers, 1958–77), 10: 290.

33. See Richard Neitzel Holzapfel, T. Jeffrey Cottle, and Ted D. Stoddard, *Church History in Black and White: George Edward Anderson's Photograph Mission to Latter-day Saint Historical Sites* (Provo, Utah: Religious Studies Center, Brigham Young University, 1995), 80–84.

34. Caldwell County, Missouri, property records, book 70, 103, Kingston, Missouri. The parcel was in Section 11, Township 56, Range 29 and cost seven thousand dollars. Although the transaction was recorded on April 2, 1909, the actual sale did not take place until May 31, 1909, nearly two months later.

35. Caldwell County, Missouri, property records, book 134, 522–23, Kingston, Missouri.

36. In 1960, Dyer published *The Refiner's Fire: Historical Highlights of Missouri* (Salt Lake City: Deseret, 1960). The book was republished in 1968 and 1972 under the title *The Refiner's Fire: The Significance of Events Transpiring in Missouri.*

37. Alvin R. Dyer, Journal Record of the Visit of President David O. McKay to Adam-ondi-Ahman, typescript, 1–30, LDS Church Archives. The account of the visit to Far West is recorded on pp. 15–28. See also Joseph Fielding Smith and John J. Stewart, *The Life of Joseph Fielding Smith, Tenth President of the Church of Jesus Christ of Latter-day Saints* (Salt Lake City: Deseret, 1972), 335–41.

38. See "Center Stake of Zion," *Church News* (Salt Lake City, Utah), August 10, 1968, 6–7, 10. That day, the same Church officials broke ground in Independence, Missouri, for the Independence Visitors' Center. The August 3 date was chosen for the Far West dedicatory services and the Independence groundbreaking because the date also marked the 137th anniversary of the dedication of the Independence temple site by Joseph Smith on August 3, 1831.

39. See Caldwell County, Missouri, property records, book 151, 82, 545, 629.

6

"Was This Really Missouri Civilization?"

The Haun's Mill Massacre in Missouri and Mormon History

Thomas M. Spencer

The three-month-long "Mormon War" in northwest Missouri during 1838 has been viewed by Mormons and scholars of Mormonism as a trying time in the history of the LDS church. As Alexander Baugh, the eminent scholar of the Missouri period of LDS history, put it, "For a period of three agonizing, painful, and eventful months, this disproportionate religious minority defended their rights, liberties, and property, against an overwhelming intolerant majority."[1] One of the pivotal events in the Mormon War was the Haun's Mill Massacre, the killing of seventeen Mormon settlers by the Livingston County militia at Jacob Haun's mill on October 30, 1838. The Haun's Mill Massacre is viewed as a seminal event by many Mormons today, who still speak with outrage and contempt for the acts of those Missourians nearly 170 years ago. The event and its aftermath have become a major part of Mormon history and culture.

Some scholars of Mormonism contend that the massacre convinced Joseph Smith to surrender at Far West two days later and agree that the Mormons would leave Missouri. Other scholars have maintained that the massacre led to a greater militancy later on the part of Smith and the Mormons, culminating in the forming of the Nauvoo Legion in the 1840s, an imposing military force that was half the size of the U.S. Army at the time. At the very least, this tragic event confirmed the worst fears Mormons had about frontier Missourians.

While some early accounts by local historians were relatively accurate, Missouri history scholars over the past fifty years have seemingly tried their best to forget the Haun's Mill Massacre even took place. In the most frequently used textbook for the Missouri history course in colleges across the state, *Missouri: The Heart of the Nation,* authors William E. Parrish, Charles T. Jones Jr., and Lawrence O. Christensen do not mention the massacre in their three-page treatment of the 1838 Mormon War—and the same brief account appears in all three editions of the book published between 1980 and 2004. Nor is the massacre mentioned in the University of Missouri Press's History of Missouri Series by Perry McCandless. The massacre merits only three sentences in Duane Meyer's 830-page magnum opus, *The Heritage of Missouri,* a book that devotes more than two pages of space each to such topics as the Missouri mule and famous professional and amateur sports teams of the nineteenth century.[2] Missouri's academic historians are not interested in recounting the events at Haun's Mill or pondering their significance. Worse than this sin of omission is that some Missouri history scholars have gone so far as to blame the victims themselves for the events of the Mormon War. Focusing on the July 4 sermon of Sidney Rigdon, they argue that the words and actions of the Mormon leaders were to blame for the events that followed.

This essay will recount the events of the Haun's Mill Massacre and its aftermath as well as focus on how the event has been interpreted by Mormons and Missourians. Ultimately, the Haun's Mill Massacre has several important causes. First, both sides in the conflict viewed violence as a proper regulatory response to remove people they considered dangerous members of society. Second, both Missourians and Mormons took aggressive actions that served to escalate tension during the fall of 1838, ultimately contributing to the outbreak of violence. Finally, Mormon historians have always argued that Missourians' land hunger was the primary cause of the massacre. Using a recently indexed original plat map of Daviess County, this study finds evidence to support these claims as a cause of the Haun's Mill Massacre.

The Haun's Mill Massacre took place on October 30, 1838, when a group of soldiers from the Livingston County militia attacked a group of Mormon settlers at a small settlement called Haun's Mill on the banks of Shoal Creek in southeastern Caldwell County, sixteen miles east of the main Mormon settlement at Far West and only four miles west of the Livingston County line. The Haun's Mill settlement never included more than ten to fifteen families. Local settlers referred to the area, which included two mills, one owned by Jacob Haun and the other by Robert White, as "the mills." By the time of the Mormon War, White had become an apostate Mormon. White had by October left the area and moved to Livingston County, and he apparently participated in the massacre, helping the Livingston County militia to kill his former neighbors.[3]

The settlers at Haun's Mill had been harassed by non-Mormons for several weeks. A group of regulators from Livingston County—including several members of the Livingston County militia—had been harassing the Mormons in the area since the middle of October. These men drove the Saints' livestock away and threatened to burn down the two mills. Jacob Haun, concerned about his village's safety, eventually went to Joseph Smith asking for his counsel. Smith told Haun that his people should move to Far West. Smith said that Haun refused, saying he thought the settlers in the village could defend themselves. Smith furthermore contended that Haun misled the community into thinking it was Smith's idea that they remain there and defend the village. Later Smith would contend that "None had ever been killed who abode by my counsel; if they had not, their lives would have been spared."[4]

Many prominent Mormons have repeated this story over the past 170 years. It seems unlikely, however, that Jacob Haun, who had already moved from Wisconsin to Missouri in order to follow Joseph Smith, would refuse

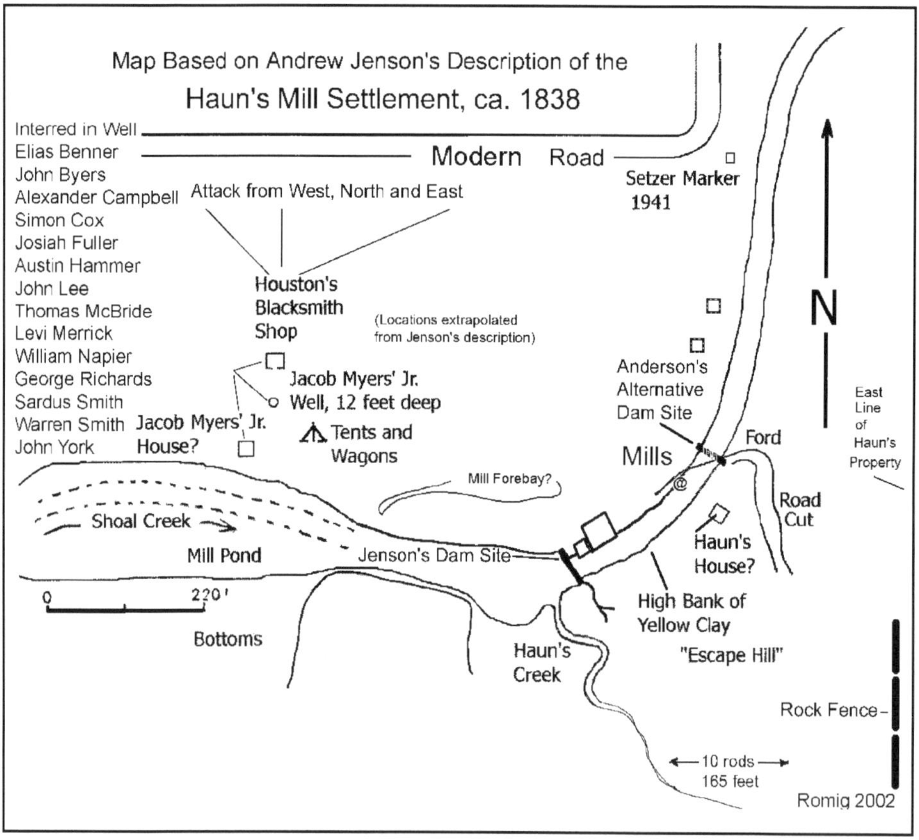

to move sixteen miles west on the direct word of the Prophet. The fact that Haun never told the people in the village of Smith's directive casts further doubt on Smith's story. By this point in November 1838, a few Mormons had already been killed in actions that had been approved by Smith. While they might not have been "counseled" by Smith directly to undertake these actions, they died while following Smith's orders, thus making his statement untrue. This statement is so transparently designed to encourage faithfulness to his dictates as to make it suspect. Smith's version of the story implies that the people at Haun's Mill were being punished by an angry God for ignoring Smith's word.

Many historians contend that the Battle of Crooked River on October 25 was the cause of both the extermination order and the Haun's Mill Massacre: when the Mormons responded with such force and attacked state troops, the governor had no choice but to react strongly. It was in response to Crooked River that the governor issued his infamous extermination order on October 27 that stated the "Mormons must be treated as enemies, and must be exterminated or driven from the State if necessary for the public peace—their outrages are beyond all description."[5] While one can find no solid evidence that the regulators—vigilantes—from Livingston County at Haun's Mill were retaliating for the Battle of Crooked River, some historians have argued that was the case.

On the day of the battle, October 30, a group of twenty men led by Nehemiah Comstock of Livingston County rode into the Haun's Mill settlement and demanded that the Mormons turn over their weapons. Most of the men in the village complied. Mormon migrants to the area were also harassed by regulators and made to turn over their weapons. The regulators entered into three separate peace negotiations with the settlers, all of which ended (the last apparently concluded within a few hours of the attack) with amicable agreements. The Mormon settlers, however, were still concerned that they were in danger and kept a small supply of arms. Alexander Baugh has concluded that this evidence points to a calculated plan to give the Saints a false sense of security so they would let their guard down. This premeditation is further evidenced in the fact that a few days before the massacre, two different groups of Mormon migrants who were intercepted on the way to Haun's Mill were told to turn around or they would be killed. The Haun's Mill Massacre was not some impulsive attack gone wrong but a meticulously planned attempt to eradicate the Mormon community there.[6]

The attack had no connection to Governor Lilburn Boggs's infamous extermination order, which was not received by the commanders in the field until the day the assault took place and was not disseminated to the troops. Thus, the attack on Haun's Mill was not in response to the extermination order. Daniel Ashby, a state senator and participant in the attack, provided a firsthand account of what Missourians called "the Battle at the Mills." Ashby claimed in a speech to his fellow senators in December 1838 that the attack took place because the soldiers involved wanted to stop the Mormon settlers from moving into Livingston County. "We thought it best to attack them first," Ashby said. "What we did was in our defense, and we had the right to do."[7] The local commanders at Haun's Mill were acting on their own authority, although a local history account claimed that "the Governor afterwards approved what was done."[8] However, there is no evidence that Boggs ever said anything about the propriety of the Haun's Mill Massacre.

Whether the people negotiating with the Mormons on the day of the attack were coordinating their efforts with those who attacked the village cannot be proven. The fact that participants in the massacre were involved in some of the earlier negotiation sessions as well as stories about the same men disarming the Mormons and turning back new migrants to the area in the days before the massacre suggests that there was a plan afoot to destroy this village and end the "Mormon threat" to Livingston County. It is possible that the negotiations on October 30 were a ruse to make the Mormons not suspect that an attack was coming.

By all accounts, most of October 30, 1838, was an idyllic day in the settlement. Two leaders in the village, David Evans and Jacob Myers, returned at around 3:30 from the aforementioned meeting with local citizens that had produced another agreement in writing between the two groups to leave each other alone. However, the Mormons did not believe these men would keep their word. About half an hour after Evans and Myers's return, those in the village who had doubted the Missourians' word were proven right.[9]

The attack on Haun's Mill began about four o'clock in the afternoon. Between two and three hundred men in three companies attacked on horseback. The commander of the attack was Thomas Jennings, and the companies were commanded by William O. Jennings, Nehemiah Comstock, and William Gee. Men were from Livingston, Daviess, Caldwell, and Carrollton counties, with the majority coming from Livingston County. The three companies approached the village from the west, north, and east. The force was largely undetected until they were within a few hundred yards of the village. At that point, the Mormons could tell the men were hostile and quickly hoisted a white flag. Once the attacking force was within one hundred yards, the men dismounted. Mormon leader David Evans waved his hat and called for quarter. Comstock ignored Evans's entreaties and fired into the air, signaling to his men that they could open fire.[10]

As the attack began, the men in the village sent nearly fifty women and children southward across a plank over the creek and into the woods. Only one woman was injured in the attack. As the group approached, Mary Stedwell raised her hands in a gesture of peace and was shot in the hand. After running across the plank, she fell down and hid behind a log. She was not further injured but that was due to good fortune. Since a part of Stedwell's clothing was visible over the top of the log, the attackers continued to shoot at her for several minutes. After the attack, the log she hid behind was examined and there were more than twenty bullets in it.[11]

Meanwhile the male settlers—including thirty-two men and three boys—went into the blacksmith shop where the weapons were stockpiled. The men were hopelessly outnumbered, and they had picked a poor place from which to mount a defense. Nathan Knight and David Evans ran out of the building to call for a cease-fire. Unable to persuade the vigilantes to stop firing, Knight and Evans ran south across the creek and into the woods. Knight was shot three times while making his escape while Evans managed to escape uninjured.

By this point, the situation in the blacksmith shop had become grave. The vigilantes closed in from the north, east, and west sides and were firing through large spaces between the logs. According to Daniel Ashby, some of the militiamen made it all the way up to the cabin and were firing through the holes in the logs at point-blank range. As it became obvious that there was no hope of defending the cabin, the men still there began one by one to try to escape by running south, crossing the creek, and seeking shelter in the woods.

Approximately nineteen men were able to escape this way, but thirteen of them were injured and three later died from their injuries. Most of the remainder were disfigured or significantly disabled for the rest of their lives. Thomas McBride, a veteran of the U.S. Army during the War of 1812, was wounded making his escape and sought shelter in a cabin near the creek. He was discovered there by the militia and surrendered his weapon to one of the militiamen, Jacob Rogers. Instead of taking him prisoner, Rogers shot him in the chest with his own gun. Rogers then mutilated McBride with a corncutter and left him in a shallow pool in Shoal Creek.

After this group escaped from the blacksmith's shop, the vigilantes stopped firing and approached the cabin. Inside, eight men were dead and four were wounded. One man and three boys were uninjured but hiding. The militiamen began to abuse some of the most severely injured men and apparently killed some.

The most shocking actions involved two boys. One boy, Charles Merrick, was shot while trying to escape and died four weeks later.[12] A second boy, Sardius Smith, pleaded for his life when he was discovered. Appallingly, one of the members of the militia, apparently William Reynolds of Livingston County, put the muzzle of his gun up to the boy's head and discharged it, killing him instantly. When asked why he shot the young boy, Reynolds replied, "Nits will make lice, and if he had lived he would have become a Mormon." Nathan K. Knight, a survivor of the massacre, claimed that attackers shouted "Kill them, damn them. Kill them. Nits Make Lice!" According to Knight, two men robbed the dead and kicked some of them, saying, "If God did not send all the Mormons to hell, they should take Jesus Christ and serve him the same way."[13] The only uninjured man in the shop, William Champlin, was taken prisoner, held for three days, and then released. After the attack, the vigilantes robbed the dead and wounded of their possessions and took everything of value they could find in the village. Only three vigilantes were wounded, the worst injury being a gunshot wound to the thigh.[14]

Ultimately seventeen Mormon men were killed in the Haun's Mill Massacre. The next day, under the direction of Joseph Young, fourteen or fifteen of those killed in the attack were buried in an unfinished well on the property. Comstock and his men returned to the scene of the crime on October 31, claiming they wished to help bury the dead. They also spread word of the just-received extermination order from the governor. Comstock and his men left after discovering that the dead had already been buried. They spent the rest of the day visiting Mormon settlements in eastern Caldwell County and gleefully telling them of the extermination order.

After the news of the massacre reached the besieged Mormons at Far West the following day, Joseph Smith realized that resistance was futile against an enemy that would perpetrate such a crime and began to seek some sort of peace settlement with the Missouri state militia surrounding him at Far West. The Haun's Mill Massacre convinced Smith that he could not win a war with the Missouri state militia. Consequently, he and the Mormons surrendered on November 1, 1838. The events of the Haun's Mill Massacre effectively ended the Mormon War in Missouri.[15]

The event tells us a great about the prevalence of violence at the time. By 1838, many Mormons—like their frontier Missouri Gentile counterparts—believed that violence was sometimes necessary. While the Mormons had responded, to use scholar D. Michael Quinn's words, with "Quaker-like pacifism," in the early 1830s to the violent actions of their enemies in New York and Ohio, and in their first few months in Jackson County, Missouri, this quickly changed. In August 1833, Joseph Smith had a revelation in which God told him that the Mormon people should endure three attacks and "bear [them] patiently." On the fourth attack, Smith told his people, "the Lord will avenge thee of thine enemy an [*sic*] hundred-fold" and vengeance may be pursued against the transgressors until the third or fourth generation.[16] The Mormons endured three separate attacks after Smith issued this revelation and began to launch counterattacks against the Missourians in Jackson County in November 1833.

In February 1834, after further atrocities in Missouri and Ohio, Smith issued another revelation in which he told the Mormon people that God had told him that they might freely take vengeance against their enemies.[17]

These events created a Mormon leadership that, in Quinn's words, "has rarely been far from a siege mentality." By the fall of 1834, Smith was choosing members of his Quorum of the Twelve Apostles and the Seventy based on their perceived military abilities. In September 1835, John Whitmer, the Church historian, recorded that the Quorum of the Twelve had appointed the church president as head of the War Department of the "Lord's Host." Quinn contends that by the time Joseph Smith arrived in Missouri in 1838, a "Culture of Violence" already existed in Mormon society. Smith and most Mormons believed that Mormonism faced a life-or-death struggle with its anti-Mormon and apostate enemies. This perception shaped Mormon society for the next several decades, creating a militaristic, standoffish, and, at times, violent society.[18]

One should keep this worldview of Mormons, forged by several years of violence and persecution at the hands of their enemies, in mind when one examines the events of the Mormon War of 1838 that led to the massacre at Haun's Mill. By the summer of 1838, Mormon settlers had been forced out of Jackson County, Missouri, and were beginning to create settlements in Caldwell and Daviess Counties, most notably Far West and Adam-ondi-Ahman. The number of Mormons in Missouri grew to perhaps as many as eight thousand by mid-summer of 1838. As their population grew, the Mormons moved out beyond Caldwell County, the county that had been set aside for them by the state legislature in December 1836. This movement into other counties frightened frontier Missourians, who began to form vigilance committees in response and to talk openly about expulsion. However, the Mormon settlement was legal, and by all accounts Mormons followed the law in filing claims and purchasing lands in other counties.[19]

While most of the blame for the events of the Mormon War rest on the Missourians, the Mormons did do some provocative things during the summer of 1838. In June 1838, a group of ultra-loyal Mormons formed a self-defense and security group called the Danites that provided security for Mormon leaders and sent letters containing death threats to prominent ex-Mormons and anti-Mormons in the area who were raising doubts about the Mormon leadership's wisdom. As Quinn and other scholars have contended, this militaristic and martial approach to dealing with threats was certainly a product of the Mormon experience and not an aberration.[20]

The Danites were apparently supported by Joseph Smith and were intimately involved with most of the Mormon depredations during the Mormon War including the election day battle and the pillaging of Millport and Gallatin. It was widely believed that some in Daviess County were planning to try to stop Mormons from voting, so Sidney Rigdon gave a fiery sermon at Far West on July 4 which included the following words:

> We have not only when smitten on one cheek turned the other, but we have done it, again and again, until we are wearied of being smitten, and tired of being trampled upon. We have proved the world with kindness, we have suffered their abuse without cause, with patience, and have endured without resentment, until this day, and still their persecutions and violence does not cease. But from this day and this hour, we will suffer it no more.
>
> We take God and all the holy angels to witness this day, that we warn all men in the name of Jesus Christ, to come on us no more forever, for from this hour, we will bear it no more, our rights shall no more be trampled on with impunity. The man or the set of men, who attempts it, does it at the expense of their lives. And that mob that comes on us to disturb us; it shall be between us and them a war of extermination, for we will follow them, till the last drop of their blood is spilled, or else they will have to exterminate us: for we will carry the seat of war to their own houses, and their own families, and one party or the other shall be utterly destroyed.[21]

Joseph Smith and church leaders duplicated this sermon and distributed it widely. Smith even claimed that Rigdon spoke for the entire church in threatening vengeance for further acts of violence. Predictably, some scholars have maintained that this sermon was the rhetorical shot that began the Mormon War.[22] This argument ignores the provocative actions of the anti-Mormon mobs in Caldwell and Daviess Counties. A more reasonable position would be that, while Rigdon's sermon aroused passions among Missourians and ultimately may have led to the election-day incident, he cannot be blamed for all of the events that followed.[23]

Regardless of who was to blame, much of northwest Missouri was in ferment within a few weeks of Rigdon's sermon. Throughout the remainder of July, citizens in the counties surrounding Caldwell County began to hold vigilance committee meetings and prepare to stop further Mormon migration into northwest Missouri. Daviess County is where the Mormon War really got its start. By August 1838, Mormons made up half of that county's settlers. As the summer wore on and the Mormon settlement of Adam-ondi-Ahman grew larger and larger, non-Mormons in the county were concerned that Mormons would soon control the county's government and the courts—as they already did in Caldwell County. As the county prepared to hold its first elections in August, rumors spread that non-Mormons in the county would try to stop the Mormons from voting. An election-day conflict in Gallatin on August 6,

1838, involving as many as sixty men was won by the Mormons, although it is unclear whether any of the Mormons actually voted after the melee.

In response, Joseph Smith, Sidney Rigdon, and Hyrum Smith rode to Adam-ondi-Ahman with a force of 150 men—including several Danites—the next day. When it became clear there would be no vigilante actions against the settlement, the group then went to intimidate Judge Adam Black, who had already been vocal in his opposition to Mormon settlement in the county, into signing a statement of loyalty to Joseph Smith. In the document, he claimed he was "not attached to any mob" nor would he "attach himself to any such people and so long as [the Mormons do not] molest me, I will not molest them."[24] Not surprisingly, Black would not keep his word. Black spent much of the Mormon War period writing letters—some with dubious charges—to newspapers across the state. His prominent role in getting state and local officials involved led some in the state to refer to this expensive undertaking (the Mormon War cost the state at least $150,000) as "Squire Black's War."[25]

Missourians were suspicious of the Mormons and their views—particularly their beliefs that they were God's chosen people, that western Missouri was Zion, their closed society—and, in the non-Mormons' opinion, their fanatical devotion to their leaders. They were especially suspicious of Joseph Smith and felt that the Caldwell County government, now controlled by the Mormons, could not be trusted. As Thomas C. Burch, a prominent citizen from Richmond, put it in a letter to Governor Boggs:

> Jo[seph Smith] infuses into the minds of his followers a spirit of insubordination to the laws of the land, telling them that the Kingdom of the Lord is come, which is superior to the institutions of the earth, and encourages them to fight, and promises them the spoils of the battles . . . I have no doubt but that Jo Smith is as lawless and consummate a scoundrels as ever was the veiled prophet of [Khorassan]. I believe the criminal law in Caldwell county cannot be enforced upon a Mormon. Grand Juries there will not indict . . . I have hoped that the civil authorities would prove sufficient for the exigency of the case, but I am now convinced that it is not, so long as indictments have to be found by a jury of the county in which the offence may be committed.[26]

As the conflict raged on into the fall of 1838, it became easy for Missourians to convince themselves that the Mormons had truly evil designs. General Robert Wilson maintained "my feelings have been shocked with the gross brutality of these Mormons, who have acted more like demons from the infernal regions than human beings."[27]

During the Mormon War, it became routine for Missouri newspaper editors to characterize Mormons negatively as "degraded," "foolish," "deluded" people or "fanatics" or even "savages" who had "absurd notions [about] what the future has in store for them." Mormons were described in the pages of the *Missouri Republican* in early September 1838 as "a troublesome and dangerous set of people, and a curse to any community in which they may be located. We have known many of them personally; they are generally a low, dirty, ignorant and degraded class, who look upon their leaders with the most implicit confidence."[28] It seems likely that these attitudes reflect those of the readers of the paper as well. By characterizing Mormons using these terms, these newspaper editors made it easier for their readers to view Mormons as subhuman, thus making atrocities like the Haun's Mill Massacre more likely.

Missourians of the 1830s viewed extralegal violence as a normal part of life.[29] If it reflected the popular will, it was viewed as a right of the populace to perpetrate violence against those they saw as transgressors or threats to public order or communal values. However, one should stop and note the difference with regard to tactics. For Mormons, the conflict was largely about being left alone to live and worship as they pleased. During the Mormon War, Mormons primarily wanted to drive Gentile settlers out of areas where they wished to settle. Mormons during the conflict often burned down the homes and farms of their enemies to drive them out of the areas they wished to settle in. Missourians, on the other hand, were interested in keeping the improvements the Mormons had made to their land, so they would try to avoid harming the buildings, preferring to convince the Mormons to leave through intimidation or, if worse came to worst, through killing them. This means that Missourians were actually more likely to kill Mormons than to destroy their property, suggesting once again that this conflict was more about gaining control over the Mormons' property than anything else. One sees this at Haun's Mill where the Missourians killed the Mormons but left all of the buildings standing.

As thousands of Mormons moved into the area during the summer and fall of 1838, many Missourians apparently felt they had to do something. As Stephen C. LeSueur has argued, the Missourians viewed their extralegal violence to expel the Mormons from northwest Missouri as a "supplement to, rather than a rebellion against, constituted law."[30] It also seems likely that violence would be viewed more positively in a society that officially sanctioned a violent and coercive labor system like slavery, as Missouri did at that time. Ironically, both Missourians and Mormons viewed violence as a reasonable response to violence perpetrated by their enemies. Mormons saw their actions in the Mormon War as a warranted response to depredations by the Missourians and the actions of apostate Mormons, both of whom they viewed as a threat to their community and property. Missourians saw their actions in a similar light, as a response to the Mormons' perceived threat to their communal values and economic security.

Both groups believed that it was perfectly legitimate for a community to use force or violence to expel people with different values, beliefs, or customs from their community. Both groups attempted to do just that in the summer of 1838. Ironically, both groups also accused the other of violating the civil liberties of their fellow Americans. These attitudes toward violence provided the justification for the actions and reactions of both sides in the Mormon War and led directly to the tragedy of the Haun's Mill Massacre in October 1838. Mormons saw their actions against apostate Mormons and mobbers as justified and some in the party of non-Mormans that attacked Haun's Mill probably felt the same way about their actions.[31]

One of the major cultural conflicts apparent in the Mormon War is that of Mormon communalism versus frontier individualism. Missouri was the westernmost territory of the United States in 1838. The two groups of pioneers were quite different from each other culturally. Frontier Missourians tended to be poor migrants from Kentucky and Tennessee who, while they seldom owned slaves, certainly supported the institution. These frontier Missourians would have believed in individualism, although their persecution of the Mormons revealed just how willing they were to defend their fellow Americans' civil liberties. By the summer of 1838, many Missourians viewed the Mormons as pawns of Joseph Smith who were incapable of independent thought. The use of the Danite organization to drive out apostate Mormons and enforce religious orthodoxy struck frontier Missourians as distinctly unfair and, as LeSueur has put it, "un-American."[32]

The Mormon pioneers, on the other hand, tended to be people from the Northeast who were against slavery. As Alex Baugh put it, the two groups were like "oil and water" that "did not mix well."[33] Mormons were much more communally minded, which upset the more individualistic settlers. Mormons tended to interact only with other Mormons and largely kept to themselves, preferring to remain in their tightly knit communities.

Ironically, the Mormons' commitment to communalism was a great strength as well as a great weakness. By staying together, the Mormons caused consternation wherever they moved, creating fears in Gentiles that they would dominate the government. Some Mormons contended in the aftermath of the Mormon War that they should scatter. General John B. Clark suggested that the Mormon people "scatter abroad, and never again organize yourselves with Bishops, Presidents, etc., lest you excite the jealousies of the people, and subject yourselves to the same calamities have now come upon you."[34] Clark's words proved prescient when the same sort of drama began to unfold in Illinois a few years later. The Saints were eventually forced to leave the settled

United States in order to find true freedom of worship and a place where the locals would not covet their land and property.

While not prominently mentioned by many Missouri historians or contemporary commentators, the Mormons posed an economic threat as well. Mormons purchased large tracts of land in Caldwell and Daviess Counties. Some have contended that the Mormon War was, at its core, a struggle for land in northwest Missouri between the Mormons and their neighbors. Missourians also worried that the rapidly growing Mormon towns threatened to gain more political power than older settlements in the area like Gallatin or Millport.[35] While some at the time contended that the Mormons who settled outside Caldwell County were breaking their agreement to stay in that county, some Saints had been in Daviess County for nearly two years by the time of the Mormon War. They were living on preemption land, meaning that it was legal for them to live there, and they had the first claim to it when it legally went on sale.

The events of the Mormon War, and in particular the Haun's Mill Massacre, seem timed to coincide with one particular event: the first public sale of land in central Daviess County on November 12. It was well-known that these lands would be sold, and the Mormons would have the right to buy large tracts. Local authorities ordered the Mormons at Adam-ondi-Ahman to leave on November 5, thus preventing them from buying the land they were living on at the sale a week later on November 12. Furthermore, during November 1838 the state of Missouri forced the Mormons at Far West to deed their property over to the state in order to pay reparations for the costs of the Mormon War.

At the end of 1838, the Mormons in Missouri were essentially landless and their property had been taken from them. Leland Gentry found that in Daviess County, many non-Mormons filed their preemption land claims shortly after the land went on sale—several only two or three weeks after the Mormons were made to leave Daviess County. The timing suggests that, despite all of the sound and fury about the Mormon War being a conflict involving law or religion or culture or community values, this may have simply been about a desire to gain the Mormons' land at little or no cost.[36]

An examination of the original land claims filed in Daviess County certainly suggests that land hunger played a large role in the Haun's Mill massacre. Of the fifty-seven identified participants in the attack on Haun's Mill, sixteen of them bought land in Daviess County, including two of the four commanders of the attack and Robert White, a former owner of a mill in the area who returned with the Livingston County militia. The vast majority of these purchases took place in 1838 and 1839 and the average purchase size was large, 192 acres. Also among those who purchased land in Daviess

County during this period was Wiley C. Williams, an aide to Governor Boggs who frequently carried messages to the governor during the Mormon War. Williams purchased a total of 720 acres in Sheridan, Jefferson, and Liberty Townships, apparently hoping to make money from land speculation.[37]

Seven participants in the massacre bought land in Monroe and Harrison Townships, the southeastern-most townships in Daviess County and the closest to Haun's Mill. These men may have already lived on the land and were waiting to make preemption claims once the land was put on the market. These seven would have been most interested in making sure the Mormons were no longer in the area as they did not want to compete for land with them. This self-interested group included Thomas and William Jennings, both of whom played prominent roles in the attack, and John Conner, Jacob Rogers, Elijah Trosper, James Trosper, and Nehemiah Woolsey, upon whose property in Caldwell County the attack was purportedly planned.[38]

There is not much evidence of the reaction around the state to the Haun's Mill Massacre. The legislative committee charged with investigating the actions of the state with regard to the Mormon War says next to nothing in its report about the event other than to include one vague and largely inaccurate account by Daniel Ashby of what Missourians called "the Battle at the Mills." The *Missouri Republican* was the only newspaper to express outrage at what they called the "bloody butchery" at "Splawns Creek." The editors pointed out that "two children were killed, we presume by accident." They understood that the attackers were "not attached to any division of the army, but w[ere] fighting on [their] own hook." The editors of the *Republican* closed their account with what turned out to be a rhetorical question: "Will the actors in the tragedy be suffered by the Courts of that District, to go unpunished?"[39] For that is exactly what happened. No investigation was ever undertaken into what happened at Haun's Mill. No one was ever brought to justice for the outrages perpetrated there.

The Mormon War had a major impact on the Mormon community. In April 1854, reacting to a Missouri newspaper editor's quip that "Mormons have learned, by sad experience, that they cannot live in the midst of civilized society," Parley P. Pratt summed up the Mormon view of the Missouri experience this way:

> Think of Shoal Creek, Crooked River, Far West, Diahman, and Haun's Mill. Was this really Missouri civilization? Yes; and the horrid perpetrators acted under executive authority and were paid for committing these crimes out of the public treasury of Missouri, by special act of the legislature....
>
> Now, for the special information of such editors and their readers, we would inform them that the laws of the United States are already in operation in this territory; that they are here for the protections of Mormons and

> all other good citizens; and the Mormons and good citizens in general in Utah hope to live to see a just administration of those laws extended over Missouri and Illinois, which would naturally result in the hanging of a few thousand robbers and murderers, who have occupied a seat in the executive, legislature, and judicial departments of those two states; and would teach the remainder a better civilized policy than they have heretofore learned.
>
> We fondly hope that the coming generation in those two states will go to school and learn that the laws and constitutions of the United States do not result, when properly administered, in murder, plunder, robbery, house-burning, rape, and exile.[40]

The Mormon War was an experience that may have strengthened the resolve of Mormons and their unity as a community facing what they felt was universal hatred and anti-Mormon bigotry. Needless to say, Mormons did not forget the experience and have historically had terrible things to say about Missourians.

For those who lost a family member in the massacre, it affected the rest of their lives—and many vowed vengeance. Upon hearing of the death of E. Dodd of Gallatin, Missouri, rumored to be a participant in the massacre, George A. Smith said, "It is believed he was the same Dodd that took an active part, and a prominent mobocrat in the murder of the Saints at Haun's Mill, Missouri. If so, it is a righteous retribution. Our God will surely inflict punish[ment] upon the heads of our oppressors, in his own due time and way." The *Journal History* also tells of how Mormons tormented a group of men they thought had played a part in the massacre in September 1849, leaving ominous funeral inscriptions bearing their names along the western trail for them to find.[41]

However, other Mormons were surprisingly charitable toward the perpetrators of the massacre. John Austin Hammer, whose father Austin Hammer was killed in the massacre, often said that he would do anything to get revenge, even "crawl through snow and ice for the distance of a mile or more if necessary." Yet, when Hammer got his chance to take revenge, he refused to do so. R. J. Hammer, grandson of Austin Hammer, told the story this way:

> It occurred while he was in the standing army, as it was called in those days. Today it is known as the U.S. National Guard.
>
> His company had been called out to protect the emigrants going to California during the Gold Rush days. After a day's forced march the Company was pitching camp close to Carson City, Nevada. (Carson City at that time was only a little more than just a stage depot.) While Father was busy up his tent, a man came up to the Captain of the Company and asked him if he knew of any Mormons in his company. The Captain replied "yes, I have

a number of Mormons in my Company." The stranger again inquired "Do you know if any of them had anyone killed at Haun's Mill in Missouri?"

"Let me think," replied the Captain, "Yes, there is a man right there" pointing to my father, "who had some kin killed there, go talk to him, he can tell you more about it than I can." The stranger came over to Father where he was busy with his tent pole, and said "Sir, did you have any of your folks killed at Haun's Mill, Missouri?" Father replied "Yes I had my Father and an Uncle killed there, why? What do you want to know for?" "Well I was one of the bunch that killed them," answered the stranger.

Father told me that his first impulse was to drive the tent ax that he was holding in his hands, right through the stranger's head, but just at that moment the Lord let me see into the very inner parts of that man's soul, and father told me that there were no words that could describe the condition of that man's suffering. As father stood looking at him the stranger said "I have been looking all this long time to find a relative of one of those that I helped to kill, so that I could die at their hands. Now, I want you to kill me, for I am powerless to kill myself. And for them I helped to kill, I hear their groans all day long, and see their forms all night long. I have no rest."

Father told him to go on his way. He said "I'll not harm a hair of your head." The poor, disappointed wretch left. From that time on, Father did not seek revenge. He felt the Lord was doing a much better job of it than he could do.[42]

John Austin Hammer claimed he was more at peace with the past after this encounter with a participant in the massacre.

Presidents of the LDS Church have told and retold the story of Amanda Smith, whose son Alma was terribly wounded in the attack on the blacksmith shop. She had lost her husband and another son, Sardius, in the attack. The skin covering Alma's hip was shot away and the joint totally exposed. Heeding a voice she believed to be that of the Lord, Amanda created a poultice from the roots of a nearby slippery elm tree. Alma experienced a full recovery. Various Mormon leaders have used Amanda Smith as a great example of the power of a mother's love, portraying it as a miracle brought about by Smith's great love for her child. This story has gained mythic proportions within the LDS church.[43]

The Haun's Mill massacre became a major part of Mormon historiography, particularly after their arrival in Utah. The massacre provided an example of how barbarous their enemies could be. It was one of several experiences of the 1830s and 1840s that convinced Mormons that their destiny lay in moving west. D. Michael Quinn has suggested that Mormons held a worldview by the middle 1830s that Mormonism was constantly "fighting for its life against conspiracies of anti-Mormons and of Mormon traitors." The Haun's

Mill Massacre certainly fits into that historical narrative of religious persecution and martydom. Thus the Haun's Mill Massacre has been embraced since the mid-nineteenth century as a major event in the history of the church by Mormon leaders. In contrast, academic Missouri historians have generally minimized the massacre's place in the state's history.

Notes

1. Alexander L. Baugh, *A Call to Arms: The 1838 Mormon Defense of Northern Missouri* (Provo, Utah: BYU Studies, 2000), 163.

2. One of the more laudable accounts of the massacre by Missourians appears in an unsigned article in *A History of Caldwell and Livingston Counties* (St. Louis: National Historical Company, 1886). The more typical approach is that taken by William E. Parrish, Charles T. Jones, and Lawrence O. Christensen in *Missouri: The Heart of the Nation* (Wheeling, Ill.: Harlan Davidson, 2004), 99–101; by Duane G. Meyer in *The Heritage of Missouri* (Springfield, Mo.: Emden Press, 1982), 200–206; and by Perry McCandless, *A History of Missouri*, vol. 2: *1820 to 1860* (Columbia: University of Missouri Press, 1972), 105–11.

3. Baugh, *A Call to Arms,* 115–16.

4. Ibid., 118.

5. Stephen C. LeSueur, *The Mormon War in Missouri* (Columbia: University of Missouri Press, 1987), 144–48 and 151–52. For the full text of Governor Boggs's extermination order, see *Document Containing the Correspondence, Orders, Etc., In Relation to the Disturbances with the Mormons and the Evidence Given Before the Hon. Austin A. King* (Fayette, Mo.: Office of the Boon's Lick Democrat, 1841), 61.

6. Ibid., 116–18. For more on the negotiations, see Nathan K. Knight's account of the massacre, *Journal History of the Jesus Christ Church of Latter Day Saints* (hereafter referred to as *Journal History*), LDS Church Library, Salt Lake City, October 30, 1838, 7, and Ellis Eamut's account, *Journal History* October 30, 1838, 12–13. Joseph Young, brother of Brigham Young, also refers to these negotiations and claims the Mormons knew of yet another mob gathering nearby in his account of the massacre (*Journal History,* October 30, 1838, 1).

7. Stephen C. LeSueur, *The Mormon War in Missouri,* 163–64. For Ashby's statement, see *Document Containing the Correspondence, Orders, Etc.,* 82–83, and the Mormon War Papers, Missouri State Archives, box 2, folder 13. For Ashby's contention that the raid was self-defense, see *Missouri Republican,* December 24, 1838.

8. *History of Caldwell and Livingston Counties* (St. Louis: National Historical Company, 1886), 151.

9. Eamut, "Reminiscence," *Journal History,* October 30, 1838, 12–13.

10. Baugh, *A Call to Arms,* 119. The map of the Haun's Mill area comes from the Missouri Mormon Frontier Foundation's Web page, http://www.farwesthistory.com/hmap.htm.

11. Baugh, *A Call to Arms,* 119–20.

12. Ibid., 120–23.

13. Ibid.; LeSueur, *The Mormon War,* 166–67; and Nathan Kinsman Knight, "Autobiographical Sketch, 1870," LDS Church Archives, MS 2852.

14. LeSueur, *The Mormon War,* 166–67; and Juanita Brooks, *Mountain Meadows Massacre* (Norman: University of Oklahoma Press, 1962), 5. Brooks insisted that this phrase from the Haun's Mill Massacre was used by the Mormons at the Mountain Meadows Massacre in 1857.

15. Ibid., 140, and LeSueur, *The Mormon War,* 167–68.

16. Doctrine and Covenants, 98: 29, 31, 37. As cited in D. Michael Quinn, "National Culture, Personality, and Theocracy in the Early Mormon Culture of Violence," *John Whitmer Historical Association Journal,* Nauvoo Conference Special Edition (2002): 166.

17. Doctrine and Covenants, 103: 25.

18. Quinn, "National Culture, Personality, and Theocracy," 167–71.

19. LeSueur, *The Mormon War in Missouri,* 23–24, 26–29.

20. Ibid., 37–47, and 117–18; and Quinn, "National Culture, Personality, and Theocracy," 172–74.

21. *Oration Delivered by Mr. S. Rigdon on the 4th of July 1838* (Far West, Mo.: Elder's Journal Office, 1838), 12.

22. Quinn, "National Culture, Personality, and Theocracy," 175.

23. LeSueur, *The Mormon War,* 52–53. LeSueur has very clearly argued that Rigdon's sermon was to blame for the bad blood that led to the conflict that followed.

24. Ibid., 54–67; and Pearl Wilcox, *The Latter Day Saints on the Missouri Frontier* (Independence, Mo., 1972), 210–15.

25. *Missouri Republican,* November 10, 1838.

26. *Document Containing the Correspondence, Orders, Etc.,* 50–51, and Mormon War Papers, Missouri State Archives, box 1, folder 41.

27. Document 78, and Mormon War Papers, box 2, folder 9.

28. *Jeffersonian Republican,* November 3, 1838; *Missouri Argus,* November 5, 1838; and *Missouri Republican,* September 3 and 29, 1838.

29. For more on this interpretation of vigilantism, see Richard Maxwell Brown, *Strain of Violence: Historical Studies of American Violence and Vigilantism* (London: Oxford University Press, 1975), 93–133.

30. LeSueur, *Mormon War in Missouri,* 3.

31. Ibid., 3–6; Quinn, "National Culture, Personality, and Theocracy," 177; and Baugh, "A Call to Arms," 35–36.

32. LeSueur, *The Mormon War,* 4.

33. Baugh, *A Call to Arms,* 6–7.

34. LeSueur, *The Mormon War,* 190.

35. Ibid., 1–3.

36. Leland Gentry, "The Land Question at Adam-ondi-Ahman," *Brigham Young University Studies* 26, no. 2 (Spring 1986): 49–53.

37. According to the *Plat Book, Original Entrys, Daviess County, Daviess County Recorder's Office,* participants in the attack who later purchased land in Daviess County included James Blakely, Nathaniel Blakely, William Bowman, John Brown, John Comer, John Conner, Thomas Jennings, William O. Jennings, Robert Lauderdale, William P. Peniston, Jacob S. Rogerts, Erasmus Sevier, Elijah Trosper, James Trosper, Robert White, and Nehemiah Woolsey. A very useful index, titled *Daviess County Patents,* has recently been compiled by Eleanor A. Bassett. Both of these sources are available in the Daviess County Recorder's Office.

38. Ibid.

39. *Missouri Republican,* November 12, 1838. For the complete papers of the Missouri state legislature's Mormon War investigation, see the Mormon War Papers at

the Missouri State Archives.

40. *Journal History,* April 2, 1854, 1. This is a reproduction of a Parley Pratt sermon given on the same date that appeared in the *Deseret News* on April 24, 1854.

41. *Journal History,* September 19, 1849, 3, and October 18, 1849, 3–4.

42. R. J. Hammer, "Reminiscences of John Austin Hammer," LDS Church Archives, MS 12048.

43. Amanda Smith, "A Heroine of Haun's Mill Massacre," in *Heroines of Mormondom* (Salt Lake City: Juvenile Instructor Office, 1884), 90–92.

7

But for the Kindness of Strangers

The Columbia, Missouri, Response to the Mormon Prisoners and the Jailbreak of July 4, 1839

Jean A. Pry and Dale A. Whitman

The unkind and unlawful treatment of the Mormons in Missouri in the 1830s has been well documented. Except for the civility and fair hand of Alexander Doniphan, a Whig attorney and a brigadier general in the Missouri state militia in a sea of Jacksonian Democrats in the western counties, the Mormons appear to have been utterly friendless. On numerous occasions Doniphan proved to be a trustworthy aid to the Mormons. Surely there were other Missourians in that region whose sympathies were similar to Doniphan's, but their names have been lost to the historical record. Thus, among Missourians of the period, the name of Alexander Doniphan stands out because of his keen sense of justice and fair play.

All other Missourians, by contrast, have too often been cast in the shadow of the anti-Mormon persecutors in the western counties, whose virulence has been well documented. The truth, of course, is not quite that simple. A case in point is the relatively brief episode of the Mormons in central Missouri in 1839. There, in Columbia, Boone County, Missouri, the Mormon experience was dramatically different from what they had endured in the western counties. This paper describes some of those differences and explores ways to account for them.[1]

When Laura Phelps left her husband in the Richmond, Missouri, jail in the winter of 1838, she did not know whether nor when she would see him again. Circumstances in western Missouri, and particularly in the Richmond and

Liberty jails, had been extremely hard on the Mormon prisoners, both physically and emotionally. Laura could not have known that she would see Morris Phelps again in a different jail nearly half a year later and halfway across the state in Columbia. The contrast in the circumstances of the Mormon prisoners' incarceration, first in Richmond and then in Columbia, provides compelling detail regarding this period of Mormon history as well as about the complexity of social-political life on the Missouri frontier.

The details of the jail break recounted here are derived from the accounts of Mary Phelps Rich and Parley Pratt; they constitute the "Mormon side" of the story. This does not necessarily render them suspicious or lacking in credibility. As Geertz explained, the value of ethnographic descriptions—and by extension, we argue, historical descriptions—is not that they are true or false but that they represent "another country heard from." Thus, the reports on which this paper rely constitute expressions of "another view," one from people who had an intimate place in the history of 1830s Missouri. Moreover, since Phelps and Pratt perceived that the Mormons had been persecuted in western Missouri, they might reasonably have been expected to depict the treatment of the prisoners and Laura Phelps in Boone County in similarly inhospitable terms. The fact that they describe the central Missourians' conduct as mainly generous and charitable lends credibility to their accounts.[2]

It was the Crooked River incident that had landed Morris Phelps, Laura's husband, in the jail. Relationships between the Mormons and other settlers in western Missouri had deteriorated rapidly during the summer and fall of 1838, particularly after a group of Missourians forcibly prevented Mormons from voting in an election in Gallatin, Daviess County, on August 6. The Mormons were determined not to be passively persecuted as they had earlier been in Jackson and Clay Counties, and they vowed to defend themselves. A series of armed raids and reprisals between Mormons and Missourians erupted.[3]

The event termed the Battle of Crooked River took place on October 25 in Bunkham's (sometimes "Buncombe's") Strip, a six-mile-wide unincorporated strip of land that was administratively attached to Ray County just south of the Caldwell County line. Just before dawn, a group of Mormon militia, about seventy-five strong and led by Apostle David Patten, encountered an encampment of Ray County militia of similar size under the command of Samuel Bogart, a Methodist minister. The non-Mormons were patrolling the Caldwell-Ray county line to guard against Mormon raiding parties they expected. Shots were exchanged, and it was initially reported that there were high casualties on both sides. These reports were greatly exaggerated; in fact, one Ray Countian and three Mormons, including Patten, died. The Mormons probably entered into the fight in good faith, believing that the Ray County militiamen were an armed mob intending to attack Mormon settlements. Nonetheless, the result of the battle was to place the Mormons in the legally untenable position of having attacked an army of the State of Missouri. This incident greatly reinforced fears of the Mormons and contributed to Governor Boggs' "extermination order," issued only two days later.[4]

By October 31, many of the Mormons in Caldwell and Daviess Counties had gone to Far West, Caldwell County, as a result of mob depredations on a number of outlying settlements. When the Missouri militia commanded by General John B. Clark, assisted by Major General D. Lucas and Brigadier Moses Wilson, disarmed the citizens of Far West, about fifty Mormon men, including Morris Phelps, were arrested. They were marched first to Independence, in Jackson County, where they were paraded before the citizens in triumph, and then to Richmond in Ray County, where they were imprisoned.

A "court of inquiry" was then convened in Richmond to consider the charges of treason, murder, and other crimes against the prisoners, stemming from the Battle of Crooked River and other incidents. The function of this proceeding appears to have been similar to that of a preliminary hearing in modern criminal procedure—that is, to assess the evidence and determine whether it was sufficient to warrant binding the prisoners over for trial. The hearing was presided over by Judge Austin A. King, and was conducted from November 12 to 18, 1838. Meanwhile, the remaining Mormons in Caldwell and Daviess Counties were being forced from their homes and across northern Missouri toward Illinois and southeastern Iowa.[5]

The prisoners at Richmond were invited to bring forward witnesses, and seven Mormons testified in their defense. There were many more witnesses willing to testify against them. There were likely some efforts to intimidate or dissuade Mormon witnesses, but it is doubtful that this made much difference in the outcome. Alexander Doniphan, who served as the Mormons' defense counsel, recommended that they not attempt to offer testimony, for, "though a legion of angels from the opening heavens should declare your innocence, the court and populace have decreed your destruction." While this advice may seem strange, it made good sense in the procedural context of the hearing. It was not a trial but a proceeding to determine whether there was probable cause to believe the defendants had committed the crimes in question. Once Judge King had heard evidence indicating probable cause, he had little choice but to bind over the defendants for trial.[6]

At the conclusion of the hearing, twenty-nine of the prisoners were released. Of the remainder, one group, consisting of Joseph and Hyrum Smith, Sidney Rigdon, Lyman Wight, Caleb Baldwin, and Alexander McRay, were remanded to prison in Liberty, Clay County, to stand trial on a charge of treason. A second group, composed of Parley P. Pratt, Morris Phelps, Luman Gibbs, Darwin Chase, and Norman Shearer, were returned to jail in Richmond to stand trial for murder, the victim being Moses Rowland, the Carroll County militiaman killed at Crooked River. The testimony of Morris Phelps may well have been responsible for the selection of the group charged with murder; he identified all four of the others as having been present at the Crooked River fight. Phelps denied that he himself participated in the battle and asserted that he was present only because of duress. Twenty-four other Mormons were charged with lesser crimes—arson, robbery, larceny, and burglary—and were released on bail. All of them evidently forfeited their bonds and left the state. No bail was offered to those charged with treason or murder, as these were capital crimes. Judge King set the second Monday in May 1839 as the date for the appearance of the men charged with murder before the Ray County grand jury, but for reasons not explained in the record, the prisoners' actual appearance before the grand jury occurred on April 24, at which time they were indicted for murder.[7]

The prisoners remaining in Richmond spent a miserable winter and spring there, sleeping on the floor, eating meager food, and often being taunted by the guards. Parley Pratt's wife was permitted several visits to him until she, like Laura Phelps, was forced to leave Missouri with the last remnants of the Mormon settlers. At some time in the spring, Chase and Shearer were released, but another Mormon, King Follett, was brought into the Richmond jail in mid-April 1839. Finally, apparently in May 1839, Judge King visited the prisoners and informed them that the venue for their trial had been changed to Columbia, in Boone County. Joseph Smith and the other men who had been charged with treason and held in Liberty were also given a venue change to Boone County, but they escaped while en route to Columbia on April 16. Thus, by June 1839, Pratt and his three fellow prisoners were probably the only Mormons remaining in the state of Missouri.[8]

Missouri had been added to the Union on August 10, 1821, a result of the "Missouri Compromise" that allowed Missouri to enter as a slave state and Maine a free state, thus retaining the balance of free and slave states represented in Congress. The county of Boone was formed nine months earlier on November 16, 1820, named for scout and explorer Daniel Boone, who had died only two months earlier at his home near St. Charles in eastern Missouri.[9]

Columbia was platted in the spring of 1821. In the early 1820s, there was a large movement of settlers into the Boonslick area, including Columbia and Boone County, from Kentucky. Family names were primarily English, Irish, Scots, and Scots-Irish, and settlers were Protestants. In general they were well off, evidenced by the fact that land prices in the area were the highest in the state. Moreover, they were highly experienced in husbandry and agriculture, and accustomed to relying on rivers to ship their production to New Orleans. Many of the immigrants were slave holders, but the system of large plantation, single-crop agriculture, which depended on slaves in the South, was considerably scaled down in Boone County. There, slaves were more typically used for general farming and household chores.[10]

In the early 1830s, Columbia saw continued growth. Its first newspaper began publication in 1830. A line of semiweekly mail stages between St. Louis via St. Charles, Fulton, Columbia, and Fayette was established in 1833. The first local theater company debuted the evening of Christmas Day 1832. In 1835 the state's first agricultural fair, a two-day event replete with entrance categories, judges, and prizes, was held in Columbia. A young artist from Franklin, George Caleb Bingham, opened a portrait studio in Columbia in 1834. He charged twenty-five dollars per portrait and eventually achieved international recognition for his paintings of everyday people involved in everyday life. Later in life he would become a well-known and influential Missouri politician.[11]

The idea of a state university had been bandied about for several years, but there was much debate among legislators about whom it should serve, how it should be governed, how to finance it, what standards should govern admittance, and where to locate it. The act of 1820 implementing the Missouri Compromise had granted the state of Missouri two full townships (roughly forty-six thousand acres) "for the use of a seminary of learning." In the early 1830s, the state began selling off these township lands. The $75,000 realized from the sales was invested by the state with the understanding that when the fund reached $100,000, it would be sufficient to endow a university.[12]

Finally, in February 1839, the General Assembly passed a bill that would locate the new state university in one of the six central Missouri counties. With the highest bid of $118,300, Boone County became the new home of the University of Missouri, the first public institution of higher education west of the Mississippi River. Pledges ranged from a few dollars to $3,000. Interestingly, of the three individuals who gave the maximum, one could neither read nor write.[13]

The picture that emerges of Columbia by 1839 is of a thriving community located in what today is referred to as the "Little Dixie" area of the state. By 1839, Boone was the second most populous county in the state next to St. Louis County. Outside of St. Louis, it was also generally viewed as the most sophisticated, urbane area in the state. Its citizens were interested and involved in the issues of the day, taking patriotism, civic responsibility, and economic development seriously while cultivating the arts to the extent possible. Town leaders had a decidedly Whig orientation. There was also a strong

Southern orientation and slavery was an assumed way of life. People were generally hard working, prosperous and, for a frontier community, remarkably future oriented. They were accustomed to the prosperity resulting from the heavy east-west traffic of immigrants on the Boonslick Trail and the trade opportunities it provided. While on the one hand citizens were concerned for their physical security and the rule of law, they also made time for theater, newspapers, and agricultural improvements. In particular, they took education seriously and recognized the economic and cultural benefit to be had for both the town and county economy by securing Columbia as the location of the new University of Missouri. The announcement that Boone County had been successful in securing this prize was made in June 1839, about a month after Morris Phelps, King Follett, and Parley P. Pratt were safely ensconced in the jail in Columbia. From the perspective of the prisoners, Columbia would surely prove to be a more favorable surrounding than the raw hostility of western Missouri.

Morris Phelps and Laura Clark Phelps both came from New England families who moved west. Morris met Laura while he was visiting friends in Illinois and they married in 1825, settling in Tazewell County, Illinois. One day Morris received a letter from relatives in northern Ohio telling him about Joseph Smith and the Mormons who had moved into that region. Shortly thereafter, two Mormon missionaries passed through the Phelps' Illinois neighborhood and stopped at his home. Morris, previously a self-avowed atheist, and his wife were quickly converted. In March 1832 they moved to Jackson County, Missouri. The next year they relocated in Clay County and eventually settled with the other Saints in Far West.[14]

During the 1838–1839 winter, while her husband was in the Richmond jail, Laura visited him every two weeks, "taking with her provisions, he not having anything provided for him that was fit to eat." However, in the spring of 1839 Laura was forced to leave her husband in Richmond and head east for Quincy, Illinois, along with their children. Mary Phelps Rich, Laura and Morris Phelps' second child, wrote in her autobiography, "We left our home and everything; we just packed up what few things we could and came away. We never got a cent for our property." Laura got her children settled west of Montrose, Iowa, near other family members. Once Laura learned that the prisoners were being moved to Boone County, she made plans to be there in time for the trial.[15]

According to Mary, while her father was in the Richmond jail he was "told many times if he would burn his Book of Mormon and quit the Mormon Church he could go free; they said he had no business there, but he chose to be firm in his religion." After the change of venue from Ray County to Boone

County, the prisoners departed Richmond on May 22, 1839. The four prisoners were Morris Phelps, King Follett, Parley P. Pratt, and Luman Gibbs. Luman Gibbs's wife was also in the party. Pratt, Phelps, and Follet believed that although Gibbs had publically denied the faith, he continued to be held in order to spy on the others. This also allowed the Missourians to avoid charges of religious persecution. As a prisoner, in Richmond he enjoyed privileges not available to the other three.[16]

After a difficult four-day trip from Richmond, the prisoners and their guards arrived in Columbia. On their arrival at the jail in Columbia, they were consigned to a dungeon, which Pratt described as being "filled with darkness, filth and cobwebs; the naked floor was our lodging. . . . We were extremely hungry and weary, but received no refreshment, not even a drink of water, till late in the evening, when our new keeper, Mr. John Scott, visited us with some buttermilk and bread; but we were now too much exhausted and too low spirited to eat. We thanked him for his kindness, and sank down exhausted on the floor, where we rested as well as we could till morning."[17]

The trial was expected to occur on July 1, leaving the prisoners in jail in Columbia about five weeks prior to that date. Pratt reported that after the first night in the dungeon, the sheriff moved the prisoners into more amenable quarters and they were "treated with some degree of humanity," being "no longer troubled with guards." Meanwhile in Iowa, now living near other family members, Laura received a letter from Morris in which he commented on how difficult life was now that he could not see her. After receiving Joseph Smith's blessing, she decided to go to Columbia for the trial. Laura Clark Phelps and her brother, John Wesley Clark, left Iowa and traveled the 150 or so miles to Columbia, arriving there on June 30, in time for the start of the trial the next day. Orson Pratt, Parley Pratt's brother, also arrived in time for the trial. Thus, although family was present at the trial, no one related to the charges on which they were being held appeared to testify against them, and their case was, once again, continued.[18]

Disappointed by yet another judicial continuance and with no end of their imprisonment in sight, the prisoners began to consider the prospect of an escape. They chose July 4 as the day to effect their plan, explained Pratt, who had been very ill: as "that day had been a lucky one for our fathers and our nation, we had determined on that time as the proper one to bid farewell to bondage and gain our liberty. In short, we had determined to make that notable day a jubilee to us, or perish in the attempt. We, therefore, prayed earnestly to the Lord, that if he had determined to favor our plan, he would heal and strengthen me, and give us all courage to act well our part. Through the ministration of the ordinance appointed for healing, I was instantly healed, and from that moment began to feel as strong and fearless as a lion." The jailer was kind and allowed the relatives, once searched, to stay in the jail with the prisoners. That certainly facilitated the planning. While a lengthy stay from visitors might have aroused suspicion, staying until the upcoming holiday would likely not. Orson Pratt went so far as to engage a lawyer to prepare a court order that would allow affidavits to be taken in Illinois by witnesses who could not travel to Boone County when the trial went forward, and even made partial payment to the lawyer up front. All these things, Pratt said, "served as a sufficient blindfold to cover our real intentions."[19]

The details of the plan were simple. After the afternoon meal on the Fourth, Orson Pratt and John Wesley Clark would appear to start for home, taking Laura Phelps's horse with them. Meanwhile, Laura had made arrangements with the jailer to stay in Columbia with her husband indefinitely and board with them at the jail. "They told the jailer they were going to leave mother there to visit with her husband longer," her daughter Mary Rich explained. "But in reality mother was giving up her horse and trusting in the Lord for her deliverance, as she knew they would be so angry with her after the prisoners had escaped that they would either turn her out or hold her as a prisoner." Meanwhile, Orson Pratt and John Clark were to go about a mile and a half north of the jail and hide the three horses there in a thicket until the jail-breaking prisoners came running for them.[20]

At sundown, the jailer would bring them their supper, open the heavy outer door, and hand in their food through a slot in the top of the thinner, inner door. The difficulty was with the coffee pot, which was too tall to be handed through the available space without turning it sideways, thus spilling some coffee. The prisoners planned to ask the jailer to do something he had already done on other occasions: open the inner door to hand in the coffee pot. With the inner door unlocked, their opportunity for their own independence on Independence Day would be possible.[21]

July 4 in Columbia was, indeed, a day of celebration, and the prisoners determined to join the citizens in the festivities. They asked the jailer for a long pole on which they could hang a flag. The jailer obliged. They tore up a shirt to provide the foundation of the flag. Then they used red strips of fabric to form the word "Liberty" and fashion an eagle. They hung their somewhat crude flag from their window of the jail. Pratt noted that their jail window was "directly in front of the public square and courthouse, and [our flag] composed one of the greatest attractions of the day." Some food from the public dinner was sent in to the prisoners. The prisoners and their relatives were delighted; Pratt said, "We partook of our feast with much cheer, and with thankful as well as social feelings, which I think have been seldom if ever surpassed."[22]

Meanwhile, festivities were under way with "troops parading, guns firing, music sounding, and shouts of joy resounding on every side." The prisoners took the opportunity to compose a toast which, Pratt reported, "was read at their public dinner, with many and long cheers." The tradition of toasts at celebrations like this one was central to the day's events. Anderson explained, "The gala day of all days in Missouri was the Fourth of July, when entire communities met to commemorate the wisdom and patriotism of the fathers, and the favor of an all-wise supervising Providence. . . . The reading of the Declaration of Independence could not be dispensed with [any more] than the reading of the Bible in the religious services of the day. Thus on the outskirts of civilization, in Missouri, were all the people nurtured on that document of the liberty of the individual, the sacredness of property, and the duties of a good government."[23]

After dinner John Wesley Clark and Orson Pratt left with Laura Phelps' horse and headed toward Quincy, or so it seemed. They departed with farewells and messages for loved ones, all intended "to lull [the jailer and company] . . . into security, and to remove all possible ground of suspicion as to our intentions." In fact, Clark and Pratt proceeded only across some fields to the thicket that they had agreed to use for secreting the horses when they had surveyed the landscape from the upper floor of the jail. Meanwhile, Laura had been given "strict orders not to touch the prisoners, nor try to assist them in any way, as that was a penitentiary act." Thus, in the afternoon, Laura left the cell, having been instructed that whatever she did, she should not let the jailer bring their supper until just as the sun was going down.[24]

According to Pratt, they then "put on our coats and hats and waited for the setting sun. With prayer and supplication for deliverance from this long and tedious bondage, and for a restoration to the society of our friends and families, we then sang the following lines:

Lord, cause their foolish plans to fail,
And let them faint or die,
Our souls would quit this loathsome jail,
And fly to Illinois.
To join with the embodied saints,
Who are with freedom blessed,
That only bliss for which we pant,
With them awhile to rest.
Give joy for grief—give ease for pain,

Take all our foes away.
But let us find our friends again,
In this eventful day.

They sang in easy earshot of Luman Gibbs and the jailer, neither of whom paid them—nor the message of freedom proclaimed in song and on their flag—any attention.[25]

Morris Phelps, skilled in wrestling, was to lead the charge and take on the jailer. Parley Pratt was to come next, followed by King Follett. Laura Phelps's assignment was to pray. As the sun was going down, Laura heard the jailer say, "Well, I must go up and give the boys their supper." She soon heard "steps and a rumbling noise." The escape was on, and pray, Laura Phelps did! Mary's journal records, "Mother said she did not feel that father would be overpowered. She thought she could pray if she could do nothing else. She thought she was whispering a prayer, but they said she hollered just as loud as her voice would let her, and she said, 'Oh! Thou God of Abraham, Isaac and Jacob, deliver Thy servant.' Father said he felt as strong as a giant when he heard those words. He just pushed the jailer and his wife off as if they were babies and cleared himself."[26]

Soon the three prisoners were flying through the fields on foot toward the thicket. Pratt reported the chaos in town:

> By this time the town was all in motion. The quietness of the evening was suddenly changed into noise and bustle, and it was soon evident that the thrilling scenes of the great drama of the 4th of July, and of the Columbian celebration of liberty were yet to be enacted. The streets on both sides of the fields where we were running were soon thronged with soldiers in uniform, mounted riflemen, footmen with fence stakes, clubs, or with whatever came to hand, and with boys, dogs, etc., all running, rushing, screaming, swearing, shouting, bawling and looking, while clouds of dust rose behind them. The cattle also partook of the general panic and ran bellowing away, as if to hide from the scene. The fields behind us also presented a similar scene. Fences were leaped or broken down with a crash; men, boys and horses came tumbling over hedge and ditch, rushing with the fury of a whirlwind in the chase.[27]

In the end, Morris Phelps and Parley P. Pratt were successful in finding their way back to Quincy and ultimately to Nauvoo. King Follett was less fortunate; he was captured almost immediately and returned to the jail in Columbia.[28]

Laura Phelps was left surrounded by very angry people. According to her daughter, the jailer called her names and told her to get out of his sight. Intrepid woman that she was, she asked him to retrieve her shawl and bonnet from the jail first. She feared that if she went back upstairs, they might try to push her out the window. Mary recorded that a man who had delivered some of the public feast to the prisoners earlier in the day, "seeing the doorway crowded with men and boys, said to the jailer, 'How do you expect this lady to get out of this place?' The jailer said he did not care how she got out. He wanted her out of his sight, and if she did not get out of his way before dark, he would soon put her out of the way. This gentleman said he would see her safely out, so he took her by the hand and led her. As they went out, she picked up father's hat."

Once outside the courthouse, two young men approached her and encouraged her to go to a hotel. "They said they would pay her fare, and for her not to stay there and suffer the abuse of the jailer. But she said she felt that people might think she was not just what she ought to be if she went to the hotel, so she did not go."[29]

Then someone else approached her. Pratt said it was "a certain young man . . . who declared that he was not accustomed to seeing a female treated thus in America, and that if she had no home his father and mother would receive her kindly and give her protection under their roof till she could return to Illinois." Mary Rich's version, however, is somewhat different:

> During this time there was a little boy who had been there and had seen all that was going on. He ran home to his mother and told her that the prisoners had broken jail, and that the young man's wife was down there and the jailer had thrown her out of doors. He said he wished it would get dark so he would get her out of the way. The little boy was crying as though his heart would break. His mother told him to go out and tell his father. The father came in and wanted to know what his boy was worrying about, and when he found what the trouble was, he and his wife and the little boy went down to the courthouse, where mother was. When they saw mother, he said to his wife, "Elizabeth, you take this lady by the hand and take her home to our house. If her husband was the greatest murderer in the world, we could not see anyone in our town treated with such cruelty as this." Mother said she thought they were true friends, and so she got up and thanked them and told them she would go with them. As she was going, she saw the enemy throw the side-saddle off her horse, and put a man's saddle on it to go after the prisoners. The gentleman and his wife, who had thus aided her, were named Richardson.[30]

The Richardsons took Laura Phelps to their home and treated her kindly. The next day they went to the jail to retrieve anything that might belong to Laura or the prisoners. They also retrieved her sidesaddle, repaired it, and asked others to be on the lookout for Laura's horse, which was returned in a few days. After ten days, she was anxious to leave. Mr. Richardson arranged for her to travel some of the way with the mail boy. "They had to travel late at night and start out early in the morning, but she told them she could stand it." Mary wrote: "She had preached Mormonism to them all the while she was there, and she left a Book of Mormon and a hymn book with them. She had also sung them the songs of Zion, as she was a great hand to sing. They made her promise that if ever there was any great calamity coming upon the state of Missouri, that she would write to them."[31]

They left Columbia in the afternoon and traveled thirty miles before stopping for the night. The next day they traveled thirty miles before breakfast. At some point Laura parted company with the mail boy and came to the Mississippi River bottoms. There the woods became very thick, and with darkness setting in and with another seven miles to go to find a hotel, she became frightened. "She looked into the woods as far as she could see and saw a man coming up on horseback. He was a white man, and when he came up to her he looked at her and she looked at him, and he said, "I wonder if you are not the woman I am looking for?" The man was King Follett's son, with whom she returned safely to Quincy. There Laura found her husband, Morris, in bed, ill from exposure. She, too, was exhausted.[32]

Morris Phelps recovered and lived to an old age in Utah, but less than three years after the jailbreak, on February 2, 1842, Laura Phelps died. Mary Rich's journal recorded her mother's death: "My mother was taken sick and died, leaving her five children, three girls and two boys, the baby one and a half years old, with my father heartbroken, and her children not knowing how to manage. Father took mother's body to Nauvoo to be buried." The Prophet Joseph Smith and Hebert C. Kimball both spoke at her funeral. "Joseph Smith said she had lived her life so fast. . . . He said her salvation was sure, that if she had lived until she was one hundred years old, she could not have done any more."[33]

The treatment of the Mormon prisoners in Columbia was dramatically better than the treatment they had received in the Richmond jail, about a hundred miles to the west, in terms of both living conditions and interpersonal relations. At one point, Pratt was one of about fifty Mormons imprisoned in Richmond. Conditions there produced utter misery: lack of furniture, cold temperatures, unbreathable air, inedible food, and incessant mockery, insults, intimidation, and sexual threats from the guards. Pratt described the guards as obscene, blasphemous, and vulgar. They seemed to go out of their way to be as irritating as possible to their prisoners.[34]

The food was particularly disappointing. Pratt described it as "the most unwholesome kind, and scant at that; consisting of bones, remnants of meat, coarse corn bread, and sometimes a little coffee. We generally partook of our meals in a standing position, using our fingers instead of knives, forks or plates. A tin cup served us for our coffee." Mary Rich's mother reported similar conditions when she visited her husband. To what extent such privations were common in Missouri jails in that period is not known, but in Columbia circumstances were much better.[35]

Although the Mormons were initially relegated to the dungeon when they arrived in Columbia, Pratt said that after some time, "our new jailer handed down some provisions." Laura Phelps described this food as "buttermilk and bread." More importantly, perhaps, immediately on receiving the food, Pratt noted that "suddenly the trap door opened, and some chairs were handed to us, and the new sheriff, Mr. Martin, and his deputy, Mr. Hamilton, entered our dungeon and talked so kindly to us, that our spirits again revived in some measure. This night we slept cold and uncomfortable, having but little bedding. Next morning we were suffered to come out of the dungeon, and the liberty of the upper room was given us through the day ever afterwards." The rough treatment had lasted only as long as the Ray County officials were on the scene. Pratt observed that the prisoners "now began to receive kind treatment from our jailer and from our new sheriff; for it was Mr. Brown [the Ray County sheriff] that had caused all our neglect and sufferings the previous evening." Things were looking up.[36]

Pratt recorded no specific comment regarding the quality of the food, except for the July 4 feast that the prisoners enjoyed, which suggests that the jailer and his wife provided at least reasonably appropriate meals to the prisoners and on schedule. Pratt mentioned that the hole in the inner door, which was too small to accommodate the large coffee pot, was used to pass "food and dishes" and other unspecified "articles." It is uncertain whether "dishes" meant bowls of food from which to serve themselves, plates and utensils, or both. As for the unspecified *articles*, perhaps these included soap and a towel to use with a wash basin. In any event, far more civility abounded than in Richmond.[37]

The willingness of the citizens of Columbia to share their Independence Day public dinner with the prisoners is especially noteworthy. Such a display of generosity toward the prisoners in Richmond would not have been likely. Moreover, the idea that they could participate in the July 4 celebration in any way, much less stir public sentiment by flying their flag and offering a toast, would have been nearly unthinkable in Richmond or Liberty. In contrast to armed guards milling around them and cursing, in Columbia the only impediments to their escape were the locked doors and the bars on the windows. The absence of harassment, the much greater degree of privacy, and the ability to have family share their quarters were huge improvements over their circumstances in Richmond. Life must have begun to feel something akin to normal.

It is the treatment of King Follett, after he was recaptured, that perhaps best captures the prevailing ethos in Columbia. He was initially put into the dungeon, but after several days he was unchained by the sheriff and taken, once again, to the upper room of the jail and treated as before. "They now laughed with him about his adventure, praised him for his bravery, and called him a good fellow." He remained in custody for several months but was eventually released and returned to Illinois.[38]

Finally, the many kindnesses extended to Laura Phelps should not be overlooked. These include the man who helped her exit the jail and escape the haranguing jailer, the two men who offered her lodging at the hotel so she could get off the street, the little boy so troubled by what he witnessed and his parents' trust in his report, the many acts of generosity offered by the Richardson family during the time she spent with them, and the postman who allowed her to ride with him as far as his route would permit. These were the acts of people with a sense of personal and civic responsibility and charity. That the jailer was outraged at the jailbreak is as understandable, as were the vigorous attempts to recapture the fugitives. They had broken the law. The jailer and his wife must have felt embarrassed and betrayed, and perhaps worried that they might lose their positions over this incident. They had been as accommodating as possible under the circumstances. Over the weeks the men had been incarcerated, a cordial relationship with their keepers had probably developed, and Laura's appearance on the scene likely confirmed those feelings.

How might one explain the difference in the treatment received by the Mormons in Richmond and Columbia? One cannot reasonably argue that Columbians were unaware of the negative view of the Mormons held by Missourians in the western counties. Numerous negative reports were reprinted widely in newspapers throughout the state and beyond. Yet clearly a number of Columbians felt that the treatment of the Mormons in the western counties and by the governor was unwarranted, especially given the cavalier manner in which decisions regarding them had been made. This point is demonstrated by an article that appeared in the *Columbia Patriot* in late 1838 in which the writer expressed concern for the reputation of the citizens of Missouri if the extermination of the Saints were not halted pending a legitimate investigation, an investigation the writer assumes had not yet occurred. This regard for fairness and rule of law also explains Columbians' outrage over the jailbreak and their zeal for hunting down the escapees.[39]

Perhaps personal predilections and local culture provide part of the explanation. In a letter written to his brother in Tennessee dated November

26, 1824, Walter Raleigh Lenore described the people in Columbia as "the most hospital [hospitable] and kind people that I ever happened amongst during life." The brief experience of the Mormons in Columbia lends weight to Lenore's assertion. What we know of the people who settled Columbia in the 1820s suggests that the citizens and their leaders were not only confident of their ability to achieve personally but also felt responsible for the long-term growth and welfare of the community in general.[40]

By comparison, the settlers in western Missouri seemed rough. Joseph Smith, while certainly not an unbiased observer, referred to the Jackson Countians as sitting "in darkness": "How natural it was to observe the degradation, leanness of intellect, ferocity and jealousy of a people that were nearly a century behind the time, and to feel for those who roamed about without the benefit of civilization, refinement, or religion!" This view of the people of Jackson County was not confined to the Mormons. The first clerk of the Jackson County Circuit Court, Robert Wilson, was assigned to go to Jackson County in March 1827, just months after the county was established. "He was so unfavorably impressed with what he regarded as the roughness and uncultivated manners of the people that he resigned the position in disgust."[41]

More important, perhaps, is the fact that citizens of Boone County were dealing with a handful of Mormons who were passing through, not thousands who proposed to settle there and thus, by their very numbers, challenge the local economic and political balance. No Mormons intended to set up shops and stores, potentially drawing away customers, either locals or travelers on the Santa Fe Trial, from existing merchants. No Mormons proposed to take control of vast tracts of land, frustrating the plans of local speculators. There was no potential in Boone County for Mormons to become a dominant voting bloc, secure political office, or press their antislavery bias. Thus, most of the conditions that precipitated conflict in the western counties simply did not exist in Boone County.

So, were Columbians really different from the Missourians on the western edge of the state? We believe that by and large, they were. If several thousand Mormons had purchased land just south of Columbia with the expectation that Boone County would be their eventual inheritance, would events have proceeded differently? Again, we think the response to the Mormons would have been different, at least in the beginning. According to Viles, "An overwhelming majority of the leading families in Columbia in 1840 have been traced definitely to central Kentucky. These 'better people' were Whigs and largely Presbyterian." Viles observed this in explaining why "these two badges of respectability" would be a handicap in locating the state university in Columbia "in a state consistently democratic in politics and in religion distinctly western, i.e. Baptist, Methodist, and Campbellite."[42]

In his work on Alexander Doniphan, Roger D. Launius noted that the Missouri Whig Party never competed well with the Jacksonian Democrats and was, in fact, "successful enough to achieve a consistent majority in only eighteen of the state's counties." Boone County was one of those counties. It is not accidental that Launius's description of Doniphan's Whig orientation is consistent with the picture of Columbia in 1839 that has emerged from this study:

> Doniphan represented, therefore, a cadre of young Whigs in the 1840s who embraced a system of national economic development, a strong capitalist tradition that he believed would lead both to his personal and the public's greater security and advancement. They also possessed a high-minded value system that emphasized democratic principles and responsibility. These people believed that their future, and the general welfare of the nation as a whole, did not lie in the hard money agrarianism of the Democrats. Nor did it lie with the amoral office-seeking and rascality that they believed present among too many Democrats within the state. In the end, Doniphan and his Whig comrades believed in the principle of governmental responsibility in promoting the welfare of its citizens.[43]

Like Alexander Doniphan, the inhabitants of central Missouri seem to have had a great respect for the rule of law, for negotiation and compromise, for civility and a long-term view of economic good, and for the welfare of the community as a whole. They did not see, as instinctively as did the western Missourians, that violence was the principal solution to their problems. While the popular conception of the attitudes of Missourians toward the Mormon settlers is one of hostility and fervent opposition, that image does not fit the state as a whole.

Perhaps the larger question is whether any neighbors, in Missouri or elsewhere on the frontier, could have been found in the 1830s or 1840s that could have coexisted with the socioeconomic system the Mormons sought to establish. Klaus Hansen has suggested that "Mormonism provided the essential ingredients for a potentially successful movement of revolutionary dimensions in this world—a realistic means for achieving not only a religious but a social, economic, and political millennium." The goal was not to accrue economic benefit to the individual, the mantra of Jacksonian democracy, but rather to the group, to "restore a more traditional society in which the economy was regulated in behalf of the larger interests of the group even if this entailed individual sacrifice." "Such attempts," according to Hansen, "inevitably, would bring the Mormons in conflict with their neighbors, who not only had very little sympathy for communal solidarity but more often than not perceived it as a threat to their own economic ambitions."[44]

Perhaps Hansen is correct, but had the effort been made in central Missouri instead of in the western counties, the social-political culture that dominated Columbia and the surrounding area would have likely encouraged a different sort of unfolding of events between the Mormons and their Missouri neighbors, an unfolding that would have been dominated by a genuine attempt at understanding, negotiation, and compromise.

Notes

1. Alexander Doniphan's pivotal and positive role in the treatment of the Mormons in 1830 has been well documented. See, for example, Alexander L. Baugh, *A Call to Arms: The 1838 Mormon Defense of Northern Missouri* (Provo, Utah: Joseph Fielding Smith Institute for Latter-day Saint History/BYU Studies, 2000); Roger D. Launius, *Alexander Doniphan: Portrait of a Moderate* (Columbia: University of Missouri Press, 1997); Stephen C. LeSueur, *The 1838 Mormon War in Missouri* (Columbia: University of Missouri Press, 1990).

2. *Life of Mary A. Phelps Rich, 1829–1912,* http://boap.org/LDS/EarlySaints/MRich/html (accessed September 19, 2006); Parley P. Pratt, *Autobiography of Parley P. Pratt, One of the Twelve Apostles of the Church of Jesus Christ of Latter-day Saints, Embracing His Life, Ministry and Travels, With Extracts, in Prose and Verse, From His Miscellaneous Writings,* ed. Parley P. Pratt [son of the author] (1873; Salt Lake City, 1985), 182. GospelLink.com, online LDS Library, http://gospelink.com/library/ (accessed Sept 20, 2006); Clifford Geertz, *The Interpretation of Cultures* (New York: Basic Books, 1973), 23.

3. The voting-day debacle is described in detail in LeSueur, *The 1838 Mormon War in Missouri*, 61.

4. The Battle of Crooked River is described in Alexander L. Baugh's "The Battle Between Mormon and Missouri Militia," in *BYU Regional Studies in Latter-day Saint Church History,* eds. Arnold Garr and Clark Johnson (Provo, Utah: Department of Church History and Doctrine, Brigham Young University, 1994), 85–86; the Missourians' intentions are described in a letter from Samuel Bogart to Gen. David R. Atchison, October 23, 1838, *Mormon War Letters* (transcribed from microfilm of originals housed at the Missouri State Archives, Jefferson City, Mo.), http://www.tungate.com/MorWar.htm; exaggerated claims of casualties can be found in a letter from E. M. Ryland to Amos Rees and Willey Williams, October 24, 1838, *Mormon War Letters,* http://www.turngate.com/MorWar.htm; the "extermination order" refers to Missouri Executive Order 44 (1838), stating that "the Mormons must be treated as enemies, and must be exterminated or driven from the State if necessary for the public peace—their outrages are beyond all description."

5. The record of the proceedings of the Court of Inquiry is found in "Document Containing the Correspondence, Orders, etc. In Relation to the Disturbances with the Mormons; and the Evidence Given before the Hon. Austin A. King, Judge of the Fifth Judicial Circuit of the State of Missouri, at the Court-house in Richmond, in a Criminal Court of Inquiry, Begun November 12, 1838, on the Trial of Joseph Smith, Jr., and Others, for High Treason and Other Crimes Against the State," *Boon's Lick Democrat,* 1841 (hereafter referred to as "Document"), http://www.farwesthistory.com/doc01.htm (accessed March 18, 2006).

6. Pratt, *Autobiography,* 182. This is not to suggest that the Court of Inquiry was fair or impartial. The conduct of the tribunal has been severely criticized. See Gordon A. Madsen, "Joseph Smith and the Missouri Court of Inquiry: Austin A. King's Quest for Hostages," *BYU Studies* 4, no. 7 (2004): 92.

7. The murder charges can be found in the order of Judge Austin A. King ("Document," at 150). Rowland was identified in the testimony of Wyatt Cravens ("Document," at 109) and testimony of Morris Phelps ("Document," at 109–10). Phelps testified that Charles C. Rich compelled him to be present by threats. The involvement of Gibbs, Chase, and Shearer was also attested by Addison Green ("Document," at 144).

8. Pratt places the date of their release shortly after April 24, and recounts Shearer's tearful reunion with his father (Pratt, *Autobiography,* 301). The apparent reason for their release was that the grand jury declined to indict them (*Times and Seasons* [1839]: 164–65); Follett had been indicted for robbery (certification of Roger N. Todd, clerk of the Boone Circuit Court, "Document," at 155); the Mormons generally believed that the escape had been made possible intentionally in order to rid the state of them without a trial. See Alexander L. Baugh, "'We Took Our Change of Venue to the State of Illinois': The Gallatin Hearing and the Escape of Joseph Smith and the Mormon Prisoners from Missouri, April 1839," *Mormon Historical Studies* 2, no. 1 (2001): 59–82.

9. William F. Switzler, *History of Boone County, Missouri* (St. Louis: Western Historical Company, 1882; repr. Cape Girardeau, Mo.: Ramfre Press, 1970), 151–52.

10. Information on the early history of Columbia and Boone County has been culled from several sources. These include Switzler, *History of Boone County;* John C. Crighton, *A History of Columbia and Boone County* (Columbia, Mo.: Boone County Historical Society, 1987); and Jonas Viles, *The University of Missouri: A Centennial History, 1839–1919* (Columbia: University of Missouri, 1939.)

11. The agricultural fair, which must have been seen as an enormous undertaking at the time, is described in great detail in Switzler, *History of Boone County,* 202–5; at the time this price for a portrait was set, Bingham was a young man and not nearly so well known as he would eventually become. See C. B. Rollins, editor, "Letters of George Caleb Bingham to James S. Rollins, Part 1," *Missouri Historical Review* 32 (1937): 7. Bingham's later political career is described in Lyn McDaniel, *Bicentennial Boonslick History* (Boonville, Mo.: Boonslick Historical Society, 1976), 57.

12. James and Vera Olsen, *The University of Missouri: An Illustrated History* (Columbia: University of Missouri Press, 1999), 4. According to Olsen, initial admittance standards to the University of Missouri required that students be able to "read in Latin the first book of the *Aeneid,*" have "studied the higher branches of English," and have "advanced beyond the common school level in English grammar, geography, and arithmetic." Descriptions of the process used to secure the University of Missouri in Columbia and Boone County can be found in Olsen, *The University of Missouri;* Switzler, *History of Boone County;* Crighton, *History of Columbia;* and Viles, *University of Missouri.*

13. Switzler, *History of Boone County,* 216; James S. Rollins, a Boone County attorney and state representative, was instrumental in shaping the strategy that secured the university's location in Boone County. Interestingly, he also served as a lawyer for King Follett, one of the prisoners who was recaptured almost immediately after effecting the jailbreak.

14. For information on the Phelps movement during the 1820s and 1830, see *Life of Mary A. Phelps Rich;* also see *Lyman Archives: History of Morris Phelps,* http://

lymanites.org/lyman/archives/pioneerhistory/morrisphelps/asp (accessed September 18, 2006); the story of Morris Phelps's conversion is an interesting one and can be found at "How the Clarks Came to Join the Church," *The Family Website of Ezra T. Clark,* http://ezratclark.org/projects/HowtheClarksCametoJointheChurch.asp (accessed September 18, 2006).

15. *Life of Mary A. Phelps Rich.* This source has been invaluable both for the detail provided and as a counter to the narrative provided by Parley P. Pratt.

16. *Life of Mary A. Phelps Rich;* Parley P. Pratt, *History of the Late Persecution Inflicted by the State of Missouri upon the Mormons* (Detroit: Dawson and Bates, 1839), http://www.boap.org/LDS/Early-Saints/PPratt-pers.html (accessed September 16, 2006); see Pratt, *Autobiography,* 193, 201, for his view of Lumen Gibbs.

17. Pratt, *Autobiography,* 206–7.

18. Ibid.; *Life of Mary A. Phelps Rich;* B. H. Roberts and Joseph Smith, *History of the Church of Jesus Christ of Latter-day Saints,* vol. 3 (Salt Lake City: Deseret, 1948), 382, http://gospelink.com/library/doc?doc_id'201668 (accessed September 20, 2006).

19. Pratt, *Autobiography,* 209.

20. *Life of Mary A. Phelps Rich.*

21. Pratt, *Autobiography,* 212–13.

22. Ibid., 210–11; according to Olsen, *The University of Missouri,* 5, 7, July 4 was a day of celebrations during the next few years in Columbia. The cornerstone for the first university building was erected on July 4, 1840. Three years later, on July 4, 1843, the building, known as Academic Hall, was dedicated. A procession accompanied by a band made its way from the courthouse to the new building to mark the occasion.

23. Roberts and Smith, *History of the Church,* 400; Hattie M. Anderson, "The Evolution of a Frontier Society in Missouri, 1815–1828," part 2, *Missouri Historical Review* 32 (1938): 459–60.

24. Pratt, *Autobiography,* 211; *Life of Mary A. Phelps Rich.*

25. Pratt, *Autobiography,* 213.

26. *Life of Mary A. Phelps Rich.*

27. Pratt, *Autobiography,* 215.

28. Ibid., 224.

29. *Life of Mary A. Phelps Rich.*

30. Pratt, *Autobiography,* 225–26; *Life of Mary A. Phelps Rich.*

31. Ibid.

32. Ibid.

33. Ibid.

34. Pratt, *Autobiography,* 200–204. Of the Richmond experience specifically, Parley P. Pratt wrote, "Alone in a State which was wholly governed by an open banditti of murderers and robbers, we seemed abandoned to our fate, and doomed to suffer that full weight of vengeance and fury which seemed in reserve an entire people; but that people were now beyond their reach; all the fury of the storm, therefore, seemed now to beat upon our heads. We were daily threatened with assassination, without the form of a trial; and repeatedly told that we never should escape alive from the State. Our guards were doubly vigilant, while the Sheriff took every possible precaution."

35. Pratt, *Autobiography,* 201; *Life of Mary A Phelps Rich.*

36. *Life of Mary A. Phelps Rich;* Roberts and Smith, *History of the Church,* 365–66.

37. Pratt, *Autobiography,* 212–13.

38. Ibid., 225.

39. Ibid., 243. Pratt collected a number of newspaper articles that he included in his autobiography.

40. Lewis E. Atherton, "Life, Labor, and Society in Boone County, Missouri, 1834–1852, as Revealed in the Correspondence of an Immigrant Slave-Owning Family from North Carolina," part 1, *Missouri Historical Review* 38 (1944): 284.

41. Roberts and Smith, *History of the Church,* vol. 3, xx; *Political History of Jackson County: Biographical Sketches of Men Who Have Helped Make It* (Kansas City: Marshall and Morrison, 1902), 14.

42. Viles, *University of Missouri,* 20.

43. Launius, *Doniphan,* 73.

44. Klaus J. Hansen, *Mormonism and the American Experience* (Chicago: University of Chicago Press, 1981), 122, 126.

8

Lessons Learned

The Nauvoo Legion and What the Mormons Learned Militarily in Missouri

Richard E. Bennett

The story of the Nauvoo Legion begins in Missouri. What began in 1831 with eager anticipation among a people anxious to establish Zion, their New Jerusalem, in Jackson County, Missouri, ended with a solemn proclamation of expulsion in October 1838 by a governor convinced the Mormons had to leave the state. Rather then establish a place of peace and a safe refuge from the world, the Mormons were forced to take up arms and defend themselves. By the time they quit Missouri for Illinois in the winter of 1838–1839, they had learned bitter lessons in how to survive in an American frontier setting, lessons they would put to use in establishing the Nauvoo Legion. Here we identify what some of those lessons were, especially those of a military nature, and argue that two of the well-known Mormon military expressions in Missouri—Zion's Camp and the Danites—were models for how *not* to run a militia. In other words, we will explore the salient differences between these two earlier Mormon military efforts and the Nauvoo Legion.

In April 1830, Joseph Smith Jr. organized what became the Church of Jesus Christ of Latter-day Saints in a small township in upstate in New York. Preaching the message of a restored primitive Christianity, the Book of Mormon as a new book of scripture, and the expectation of the imminent, premillennial return of the Lord Jesus Christ, Smith and his rapidly growing number of followers preached Mormonism with notable success first in New York, then in Ohio, and later in New England, Upper Canada, and Great Britain. Central to Smith's theology was the belief that Zion, their prophesied New Jerusalem, must be established before Christ's return. By revelation he identified "the center place" of Zion as Independence, Missouri, which in 1831 was a fledgling frontier river town on the upper Missouri River not far from Indian lands in the western frontier of the United States. Convinced as well that the American Indian was a remnant of God's ancient chosen people and the primary audience of the Book of Mormon, Latter-day Saints began to congregate in western Missouri in the summer of 1831.

Jackson County may have been Zion in Mormon parlance, but in the vocabulary of the rapidly expanding local populations it represented an exciting new commercial opportunity. By 1832 Independence so dominated the southwest trade as an outfitting point for the Santa Fe Trail that one visitor described it as a town "full of promise . . . consisting of nothing but a ragged congeries of five or six rough log-huts, two or three clap-board houses, two or three co-called hotels (alias, grog shops), and a few stores . . . but nevertheless a thriving and aspiring place."[1] One would be hard pressed to find any other place in America where the divide between a religious dream and cultural reality was wider than Independence in 1830.

Eagerly anticipating establishing their Zion in this far west community, the Mormons were entirely unprepared for the clash of cultures that awaited them. Most western Missourians in the early 1830s hailed from the upper South and had brought with them much of Southern culture. Predominantly Protestant, they, too, believed in God and in such values as industry, integrity, and the common good. Fierce individualists, they were committed to the Jacksonian American ideals of free enterprise, democracy, and a strong capitalist work ethic. They deeply distrusted religious zealotry, especially the kind that looked upon their own backyards as temple lots and hallowed ground. As Southerners, they also revered the "peculiar institution" of slavery, and reflected other Southern cultural characteristics in their way of life.

No less a scholar of the South than W. J. Cash has argued that the Southern character of individualism and independence likewise contributed to the "perpetuation and acceleration of the tendency to violence which had grown up in the Southern backwoods . . . conflict with them could only mean immediate physical clashing, could only mean fisticuffs, the gouging ring, and knife and gun play . . . the tradition of vigilante action."[2] Such individualism contrasted markedly with the group mentality of the newly arrived Latter-day Saints who in 1831 were pooling all of their resources and energies into living a new economic order, what they termed the "Law of Consecration." Trading among themselves and shunning so-called Gentile merchants, the Mormons looked primarily to themselves for economic support. Their banding together in matters of religion, trade, and community made their "outsidedness" all the more pronounced—and suspicious.

Warren A. Jennings, a careful Mormon scholar, has identified several other reasons for this almost inevitable confrontation. They include the Mormon penchant for purchasing lands on a large scale for future immigrants and the existing residents' fear of a Mormon takeover, the rapid influx of new Mormon settlers and the non-Mormon fear of losing political control, and articles in the Mormon-owned Independence newspaper *Evening and Morning Star* over importing "free people of color." Jennings adds yet another, perhaps more basic reason: the Latter-day Saints were as politically naïve as they were religiously motivated and were, frankly, unprepared for as violent a society as western Missouri turned out to be.[3]

When the local citizenry banded together to drive the Mormons out of Jackson County, the Saints "were in a state of shock as a result of their treatment. They were perplexed as to why it had happened, they were dismayed by their prospects, and they were puzzled about their future."[4] Poorly equipped for this or any other kind of warfare, the Latter-day Saints "had not embodied for defense, though it appears that a number of them had guns. None had joined the local militia regiment," and they concluded belatedly "that each branch would organize into its own defenses and muster its own men."[5] Fearing a full-scale massacre in early November 1833 after killings on both sides, the Mormons were forced to sign an agreement and agreed to surrender their arms and vacate their homes and farms in the county by January 1, 1834. The refugees crossed the Missouri River and settled near Liberty where local citizens welcomed them, at least temporarily.[6]

Upon hearing of the rising tide of Missouri persecution, Smith petitioned President Andrew Jackson and Governor Daniel Dunklin for redress but without success. Frustrated, he organized a military unit of some two hundred men called "Zion's Camp" that marched from Kirtland, Ohio, starting on May 1, 1834, to the outskirts of Liberty, Missouri, arriving there by mid-June. With Smith as commander in chief and Lyman Wight as major general, Zion's Camp's immediate purpose was to deliver twenty wagons of supplies and, with the anticipated support of state militiamen, to reinstate the Mormons in Jackson County. Neither part of the regular army of the United States nor of any state militia, Zion's Camp was a paramilitary, legally questionable, yet understandable reaction to the illegal, unjust actions of Jackson County mobs on the one hand and the inactions of elected officials on the other. More than anything else, it was a statement against perceived injustices. Inadequately provisioned, poorly trained, without sufficient arms, and eventually decimated by disease, it never really intended to fight on its own.[7] Had Zion's Camp taken the field against Missouri mobs and militia, the outcome would have been one-sided indeed. While it may well have focused public attention on the plight of the Mormons—and surely everyone in western Missouri knew an armed reaction was coming—it "left a legacy of ill will." Many Missourians "who otherwise had been friendly to the Mormons, were antagonized by the intrusion of a large force of armed men from outside the state."[8] When it became clear that no state regiments would be allowed to work with Zion's camp to protect the Mormon settlers, Smith wisely disbanded it in favor of effecting a more peaceful compromise.

Thanks to the legislative action of Alexander Doniphan that led to the creation of two new counties in the northern part of Ray County primarily for Mormon settlement—Caldwell and Daviess—the Mormons began moving northward en masse in late 1837. While it was tacitly understood that they would settle primarily in Caldwell County, they lost little time in organizing new communities in both counties. Far West became their new capital in Caldwell County and Adam-ondi-Ahman further north in Daviess County.

During this period in Missouri, the Mormons responded militarily in ways much different than before. First of all, by taking full advantage of the militia laws of the state and with the encouragement of state officials, they organized themselves into a bone fide county militia—in this case, the Fifty-third Regiment of Caldwell County. Eventually placed under the titular direction of Joseph Smith as commander in chief, but essentially directed by Major General Lyman Wight, this regiment was a legitimate, relatively well-trained detachment of the state militia with full right to state arms and equipment.[9]

This militia should not be confused with that band of Mormon zealots or extremists that came to be called the "Avenging Angels" or "Danites." The Danites were secretly organized by Sampson Avard and had, as historian Alex Baugh argues, at least three purposes: to intimidate apostate Mormons into leaving Mormon society, to enforce living the Law of Consecration, and to influence state and county elections in favor of Latter-day Saints.[10] This group, as historian David March has argued, was "ostensibly formed for defense against non-Mormon aggression" and "seems to have been equally concerned with enforcing conformity among the Saints. . . . Smith, unaware of Avard's machinations, evidently knew little, if anything, about the Danite band."[11]

Other scholars have argued that Joseph Smith was much more involved with the Danites than previous writers have been willing to admit. Stephen C. LeSueur maintains that Smith "directed much of the plundering and burning committed by Mormon soldiers in Daviess County" and that the "Danite organization was the product of, not an aberration from, Mormon attitudes and teachings. The Danites represented mainstream Mormonism."[12] D. Michael

Quinn has written that "what the Danites did militarily during the summer and fall of 1838 was by the general oversight and command of Joseph Smith."[13] Both argue that the actions of a few Mormon militants like Avard and Lyman Wight are indicative of a spirit of militancy that characterized the entire Latter-day Saint movement. Richard L. Bushman in his recent biography of Joseph Smith concedes that there were "militant elements" in Missouri Mormonism, but thinks that Smith acknowledged the legitimacy of the Danites but not their violence; "When it came to violence, Joseph was a man of words" and his "military instincts were defensive."[14] At the very least, if the Mormon leader did not know of the activities of the Danites, he should have.[15]

Whatever Joseph Smith's actual role, the actions of the Danites were violent, secretive, and oftentimes illegal and should not be confused with the many legitimate efforts by the Mormons to join the state militia and to use legal means to insure self-protection and redress. Then, on October 25, 1838, some sixty Latter-day Saints led by David W. Patten fought against a regiment of the Missouri militia at Crooked River in Ray County.[16] While the Mormons carried the day, some men were killed on both sides, including Patten. This attack so alarmed those opposed to the Mormons that civil war appeared imminent. Under these conditions, Governor Lilburn W. Boggs "ordered out the First, Fourth, Fifth, Sixth and Twelfth divisions" of the Missouri militia on October 26 and the very next day issued his infamous extermination order.[17] Four days later, a militia mob of some two hundred men from Daviess and Livingston Counties attacked the Mormon settlement of Haun's Mill where they killed seventeen poorly armed men and boys. That same day, twenty-two hundred to three thousand militiamen arrived in Far West and would surely have executed the surrendered Mormon leader had it not been for the courageous objections of his lawyer and Missouri militia leader Alexander Doniphan. On November 6, General John B. Clark, a political enemy of Boggs who had assumed command of the Missouri militia regiments, ordered the Mormons to leave the state as soon as possible. Meanwhile Smith and his fellow leaders were taken into custody and sent to Independence, then to Richmond, and finally to Liberty Jail to await trail on the charge of treason while Brigham Young organized the exodus of thousands to Quincy, Illinois.[18] Thus ended the unhappy Mormon sojourn in Missouri.

Fleeing to Quincy and ultimately to Commerce, Illinois, the Mormons began to rebuild, this time in Nauvoo, on the eastern bank of the Mississippi River. Recognizing the need to obey the law as well as to defend themselves, one of their first moves was to obtain a bona fide city charter approved by the state legislature. Furthermore, they obtained state authorization to fulfill their militia obligations by organizing a city militia rather than serve in already existing county militias. John C. Bennett was successful in lobbying Springfield for both. As a result, the Nauvoo city charter and the Nauvoo Legion charter were signed into law by Governor Thomas Carlin on December 16, 1840, to take effect February 1, 1841.

The Nauvoo Legion would be significantly different from Mormon military activities in Missouri in several ways. First, unlike Zion's Camp and the Danites, everything about the Legion would be done publicly and aboveboard. The Latter-day Saints simply could not afford the public relations problem of more secret bands and parallel militias. The Legion would be well uniformed, drill on public squares, be open for review and inspection, and frequently parade in the community. Not a police force (a Nauvoo city police came into being much later), the Legion would be at the beck and call of the state. The Mormons hoped that its size and skill would serve as a deterrent against any outside encroachment. Furthermore, unlike misunderstandings in Missouri, many of which were their own fault, it would be made clear from the beginning that the Nauvoo Legion was a state, not a private religious militia. They would make much more concentrated efforts to keep in closer contact with the commander in chief, that is, the governor of the state, who by constitutional mandate commands all state militias. The records show that Joseph Smith, lieutenant general, went out of his way to defer to the governor and to keep him informed.

While some have argued that the Nauvoo Legion was but another piece in the Mormon military puzzle, a continuation of the culture of militancy and violence, the fact is that even before the formation of the Legion, the Latter-day Saints enlisted in existing local militias, both to obtain needed arms as well as to fulfill state militia requirements. As per federal law, every able-bodied man between the ages of eighteen and forty-five had a militia duty to discharge. Unlike their experience in Jackson County, Mormons moving into Illinois enlisted in the state militia almost as soon as they arrived there. The best evidence for this is the fact that many of them, pending further directions, had already joined the Illinois Fifty-ninth Regiment of Hancock County almost as soon as they took up residence. The Illinois Fifty-ninth, a company of light infantry, had been officially organized in 1835.[19] By 1840, with the arrival of so many new settlers, the Mormons constituted a significant percentage of the seventy-eight persons, rank and file, belonging to it, with Don Carlos Smith, Joseph Smith's younger brother, serving as its lieutenant colonel.[20] In September 1840 he made a formal request to Governor Carlin for "88 muskets, bayonets and accoutrements—the company being organized according to law."[21] Many joined because they eagerly volunteered or were persuaded by their peers; however, it would not be correct to call the Legion strictly a volunteer company.

As Nauvoo grew, the numbers of recruits would far outpace the Fifty-ninth Regiment's capacity. Thus to accommodate the rapidly rising Mormon population and the demands of the law, either additional county regiments would have to be formed, or provision be made for one or more "independent" city companies. As soon as the Legion was legally formed and permission granted for switching from the county regiments to a city legion, most Nauvoo citizens, including those who had served previously in the Fifty-ninth, enlisted in the Legion. This city regiment or "odd battalion" was to be independent not of the state militia but only from the local Fifty-ninth Hancock and other surrounding county regiments. Precedent for such city militias had long existed in American militia history. And as Nauvoo was to become one of the largest cities in the American West, the Legion grew in proportion with it.

State adjutant general files clearly show that the Legion was, from its inception, a unit of the Illinois state militia obeying first the orders of the city mayor but ultimately responsible to the governor, acting in his capacity as commander in chief.[22] Its officers, though selected by the rank and file, including Smith as lieutenant general, were ultimately responsible to the governor and, if ever called into action with the federal military, subordinate to commanding officers of the standing U.S. Army.

Second, unlike the Missouri debacle, Smith would here be firmly in control. While the Mormon leader languished almost six months in Liberty Jail in the winter of 1838-1839, he had given much thought to their Missouri mistakes. As historian Leonard Arrington has suggested, free as Smith was from the daily business of running the Church, "Here [Smith] had uninterrupted time to think out the wider implication of the Latter-day movement. The Liberty Jail experience brought him to ponder his course, to synthesize ideas, to formulate goals, and to communicate in an unhurried manner with the Lord."[23] While his indignation against Missouri remained constant, railing against his oppressors there as "the most beastly set of men that the earth can boast of [who] . . . steal to plunder to starve and to exterminate and burn the houses of the Mormons,"[24] there was another side to this hurtful equation. He came to the painful recognition that his own people were not without blame and that he as leader had more to learn. It is true that Smith attributed much of their distress to apostates. "Renegadoes, Mormon dissenters are running through the world and spreading various foul and libelous reports against us thinking thereby to gain the friendship of the world . . . Such characters God hates. We cannot love them the world hates them and we sometimes think the devil ought to be ashamed of them."[25] Specifically referring to George Hinkle, William W. Phelps, Sampson Avard, William E. McLellin, John and David Whitmer, Oliver Cowdery, and Martin Harris, "whose cloak of hypocrisy was not sufficient to shield them or to hold them up in the hour of trouble," Smith condemned them as "truce breakers and despisers of those who do good, traitors and tyrants," and the cause of so much affliction.[26] And in words which Mormons now accept as scripture, he reprimanded and chastened priests in no uncertain terms: "No power or influence can or ought to be maintained by virtue of the priesthood, only by persuasion, by long-suffering, by gentleness and meekness, and by love unfeigned.... Let thy bowels also be full of charity towards all men" (Doctrine and Covenants 121: 34-37, 41, 45).

Yet he also had time to consider the excesses of his own people, their secret groups such as the Danites, and the stark possibility that he had not provided as strong and careful leadership at Far West as he should have. Certainly they would learn from their mistakes. "And again I would further suggest the impropriety of the organization of bands or companies by covenants or oaths by penalties or secrecies," he wrote just a fortnight before his escape, "but let the time past of our experience and sufferings by the wickedness of Doctor [Sampson] Avard suffice and let our covenant be that of the everlasting covenant as is contained in Holy writ and the things that God hath revealed unto us. Pure friendship always becomes weakened the very moment you undertake to make it stronger by penal oaths and secrecy . . . Our religion . . . gives scope to the mind which enables us to conduct ourselves with greater liberality towards all others."[27] Troubled by the excesses of the Danites, much of which he now repudiated, as prophet-leader he knew that he bore some of the responsibility for their doings and determined that in the future Mormon military movements must abide by the law.

Joseph Smith's appointment as lieutenant general of the Nauvoo Legion has long been perceived by some as evidence of his interest in the military, if not aspirations for power. Like his grandfathers, who had distinguished themselves in the Revolutionary War, he had military interests. And as referenced earlier, in 1834 he had led Zion's Camp from Ohio to Missouri in hopes of securing the legal rights and properties of the Saints who had been driven out of Jackson County. Yet the lieutenant general job seems to be one he did not seek, as Wilford Woodruff has recorded. He quoted Smith:

> As to the military station I hold and the cause of my holding it is as follows: when we came here, the state required us to bear arms, and do military duty according to the law, and as the church had just been driven from the state of Missouri, and robbed of all their property and arms, they were poor and destitute of arms, [and] they were liable to be fined for not doing duty, when they had not arms to do it with. They came to me for advice and I advised them to organize themselves into independent companies and demand arms of the state: this they did . . . I then told the saints that though I was clear from military duty by law, in consequence of lameness in one of my legs, yet I would set the example, and would do duty myself, they said

> they were willing to do duty, if they would be formed into an independent company and I could be at their head; this is the origin of the Nauvoo Legion and of my holding office of lieutenant general.[28]

His military rank raised little or no comment at the state adjutant general's office when the returns were submitted. Although by law most other regiments were commanded by a major general or lesser officer, in practice militias were free to choose virtually whomever they wanted as leader and in what position. While it was unusual and perhaps in the long run unwise for Smith to hold such a daunting rank—one no other man in American military history had held since George Washington nor would again until Ulysses S. Grant—militarily it meant little more than a ceremonial title for a local commander, in this case one held in such esteem among his followers. However, such a ranking, tantamount to that of major general elsewhere, did not outrank any other unit's commanding officer. Indeed, the ultimate authority over the Legion and every other local regiment, battalion, or legion was neither prophet nor priest, major nor mayor, but the governor of the state. Likewise, ever since controversies stemming from the War of 1812, it was well established in law and upheld by court ruling that no officer in any state militia could ever outrank an officer of the standing U.S. Army. If some later charged that Smith was seeking power in position by the use of the title "lieutenant general," none in Springfield or in Nauvoo felt so at the time.

A third lesson: unlike Sampson Avard and the Nauvoo Legion's cofounder, John C. Bennett, Smith saw the Legion as a deterrent against aggression and would only call upon it as a military force as a last resort. While this will ever be a debatable point among those who assert that Smith saw it otherwise—and certainly he often spoke in confrontational tones—rhetoric was one thing, action quite another. Writing to James Arlington Bennett in New York about recent difficulties, he said, "Our enemies shall not have it to say that we rebel against government or commit treason. However much they may lift their hands in oppression and tyranny, when it comes in the form of government we tamely submit, although it leads us to the slaughter and to beggary."[29] In light of how the Mormon leader would eventually submit to government requests, at the expense of his life, these words are more than prophetic; they are characteristic of the man. Carry the threat of action, but seldom if ever employ it, even at the cost of their lives.

While Bennett later argued that the real purpose of the Legion was "to execute a daring and colossal scheme of rebellion and usurpation throughout the Northwestern States of the Union . . . and [erect] upon the ruin of their present governments a despotic military and religious empire,"[30] if such were the designs of the Legion, no one else knew it. Ever and always more militant than his leaders, Bennett believed in military force as a way to achieve his goals and wanted to be at the forefront of any such deliberate actions. Why Joseph Smith never used the Legion as a vengeful force against its enemies puzzled him. Why have force and not use it?

A fourth point: one argument over the Legion was that its very size bespoke an offensive military intent. Its numbers did, indeed, grow in concert with the city's rising population, but to go on the attack was not generally part of the Legion's purpose. Although it is true that at one point members of the Legion went on the offensive to rescue Smith from what the Mormons believed was unjust arrest by Missouri sheriffs, an arrest that even Governor Ford condemned, in most every other situation it acted in a defensive measure. This was certainly the case when all feared an imminent attack upon the city by outside enemies. In response to threats upon their leader's life and upon the city and its citizens, the Legion scheduled frequent musters and drills. More than a motley crew of state militiamen, it saw itself increasingly as the first line of defense in whatever troubles lay ahead.

A fifth and final lesson from Missouri: incorporated into the Legion's charter was the right to discipline and court-martial its enlistees. While there has been much discussion about the legislative and executive powers of the Legion's court-martial powers, the fact is it was in compliance with provisions for militias under the U.S. Constitution. It was terribly important to the leadership of the Legion that they be able to exercise control over those men who might disregard law and authority and, as in Missouri, bring down ruin upon the Mormon people.

In conclusion, I have argued that the Nauvoo Legion resulted, at least in part, from bitter lessons the Mormons learned from Missouri. Neither Zion's Camp nor the Danites would serve as its model. They had shown how not to operate a militia. The situation in Nauvoo would be different from Missouri on several counts. First, everything would be done publicly and aboveboard. Second, the Nauvoo Legion would be clearly established by law and chartered under the authority of the state and its constitution. Third, unlike Missouri, where Avard and others had embarrassed the Latter-day Saints, Joseph Smith would be firmly, and very publicly, in control. Fourth, the Legion would function primarily defensively. Fifth and finally, the Legion would retain and exercise the constitutional provision to discipline and court-martial unruly members. While violence would later engulf the Mormons in Nauvoo and embroil the Legion in a scenario that led to the murder of Smith in June 1844, the Nauvoo Legion should be seen as a response to much that had gone wrong in Missouri.

Notes

1. Eugene T. Wells, "The Growth of Independence, Missouri, 1827–1850," *Missouri Historical Society Bulletin* 16 (October 1959): 36.

2. W. J. Cash, *The Mind of the South* (New York: Alfred A. Knopf, 1957), 43.

3. Warren A. Jennings, "Zion Is Fled: The Expulsion of the Mormons from Jackson County, Missouri" (PhD diss., University of Florida, 1962), 20.

4. Ibid., 203.

5. Ibid., 169.

6. Of interest is the fact that the state did not trust local militia regiments to escort the Mormons out of the state and to court proceedings but rather relied on the better disciplined, uniformed companies to carry out such tasks. John Glendower Westover, "The Evolution of the Missouri Militia, 1804–1919" (PhD diss., University of Missouri, 1948), 88.

7. Alexander L. Baugh, *A Call to Arms: The 1838 Mormon Defense of Northern Missouri* (Provo, Utah: Joseph Fielding Smith Institute for Latter-day Saint History and Brigham Young University Studies, 2000), 11.

8. Jennings, "Zion Is Fled," 293.

9. Baugh, *A Call to Arms,* 9. As Lyman Wight stated, "The county having been settled, the governor issued an order for the organization of the county and of a regiment of militia; and an election being called for . . . I was elected unanimously, receiving 236 votes in August 1837" (cited in Baugh, *A Call to Arms,* 14).

10. Ibid., 37.

11. David March, *The History of Missouri* (New York: Lewis Historical Publishing, 1967), 2: 558.

12. Stephen C. LeSueur, *The 1838 Mormon War in Missouri* (Columbia: University of Missouri Press, 1987), 4, 46.

13. D. Michael Quinn, *The Mormon Hierarchy: Origins of Power* (Salt Lake City: Signature Press, 1994), 99.

14. Richard L. Bushman, *Joseph Smith: Rough Stone Rolling. A Cultural Biography of Mormonism's Founder* (New York: Alfred Knopf, 2005), 371.

15. If Joseph Smith did not know the full extent of Danite excesses before he was incarcerated, he certainly came to know them afterwards. Six weeks following his arrest, he summarized the Danite situation as he understood it: "We have learned also since we have been in prison that many false and pernicious things which were calculated to lead the saints far astray and to do great injury have been taught by Dr. Avard as coming from the Presidency . . . which the presidency never knew of being taught in the church by any body until after they were made prisoners . . . the presidency were ignorant as well as innocent of these things" (*The Papers of Joseph Smith: Autobiographical and Historical Writings,* 2 vols., ed. Dean C. Jessee [Salt Lake City: Deseret, 1989], 2: 297). See also *History of the Church,* 3:321, and Baugh, *Call to Arms,* 42–43.

16. Westover, "The Missouri Militia," 75. The core of Mormon resistance was the Fifty-third Regiment, commanded by Col. George W. Hinkle. All of its officers had been commissioned by Gov. Boggs. However, like every other regiment in the state of Missouri, it was inadequately provisioned. Although the Fifty-third made great efforts to arm itself, it had "only 630 guns for its 700 to 1000 men when it was sanctioned" (Westover, "The Missouri Militia," 79).

17. R. J. Robertson, "The Mormon Experience in Missouri, 1830–1839," part 1, *Missouri Historical Review* 68 (1974): 289.

18. There is some disagreement over the nature of these Missouri militias. Baugh argues that they were almost certainly local regiments, almost mobs, with a strong degree of anti-Mormon feelings; "The county militia that came against the Mormons in Jackson County in 1833, and the units called out by Boggs in the 1838 conflict, were comprised almost exclusively of local and county irregulars, not volunteers . . . It was not until the 1840s and 50s that independent companies came into vogue in Missouri" (*A Call to Arms*, 28).

Missouri militia historian John G. Westover, on the other hand, seems to think otherwise. Uniformed companies were better trained and better equipped than local regiments would have been. If so, many of them may have been uniformed companies. As late as 1825, such Missouri volunteers had been allowed to form battalions and regiments of their own. When eight or more such uniformed companies of different corps existed in a brigade, they could form a legion made up of foot regiments, cavalry, and artillery. Such "Legionary battalions" may have participated in the forces that faced the Mormons in October 1838. See Westover, "The Missouri Militia," 92–93. Likely, the forces called out to fight the so-called Mormon War were a mixture of local militiamen who were stridently opposed to the Mormons and units of better-trained volunteers.

19. "Militia Regiments" ledger, 1819–1835, Illinois State Archives, Springfield, Illinois.

20. Among the many other Latter-day Saints serving in the Fifty-ninth Regiment of Hancock County were William and Wilson Law, Albert P. Rockwood, James Guyman, Amos Perry, Titus Billings, Charles C. Rich, Francis Higbee, Hiram Kimball, and Thomas Rich. See "Commission Records. Ledger Book, 1835–1846," vol. 12, 368–71, Illinois State Archives.

21. Don Carlos Smith, Lt. Col. 59th, to Thomas Carlin, September 27, 1840, executive papers, "Governors Correspondence," 1840 Military Affairs, Illinois State Archives. There is some confusion as to the date of the organization of the Fifty-ninth Regiment. If organized in 1835, it was the Latter-day Saints who, needing arms and anxious to fulfill their legal duty, revitalized it.

22. See the commission records of the Illinois State Militia, 1835–1846 ledger book, Illinois State Archives, pp. 39–44. See also "Governor Correspondence—Military—Hancock County and Nauvoo Legion, 1840–1844," Illinois State Archives.

23. Leonard J. Arrington, "Church Leaders in Liberty Jail," *BYU Studies* 13, no. 1 (Fall 1972): 23.

24. *Personal Writings of Joseph Smith*, comp. and ed. Dean C. Jessee (Salt Lake City: Deseret, 1984), 378.

25. Ibid., 379.

26. Ibid., 381.

27. Ibid., 405–6.

28. *Wilford Woodruff's Journal*, ed. Scott G. Kenney (Midvale, Utah: Signature Books, 1983), July 4, 1843, 2: 258.

29. *History of the Church*, 5: 158.

30. John C. Bennett, *A History of the Saints: An Exposé of Joe Smith and the Mormons* (Boston: LeLand and Whiting, 1842), 300, 306.

9

Between the Borders

Mormon Transmigration through Missouri, 1838–1868

Fred E. Woods

Negative Response to the Extermination Order

The infamous extermination order issued October 27, 1838, by Missouri governor Lilburn W. Boggs caused thousands of Latter-day Saints to flee the state and seek refuge in Illinois.[1] Throughout the harsh winter of 1838–1839, many Latter-day Saint families fled eastward (some 150 miles) by carts, wagons, and on foot, and crossed the Mississippi River on the Quincy ferry or by riverboat from Richmond, Missouri, to the Quincy region.[2]

After this initial exodus, however, Mormons crossed the state for the next three decades on their way west, until the transcontinental railroad made the route obsolete. This study takes a careful look at the emigration experience of Latter-day Saints who passed through the state of Missouri during the three decades following the extermination order of Governor Boggs. It reveals a neglected period in Mormon history when the Saints continued their journey over hundreds of Missouri miles by sail, rail, and trail in spite of an official government death threat to all those who dared trespass upon Missouri soil.

The forced exodus during the frigid winter of 1838–1839 deeply embittered the Mormons against Missourians and continued to fester long after the Saints had gathered in the Salt Lake Valley a decade later. Such resentment is evident through several Mormon emigrant accounts recorded during the mid–nineteenth century. The painful memory of the cruel treatment at the hand of the western Missourian mobocrats during the decade of the 1830s was deeply etched. Even before the Saints reached the Great Basin, several accounts from the mid-nineteenth century verify the migrating Saints' tarnished views of the Missourians. [3]

Prophesies of Doom upon the Heads of Missouri Mobocrats

Mormon narratives evidence that the memories of mobocracy, coupled with predictions of a just vengeance, lingered in the minds of the Saints as they encountered bleached bones strewn across the overland trail heading west. Although the Prophet Joseph Smith had publicly prayed, "Have Mercy, O Lord upon the wicked Mob, who have driven thy people . . . if repentance is to be found,"[4] he also warned, "Let the government of Missouri redress the wrongs she has done to the Saints, or let the curse follow them from generation to generation."[5]

In the summer of 1850, Latter-day Saint emigrant Nelson Whipple Wheeler described what he apparently viewed as the literal fulfillment of the curse: "Many of the bodies of those jentiles were dug up and eaton by the wolves (which were most numerous in the Platt Country)[6] . . . and their bodies lay to bleach on the Desert. This was a literal fulfillment of some of the predictions of the Prophet Joseph as vary many of these vary men ware the ones that had Driven the Saints from Missouri and murdered and plundered them thire."[7] James Madison Fisher, who also crossed the plains that summer, recalled, "I will mention a prophasy of Joseph Smith the prophet he prophesied that the mosuri [Missouri] mobocrat bones would bleach upon the plains we saw many graves where the wolves had draged the bodies out they *stunk* allong the road. We heard they were from Mosuri."[8]

The most gruesome witness was penned by British convert Thomas Steed, who crossed the Plains in 1850 with the Milo Andrus Company:

> Such a horrible scene as I beheld I hope never to see again; the graves of the cholera victims were there, with head-boards bearing their names, who were from Missouri; but the hyenas had dug open the graves, dragged the cadavers out and devoured the flesh from their bones; the ravens had plucked out their eyes, and their bloody long skeletons lay stretched out on the ground. That awful sight shocked my feelings beyond expression. I did not take note of their names, unfortunately, but I remembered many were of the mobbers of Missouri, who had so cruelly treated our people. Then I recalled the prophecy of Joseph Smith: "You shall not die a natural death; the judgements of the Almighty shall overtake you; the wolves shall eat the flesh from your bones and the ravens shall pluck out your eyes." And I saw it literally fulfilled . . . This was between Fort Kearney and the crossing of the South Platte.[9]

Attitudes and Avoidance of Salt Lake City

The acceptance of the certainty of God's awful wrath heaped upon the Missourians was widespread among the Mormons. Apparently this widely held view deterred Missouri migrants from entering the city of the Saints. For example, on July 2, 1849, James H. Humphreys of Hannibal, Missouri, wrote, "having some fear of going through Salt Lake on account of the ill feelings they the Mormans had against the Missourians, we concluded to take the Serblets [Sublette's] Cut Off."[10]

Perhaps the bleached bones prophecies and reports like Albert King Thurber's reached the ears of Missourian migrants heading west: "Arrived in G. S. [L.] City July 19 [1849]. I was riding along the street I spoke to an aged man. Well, says he, we are glad to see you if you did not drive us out of Missouri, which was all Greek to me as I knew nothing of Mormons or their history."[11] That same year, Leonard Babcock worked in Salt Lake City for a few weeks before traveling on to Los Angeles. During his brief stay, Babcock received a firsthand account of the dark days of Missouri from a Mormon named James Hendricks, who had been severely wounded at the Battle of Crooked River. Babcock wrote, "Worked for a man Hendricks who was shot in the back of the neck . . . when Mormons was driven out of Mo. on Crooked River—battle grounds."[12] Such reports no doubt influenced the perception of this emigrant regarding the difficult relationship that existed between some Mormon victims and their Missourian abusers.

One Missourian who traveled to California the following year wrote, "I went north of Salt Lake City as the Mormons we [were] down on Missourians generally many Missouri trains got in trouble If their stock got in to the gardens or any fields they were fined heavily It was charged that the mormons would turn the cattle in on purpose to make trouble I knew many emigrants that ware ruined and had to work their way to oregon or California."[13] Another emigrant wrote:

> We arrived at Salt Lake in the early part of August [1849] and stopped nearby the settlements from Friday to Sunday. . . . There was a large circular canvass suspended in the form of a great tent under which the people had their meetings and in which Brigham Young preached the Sunday we were there. I was not feeling very well and did not attend the meeting. I was told that he said that there were people coming and skulking through that place on the way to California, who had taken part in driving them out of Missouri, and if he could catch them, he would send them to Hell Across Lota. There were some Missourians who became alarmed and started on as soon as possible.[14]

On July 24, 1850, Dan Carpenter cited a Pioneer Day celebration in Salt Lake City:

> The Mormons this day cellebrate the arrival of the first settlement of this valley 3 years ago by them. We are in a hearing of their cannons, by way of jollification. The whole valley comes to this city today and have a perfect jubilee. The music waggon for today is drawn by 14 horses, large and commodious. The Mormons curse the d——d ragged Emigrant Sons of Bitches from Mo. & Ill. Traveling through their country.[15]

Notwithstanding such resentment that seemed to pollute the migrant plains, Mormon converts (mostly from Europe and the eastern United States) continued to cross Missouri borders by steam and rail during the next three decades when the extermination order was still in effect.[16]

Knowing what Utah Mormons generally thought of passing migrant Missourians, what did the Mormon migrants encounter during this tumultuous period of the mid–nineteenth century when they traveled across Missouri? What challenges did they face as they traversed this American Mesopotamia from the Mississippi to the Missouri River? The engaging story of Mormon transmigration through Missouri during the sail, rail, trail years of Mormon emigration is one worth telling and also one that has been largely neglected.

Though it is true that most Mormons fled the state at the time of the extermination order, some found refuge on the eastern edge of Missouri in the metropolis of St. Louis. This thriving city also served as an inland transmigration port for about 18,000 European Saints who crossed the Atlantic and traveled up the Mississippi during the years 1840 to 1855.[17]

Mormon Transmigration through St. Louis during the Nauvoo Years (1840–1846)

During the years when British Latter-day Saint converts emigrated to Nauvoo (1840–1846), they often stopped briefly in St. Louis. After about a twelve-day trip up the Mississippi River from New Orleans to St. Louis, most Saints picked up another steamer to travel the rest of the way to Nauvoo. Some were delayed due to sandbars, snags, currents, and ice. For example, Mormon immigrants from the Atlantic ships the *Sidney* and the *Medford* joined in New Orleans, took the steamboat *Alex Scott* up the Mississippi and were stuck for three weeks ninety miles below St. Louis because the water was so low in the river. By the time they arrived in St. Louis, the river had frozen over, forcing them to spend the winter of 1843 there.[18]

Another LDS company, which crossed the Atlantic a month later on the *Emerald,* was also detained in the river cities of Alton, Chester, and St. Louis for three winter months because of ice on the Mississippi.[19] Parley P. Pratt, the company leader of the *Emerald,* decided against St. Louis on the following grounds: "I landed with my family in Chester, Illinois—eighty miles below St. Louis. The company continued on to St. Louis. My reason for landing there was, that I would not venture into Missouri after the abuses I had experienced there in former times."[20]

The following year, a number of LDS immigrants from the 1844 *Norfolk* voyage were stuck in St. Louis for a different reason: they did not have sufficient funds to continue the journey to Nauvoo.[21] St. Louis was a place that most Nauvoo-bound immigrating Saints wanted to pass through in a hurry. There was the threat of cholera or yellow fever and a hardness in the hearts of the St. Louis Mormon apostates that seemed as cold as the ice on the Mississippi.[22] Such hardness frequently affected the Mormon migrants on their way to Nauvoo. For example, Hiram Clark, who gathered to Zion with a group of 181 Saints in 1841, noted that about thirty of his group had been "disaffected through false reports" and therefore chose to tarry at St. Louis.[23]

Thomas Wrigley, who went to Nauvoo in 1843 to prepare the way for his British family, met opposition on two fronts. When he visited his sister's non-Mormon family, he related that "they tried their best by every means to persuade me to give up my faith."[24] Returning to St. Louis the following year to bring his family up the Mississippi, he was delayed there for a season. He described the dark conditions then present in the city:

> We for some time felt afraid of the exterminating orders of Governor Boggs, which were still in force, but our numbers began to increase in that city and we took courage and a few met in a private house and organized a branch of the Church and the Lord blest the faithful but it was hard work having to contend with the prejudice of the people of the world and every apostate that left Nauvoo came there and did their best to bring persecution on us.[25]

Joseph Fielding, company leader for more than two hundred Saints on the 1841 *Tyrian* voyage, summarized in a letter his view on the apostate spirit in St. Louis:

> At St. Louis we found a number of Saints, at least who have a name among the Saints, some of these prove a trial to those who call there. They tell you many evil tales; I wish they would stop all who are like themselves. The faithful need not be troubled by them; let them talk and have all they can get, they seem afraid to suffer affliction with the people of God, and so go to Missouri, where there are none, thinking also to get a little more money.[26]

In his journal, Fielding added, "Here we saw some poor, faithless Saints something like spiders webs set to catch flies. They came to us with fair words as our best friends, but their counsel was that of enemies, but did not prevail to stay any of our company except two."[27]

Thus, during the Nauvoo years it appears that the Saints passing through St. Louis were more concerned with opposition from Mormon apostates than from those of other faiths, with whom they commingled in the marketplace.[28]

Mormon Migration on the Northwestern Border of Missouri

Once the exiled Nauvoo Saints reached the Missouri River (which also served as the western border of Missouri), they benefitted from what Mormon historian Richard E. Bennett calls "an uneasy truce" as they temporarily settled on the border of Iowa and Missouri near the "Big Muddy" (1846–1848). Here, in the Council Bluffs region, they crossed the border into settlements in northwestern Missouri, where they (of necessity) sought trade for provisions in order to continue their journey west to the Great Basin. Bennett writes, "The Bluffs were far enough away from Missouri so as not to provoke trouble yet close enough to permit trade at arm's-length."[29]

In addition, Bennett explains how the struggling Saints sought employment in diverse ways: "Many teamsters hired themselves out as laborers for nearby farmers building fences, erecting barns, repairing roads, and performing a myriad of related tasks in return for a measure of corn, flour or fodder. . . . Some, in more desperate straits, traveled disguised and incognito among northern Missouri farm sites and villages to find interim employment."[30] This combination of work and trade appears to have been crucial for the survival of a number of westward-bound Saints during the Mormon exodus throughout the years 1846 to 1850. Bennett persuasively argues that "Missouri became the lifeline to the exodus. Had it not been for this Missouri trade [and employment] most would not have gathered sufficient means to migrate to the valley of the Great Salt Lake. Once their inveterate enemy, Missouri became provider, supporter—in a word, their economic salvation."[31]

Although it certainly appears that at times either party was uneasy with the much-needed relationship, Hosea Stout wrote that as 1847 dawned, "The most opposition we have in Missouri is in consequence of the stories of the dissenters otherwise the Missourians are very friendly."[32] This desire for cooperation rather than conflict was also attested in St. Louis on the eastern border of Missouri. At the same time, in both cases, the Mormon apostates were the ones who were stirring up problems for the Saints on the borders.

St. Louis: Inland Port for Mormon Migrants (1848–1857)

In the year that gold was discovered at Sutter's Mill and for nearly the following decade, the Saints poured through the eastern border metropolis of St. Louis, which lay at an important juncture for steamboat travel on the Mississippi and Missouri Rivers. By this time St. Louis had been designated by Brigham Young as a gathering place for the transient Saints. During this period, emigrants were attended to by local priests. During the late 1840s, emigrants were assisted by Mormon agent Nathaniel H. Felt, the local ecclesiastical leader whose responsibilities included overseeing the affairs of emigration.[33] Stan Kimball wrote concerning the influx of Saints in St. Louis during this period, "So many hundred emigrants flooded into the city that President Felt took most of the Mound House Hotel for temporary housing, and rented the larger and more suitable Concert Hall on Market Street . . . for Sunday services. He divided the Gravois branch into four units, one of which was Welsh and found himself by September 1849 shepherding from 3,000 to 4,000 members—the largest district in the Church."[34]

The bulk of the membership consisted of emigrants who were trying to work their way to the Valley of the Great Salt Lake. Besides the constant drive to obtain employment, these St. Louis Saints faced challenges on two fronts: the threat of cholera or yellow fever and the venom of apostates. For example, Latter-day Saint migrant William Booth Ashworth wrote, "We arrived in St. Louis in the spring of '48 when there was a terrible epidemic of cholera raging. My aunt was taken by this terrible disease."[35] The following year, John Martin, who was at this time recovering from illness at St. Louis, wrote, "The cholera in the summer of 1849 was so bad that they had to have eight hospitals in St. Louis."[36] During this same sweltering season, Charles Sansom described the dreaded St. Louis scourge:

> The cholera broke out again with redoubled fury, until its victims numbered over 1000 in a week; all labor seemed suspended except coffin making and grave digging. . . . During the raging of the cholera many of our folks the Latter Day Saints were called to lay their bodies down. I was many times called on to assist in waiting on the sick and assisted in preparing for burial the bodies of those who were called away, but escaped myself from any attack of that fearful scourge.[37]

The Latter-day Saint dissenters proved a different kind of threat. LDS member Charles Dutton Miller wrote upon his arrival in St. Louis in 1849, "I found St. Louis abounding with Saints & apostates."[38] In this same year another emigrant remarked, "I found the Saints in the sixth ward meeting in Bywardrobe [St. Louis area]. They locked the door for fear of the apostates."[39] The opposition from apostates continued for several years, as described by William Gibson, who recalled an experience in St. Louis three years later: "We had a good number of the apostates from Nauvoo to contend with who tried by every means to prevent the emigrants from going farther."[40]

St. Louis thrived in the mid–nineteenth century, and by 1850 had a population of 82,744. By 1853, St. Louis had thirty-five churches and was exporting goods estimated at $50 million per year. River travel brought a great deal of revenue, with 266 steamboats being launched from this inland port. *Conclin's New River Guide* (published in 1853) told of the international makeup of the city and its unique position for commerce: "The population is made of emigrants from all parts of the world. There is no town in the western country more favorably situated, as the seat of an immense trade. It is nearly in the center of the Mississippi valley, commanding the trade of the Missouri, the upper Mississippi and the Illinois."[41]

A portion of the city was made up of Latter-day Saints. A widely read newspaper, the *Missouri Republican,* wrote on May 8, 1851, the following:

> Although we have no Mormon Church in St. Louis, and though these people have no other class or permanent possession or permanent interest in our city, yet their numerical strength here is greater than may be imagined. Our city is the greatest recruiting point for Mormon emigrants from England and the Eastern States, and the former especially, whose funds generally become exhausted by the time they reach it, generally stop here for several months, and not infrequently remain among us for a year or two pending the resumption of their journey to Salt Lake. . . . There are at this time in St. Louis about three thousand English Mormons, nearly all of whom are masters of some trade.[42]

With thousands of migrant Saints in St. Louis, by 1854, St. Louis became a church stake.[43] The following year, the LDS periodical *St. Louis Luminary* published an article explaining that "this city has been an asylum for our people from fifteen to twenty years. . . . There is probably no city in the world where the Latter-day Saints are more respected."[44] During the mid–nineteenth century, St. Louis LDS emigrating agents met Mormon migrants to arrange for local lodging and transportation for the next segment of the journey, which meant a trip on the Missouri River. The agents were also consulted concerning financial needs and employment opportunities.

Mormon Migration on the Missouri River (1848–1855)

After Brigham Young and the vanguard company of Saints reached the Salt Lake Valley in the summer of 1847, a new gathering place emerged. Various outfitting posts were selected each year where the incoming emigrants could assemble before crossing the Plains to the Mecca of Salt Lake City. During the years 1848 to 1855, the posts were reached via the Missouri River, and all were near the river: Kanesville, Iowa (1848–1852); Keokuk, Iowa (1853); and the Town of Kansas Landing, near Westport, in Jackson County, Missouri (1854).[45] The designated post for the year 1855 was Mormon Grove, which lay only a few miles from Atchison, Kansas. Changes in outfitting posts and routes were influenced by concern for the incoming converts, and arrangements were made according to the safest and most economical routes possible on the Missouri River.

Although it appears that the Missourians were not an obstacle along the "Big Muddy," there was another enemy to be feared, cholera. As previously noted, at St. Louis and along the western rivers, this dreadful disease was a continual threat to emigrants who traversed America during the mid–nineteenth century. This was certainly true for the 249 Saints who left Liverpool for New Orleans on the *Buena Vista* in the spring of 1849. By the time they disembarked at Council Bluffs, Iowa, this group lost sixty Welsh Mormons, nearly a fourth of their company, while traveling on the steamboat *Highland Mary.*[46]

A chief factor behind changing the migration route from Kanesville to Keokuk in 1853 was to avoid the dangers of the Missouri River, where there had been another serious outbreak of cholera in 1852. An additional reason was news of the explosion of the steamboat *Saluda* near Lexington, Missouri. For that reason, the frontier outfitting post was relocated two hundred miles north of St. Louis on the Mississippi River.[47]

However, the explosion of the *Saluda* seems to have carried a silver lining in an act of compassion that may have helped to atone for the memories of mobocracy witnessed on the western Missouri border in the 1830s. In what some historians consider the worst steamboat disaster in Missouri River history, the steamboat *Saluda* blew her boilers on Good Friday, April 9, 1852. Twenty-six Latter-day Saint emigrants were killed and many others injured at a river bend near Lexington. Lexington citizens hastened to the dismal scene and rendered needed aid as modern-day good Samaritans. Not only did they raise money to bury the dead, they also gathered funds to help the survivors continue their journey to Utah. The local townspeople created an orphan fund, and some even adopted the destitute Mormon children.[48]

Abraham Smoot, an eyewitness, wrote, "I shall never forget the kindness of the citizens of Lexington in caring for the living and burying the dead. The Lord certainly inspired them to do all that sympathy and benevolence could suggest in aid of the afflicted."[49]

Rerouting the Migrating Saints through the East Coast

Commencing in the spring of 1855, Latter-day Saint immigration was rerouted by Brigham Young to the East Coast, primarily because of the threat of cholera and yellow fever along the Mississippi River.[50] President Young had given the option of using Philadelphia, Boston, or New York, but during the nineteenth century, most Latter-day Saint voyages disembarked at New York because of the immigration depot housed there, called Castle Garden.[51]

During the Latter-day Saint immigration in the nineteenth century, New York Mormon migration agents such as George Q. Cannon met the incoming Latter-day Saint voyages and arranged for the groups to continue on their journey west by rail, sail, and trail. While most groups could proceed directly, the agents aided those who could not afford to move west immediately with employment and housing.[52]

Mormon transmigration through Missouri by rail came as a result of a letter written to Brigham Young by Cannon. At the time, Cannon was serving as the Latter-day Saint immigration agent in New York on the eve of the 1859 migration season. After Cannon made a trip from the East to St. Louis, he discovered a better, more economical route to channel the gathering Saints through Quincy to Florence, Nebraska, rather than sending them to Iowa City on the Chicago and Rock Island Railroad, which had been the established route ever since it reached Iowa City in the spring of 1856.[53] Cannon wrote the following:

> After making more extended inquiries in regard to the best and cheapest route by which to send the Saints to the West, we have ascertained that we can make an arrangement to have through tickets furnished them from New York to Florence at about $3.20 per head in advance of the rates to Iowa City, and for every extra 100 lbs of baggage over the allowance $1 *less* than the rates to Iowa City, a distance of three hundred miles or thereabouts from Florence. The route proposed is by the N. Y. Central R. Road from N.Y. City, via Albany, to the Suspension Bridge (Niagara Falls), thence by the great West R. Road to Detroit, thence by the Michigan Central to Chicago, thence by the Chicago, Burlington & Quincy route to Quincy on the Mississippi, thence to Hannibal, Mo., and from there by the Hannibal and St. Joseph Rail Road to St. Joseph, where packet is taken to Florence. . . . It avoids

St. Louis entirely, and is a much shorter route than that by St. Louis and the Missouri river, even if it were wisdom to send the Saints by that route.[54]

President Young incorporated Cannon's suggestion, and the rail routes for the 1859–1866 migration seasons changed. Although the rail routes from the East Coast to Chicago sometimes differed, once the Saints reached Chicago they took the Chicago, Burlington, and Quincy Railroad (hereafter cited as CB&Q) from Chicago to Quincy.[55] The migrants then crossed the Mississippi and traveled across the state of Missouri from either Hannibal (1859-1863) or West Quincy (1864–1866) via Palmyra to St. Joseph on the Hannibal and St. Joseph Railroad (hereafter cited as the H & St. Joe). The emigrants then traveled north on the Missouri River to outfitting posts at Florence, Nebraska (1859–1863), and Wyoming, Nebraska (1864–1866).[56]

During this period (1859–1866), it is estimated that about eighteen thousand Latter-day Saint immigrants crossed the Atlantic and the Mississippi River (via Quincy, Illinois, or Hannibal, Missouri) to gather in the Salt Lake Valley. The immigrants who made the voyages were primarily British and Scandinavian, although a much smaller representation of foreign converts were Swiss/Germans, South Africans, and French. Of an estimated fifty-five voyages carrying foreign converts, thirty-one of them left from Liverpool, with others coming from such ports as Port Elizabeth (nine), Hamburg (eight), and London (five), with Calcutta and Le Havre each having one. Six of the voyages arrived at Boston, while the other forty-nine landed in New York City.[57]

Newspaper Accounts of Mormon Transmigration across the Mississippi into Missouri

For the years 1859 to 1866, thousands of Latter-day Saint migrants who went west by rail passed through the river cities of Quincy, Illinois, and Hannibal or later West Quincy, Missouri, twenty miles north of Hannibal. Through first-person accounts and from several newspapers, their migration experience through this area emerges with striking color and detail.[58] For example, the *Daily Quincy Whig and Republican* reports the passing Saints in eight separate accounts for the years 1860 to 1862, while the weekly *Quincy Whig Republican* mentions them twice during the migration seasons from 1860 to 1865. The weekly *Quincy Herald* noted the Mormon migrants in nine features in the years 1860–1862 and 1864–1865, while the *Quincy Daily Herald* featured the Mormon immigrants in fifteen different articles for the years 1859, 1861–1862, and 1865–1866. While no known newspaper was published in the small river town of West Quincy, the Hannibal newspapers covered events in the local region, which included West Quincy.[59]

Although only three years are available from the local Hannibal newspapers for this period of study (1859–1861), the Mormon migrants are mentioned in sixteen articles in the *Hannibal Weekly Messenger* and in thirteen accounts in the *Hannibal Daily Messenger;* the Hannibal papers mentioned the Mormon transmigrants more frequently than did the Quincy papers during these years.

These river newspapers often expressed opinions and tones that sharply contrasted with one another. Although sarcasm creeps into articles published on both sides of the Mississippi, generally the newspapers in Quincy (which had a population over twice that of Hannibal) reflect a much more civil, objective, and educated professionalism than the papers from Hannibal, Missouri.[60] Reports from Quincy publications indicate that journalists took more time and effort to give detailed accounts of dress and cultural aspects of the migrants, and their attitudes were much more favorable and genteel than the journalists in Hannibal. The emigrants themselves provide accounts of contrasting moods from one side of the river to the other.

In light of the prior Mormon-Missouri conflict, it is understandable that the Hannibal publications more often reported antagonistic and hostile accounts of the migrants. Apparently Hannibal had earned a reputation of being inhospitable to passing Latter-day Saint migrants during the Nauvoo period. According to tradition, "News came one day that a Mormon boat was on its way up the river, and some of the Hannibal citizens rigged up a shotted cannon, for the purpose of salute and reception, but the Mormon boat was advised of the danger, and it found a channel east of Glascock's Island near the Illinois shore."[61] The story relates that the cannon continued to be used "so as to compel [other] Mormon steamers to hug the Illinois shore."[62]

As the 1859 migration season dawned and the Latter-day Saint migrants drew near the Mississippi on their journey west, the *Hannibal Daily Messenger* printed an article entitled "UTAH AND THE MORMONS." Among other things, this account reported that "the hypocritical, traiterous [*sic*], and adulterous Brigham" had been replaced by another, Governor Cummings, but it noted that "Brigham Young is really, Governor of Utah; as much so, as so far as influence for evil is concerned."[63] Four days later, this newspaper printed the first announcement of the Latter-day Saints who had recently crossed the Mississippi to begin their rail journey from Hannibal across Missouri:

> MORMONS. — On Thursday morning, about 200 deluded followers of Brigham Young, men, women and children, took the cars of the Hannibal and St. Joseph Railroad, at their depot in this city, for St. Joseph, their destination being Salt Lake City. We learn another large reinforcement is

> just behind. They are principally foreigners of the humbler class. Poor, silly dupes of the greatest scoundrel that walks unhung![64]

Five days later, the *Hannibal Weekly Messenger* reprinted this article on the front page of the paper, alongside another article on the Saints entitled "Mormon Civilization." This entry contained a damaging letter written by an army officer at Camp Floyd, Utah. Among other things, his account purports how a mutilated Danish Mormon immigrant had "fled for protection all the way from San Pete to our camp." The officer notes, "I could fill whole sheets with instances of other cold blooded deeds of brutality."[65] Such was the hostile tone of the Hannibal media as they reported news from Utah while the Mormon transmigrants were passing through Missouri.

During this same month, a bold caption entitled "Arrival of Mormons" ran in the *Quincy Daily Herald,* which reported the Latter-day Saint transmigration in a different tone:

> On Thursday last, seven hundred and twenty-five Mormons arrived in this city from Chicago, on their way to Salt Lake. They came down by railroad, filling up some fourteen cars, and left on the morning packet for Hannibal, where they were to take the cars on the St. Joseph railroad yesterday. They were direct from Europe and embraced the following nationalities: — English, 233; Scotch, 31; Irish, 7; Welsch, 30; Swiss, 4; Danish, 224; Swedish, 108; Norwegians, 16, the remainder being infants, under one year of age.[66]

The article continued with the list furnished by the head of the group of the occupation of each member of this company. On the same day (May 21, 1859), the *Hannibal Daily Messenger* noted that it was necessary for this large Mormon group to make a one-day layover at the depot in Hannibal. This, the reporter noted, not only gave the Latter-day Saints a chance to "stroll through town," it allowed the citizens of Hannibal to have a closer look at the passing Latter-day Saint migrants:

> An opportunity was thus afforded us of learning something more of the character of this emigration; of their newly fangled ideas, and of the hold this infamous system hell-born and begotten by the devil, has upon them. We ascertained that there were some five or six different nations represented in this motly crowd, but by far the larger portion were English and Welch. As a general, we might almost say universal rule, they were of the lowest, humblest and most ignorant class of peasantry, giving little or no evidence of intellectual culture, and many of them, by their stupid, brutish and sensual look, indicating unmistakingly that they were the slaves of more vices than one.[67]

The Quincy newspapers generally reflected a more broad-minded community. The passing Saints thus probably felt more secure as they stopped on the Illinois border before crossing the Mississippi River. Once the Mormons entered Missouri (usually at Hannibal), a heightened sense of tension arose, a result, in part, from past and current events. The dark memories of the injustices incurred by the extermination order were not yet dim in the minds of both Latter-day Saints and the inhabitants of northern Missouri. The Saints also had to contend with guerrilla warfare during the years of the Civil War (1861–1865), threatening the migrants' safety as they tried to pass "east to west through north and south" to their eventual refuge in the Salt Lake Valley.[68]

Making reception more difficult for the Latter-day Saints, negative reports flowed into these newspapers during the mid–nineteenth century on such controversial issues as polygamy, the Mountain Meadows Massacre, the Utah War, and Brigham Young's view of the Civil War.[69] Some newspaper accounts were also based on interviews with passing Mormon migrants, which would probably have prejudiced some gentiles in northern Missouri communities.

For example, after the Civil War had dawned, the *Hannibal Weekly Messenger* ran the following article on Independence Day, 1861, from an overland traveler on his way to California:

> MISSOURI THREATENED BY MORMONS IN CASE SHE SECEDES.— . . . We met a large party of Mormons at Scott's Bluff, [Nebraska,] numbering about four hundred, going to the States to purchase goods and get recruits. Some of the elders informed me that they intended at no distant day, in case Missouri secedes, to march an army against her, and recover their lands.[70]

Such a report during the war must have sent additional sparks flying in Hannibal, and they may have ignited additional brush fires for the migrating Saints who were yet to cross war-torn Missouri.[71]

Three years later, a reporter for the *Quincy Weekly Herald* interviewed Elder John M. Kay, who had recently brought 863 immigrants across the Atlantic to New York on the *Hudson.* The journalist reported that the group "fear they will be detained owing to the operations of the guerrillas in Mo. Until allowed to proceed they expect to encamp in the woods near West Quincy. They seem to want to press ahead however, declaring they have no fears of being molested, but have a firm trust that the same Providence that has so far safely guided and guarded them on their way will continue His fatherly protection to them."[72]

The turmoil of the war seems to have increased attitudes of suspicion. For example, just six weeks after the first shots were fired at Fort Sumter, a rumor circulated among Confederate sympathizers that a large group of federal soldiers would be crossing the Mississippi on the steamboat *Black Hawk.* A large crowd of sympathizers who gathered at the Hannibal levee were surprised to discover that the supposed soldiers were in reality a group of about four hundred Latter-day Saint immigrants (including an infantry of children) on their way to "the promised land."[73]

A week later, the *Hannibal Weekly Messenger* referred to the mistake in an article about more immigrants, entitled "MORE MORMONS. — Mr. Hall, the second clerk of the Black Hawk, informed us yesterday that they would bring down another large company of Mormons this morning. We make mention of the fact now that our secession friends may not think they are U. S. Soldiers again in disguise."[74]

Thus, although the mid–nineteenth century Latter-day Saint migrants shared a variety of travel-related challenges with other passing migrants, their religion presented additional obstacles as they journeyed through Illinois and Missouri. When the Saints left Quincy and traversed the Mississippi, they not only left a larger, more refined community, but also a city that had matured in tolerance, influenced no doubt by the large number of European immigrants there. As they entered the Hannibal region, they encountered not only different demographic circumstances but faced a tumultuous environment influenced by past and current episodes of discord. The newspapers fueled local prejudices by their interpretation of prior Latter-day Saint incidents as well as beliefs and practices. The Mormon-Missouri conflict and the Utah War, combined with the advent of the Civil War, all sparked a press that smoldered with enmity.

Crossing Missouri on the Hannibal and St. Joe Railroad during the Civil War

As noted, during the Civil War, the journey through Missouri was even more challenging than through Illinois because of unpredictable guerrilla warfare.[75] Quincy was a lull before a storm as described by Mary Ann Ward Webb, who provides a glimpse of the contrast of travel for Mormon immigrants once they reached the other side of the Mississippi River:

> The trip from Chicago to Quincy, Ill., was a pleasant one. We arrived there on July 26th [1864]. We crossed the Mississippi River and had to walk from the landing to the railway station over a very rough road. We had to stay for

> two days waiting for a train. A heavy storm came up; there was not room for all in the station so we had a most miserable time. Some of us went down to the river where some men tried to drown us. They were very bitter against the Mormons.[76]

Andrew Christian Neilson, who also passed through this turbulent region in 1864, wrote, "In Quincy, Illinois we stopped several days and then had to take cattle cars for St. Joseph through Missouri. We had some trouble in getting through the wars. Here was the ruins of whole towns as had been laid waste by the terrible struggle."[77] In 1862, another Saint summarized his journey through Missouri as a "mournful picture. In many places houses were burned down, fences destroyed, and crops unattended. All the bridges were well guarded by Union troops to prevent the Secessionists from burning them. The fulfillment of Joseph Smith's prophecies concerning Missouri can be visibly seen in passing through the state."[78]

The Saints had their initial glimpse of the Civil War in the Hannibal region. Federal troops were stationed there as early as 1861, and they stayed for the duration of the war.[79] In 1862, Thomas Memmott wrote, "Left Hannibal. . . . Saw first signs of the Civil War, passing a party of soldiers guarding a bridge."[80] In June 1862, Jens Christian Anderson Weibye indicated, "We left Hannibal, . . . where we saw American soldiers who had raised their tents, partly at the towns and partly at the bridges to prevent the Southern people to break up the railroad or the bridges."[81]

One immigrant noted after crossing over the Mississippi to Hannibal, "We had to change into a train of cattle cars and the car I got in was a car that hogs had been shipped in. Everything was dry. The dust from the hogs' excrement was something very unpleasant. We could smell and taste hogs for two or three days afterwards."[82] Another migrant explained his 1864 rail ride saying, "The ride was very bad as the cars were terrible."[83]

Tales of riding in cattle cars are common in the migrant accounts. In 1862, William wrote that "some of us [were] packed in cattle cars as though we were but beasts."[84] Mary E. Fretwell Davis, who journeyed west a year later, remembered, "We rode three days shut up in cattle cars with nothing but straw to sit on."[85] An immigrant from another 1863 company related:

> All of the passenger cars had been burned as [so] they locked us up in cattle cars which had straw floors. There were no seats. We passed a soldiers' camp and it was here we ran into a place where logs had been placed to disrail the cars. I happened to be standing up when the cars struck the logs and the jolt threw me head foremost to the other side of the car among the women and children. Everyone was crying and screaming. A few were hurt.[86]

Although the cattle cars were at times dangerous, they were actually safer than the passenger cars, which carried Union soldiers and thus became the target of Confederate attack. The passage through the "North" (a rail route usually from New York to Chicago) did not have the threat of warfare found in Missouri.

Not only were the migrants consigned to cars fit for beasts, but the roads were of very poor quality. One migrant remarked, "We had a rough ride through the State of Missouri. The H. & St. Joseph's Railroad was new but not finished. Appeared to be the most uneven road for a railroad I ever traveled on."[87] At times the threat of destruction to the tracks posed an additional challenge. One migrant wrote, "To Quincy. Got over the Mississippi River to an grove of trees and laid there to the 11 of June 64. (All the cars was in the South with the soldiers) Then to Palmyra [just north of Hannibal], we saw 1000 of soldier. They tore the track."[88]

In 1864, Joseph A. Young (the eldest son of President Brigham Young) was given general charge of Latter-day Saint migration through America by his father. As Joseph A. crossed the Missouri border to make plans for the 1864 migration season, he noted that "the whole face of the country from where we crossed the Mo line to St. Joseph, bears the impress of the judgments of the Almighty."[89] He recorded that there was more evidence of the Civil War in Missouri along the Hannibal and St. Joseph tracks than anywhere else in Missouri. Joseph observed "every few miles the debris of a 'wrecked' train" and summarized the situation by stating, "Were it not that 'God is with his people' the thought of the saints traveling over such a road would be almost unbearable."[90]

One emigrant recalled a close call for some who chose to ride in the passenger cars during their trip through war-torn Missouri:

> Just before we arrived in St. Joseph, Missouri, the rebels, or bushwhackers, fired two cannon balls through our train, one shot went through the passenger car exactly eight inches above the people's heads and the other through the baggage car destroying a great amount of baggage. We stayed three or four days, afraid to go on because of the rebel soldiers being all throughout the country. While we were there, some fifteen rebel soldiers were taken prisoner, right from among [meaning near] our company, by the northern soldiers. Two companies of Union soldiers surrounded the depot and made the rebels surrender or they would have killed them. I can truly say I saw a little of the war between the North and the South.[91]

Elizabeth Staheli Walker also saw a little of the war. She wrote of her experience traveling from east to west: "We could hear the boom of cannons and firing of guns as we rode along. Shutters were up at the window and the people on the trains were asked to be very quiet. When we passed through Missouri the people were very bitter against the Mormons and set a bridge on fire to retard our progress."[92]

Charles Henry John West recalled his memorable journey across the States. He intimates that after a rough train ride, the boat ride up the Missouri River was not much better: "We traveled by cars day and night for seven days. On account of the Civil War going on we had to rough it, traveling part of the time crowded in sheep cars. They said they were afraid of their good cars being burned by the Confederates. We took a steamer up the Missouri River as far as St. Joseph. It was a flatboat and we were very crowded."[93]

Another Latter-day Saint migrant recalled, after having reached the end of the tracks, "We then went on a flat boat for three days on the Missouri River, and it was crowded, and we had to sleep just where we could sit down. We was cramped and very uncomfortable and the sailors were a rough set of men, and we were quite afraid of them for we seemed to be in a rough country."[94] Thomas Henry White noted, "While sailing up the river to Florence, Nebraska, we met many Josephites[95] who were eager to tell us what would happen to us if we went to Utah and did not succeed. The emigrants were met [at Florence] by the captains of the different companies."[96]

As the war continued to drag on, by 1864 some LDS companies tried to scoot around the war as opposed to taking their chances traveling through the eastern states. Christopher Alston, an LDS immigrant on the *General McClellan,* provides a synopsis of his migration experience:

> We arrived in New York June 23rd 1864. There we took steamer and traveled up the Hudson River into Canada to avoid the Armies of Rebellion, broken bridges,[97] uptorn railways, etc. incident to war, which was raging in the States between the North and the South, with blood and rapine in all the land. We arrived in Wyoming [Nebraska] near Omaha, July 3rd, after going by rail and another steamer up the Missouri River. There we were met by the teams of oxen and teamsters from Utah.[98]

Others who voyaged on the ship *Hudson* before heading west were not as fortunate. Mary Ann Rawlins wrote in 1864:

> Some of the troops encountered by the emigrants on the way to the outfitting camp in Wyoming [Nebraska] manifested bitterness toward our company of Saints. At one point they drove us through a river, with rain falling in torrents, which exposure caused much sickness and many deaths in the company. Expostulating with the soldiers on their conduct, Elder [John M.]

> Kay said to them, "If you have no respect for the living, will you not look with mercy on the sick and the dying, and consider the sacred dead?" "If you say another word, I will rip you up, even if you were Jesus Christ Himself!" one of the soldiers replied.[99]

There was also the fear of LDS migrants being abducted by the soldiers. In 1864 Mary Ann Ward Webb learned of a young Dutch Mormon female passing through St. Joseph, Missouri, who was stolen by the soldiers, but the elders managed to get her back.[100] The year before, Thomas Henry White reported that one girl was taken by the soldiers of their emigrating company.[101] White further wrote of his company's encounter with soldiers while crossing Missouri: at every station the soldiers would ask, "When are those Mormons coming through"? The migrants were in danger, especially the boys, of being drafted into the army.[102] Notwithstanding, the Saints continued their march to the Salt Lake Valley.

Conclusion

During the three decades that followed the extermination decree issued in 1838, there is no evidence of the state of Missouri enforcing this infamous order. Yet the Mormon emigrants did face a number of adversities of a different kind. Such obstacles included disease on the Missouri River, opposition from Mormon apostates, threats resulting from military conflict during the Civil War, and an abundance of bad press. Nevertheless, Lexington's citizens rendered compassionate aid when Latter-day Saints experienced the *Saluda* steamboat disaster, and in Missouri border cities such as St. Louis and St. Joseph, the Mormons were able to gain employment and make useful trades. Thus most of them were able to successfully cross this modern-day American Mesopotamia and reach their promised land in the West.

Notes

1. Among other things, the extermination order stated, "The Mormons must be treated as enemies and must be exterminated and driven from the state, if necessary for the public good." See Joseph Smith Jr., *History of the Church of Jesus Christ of Latter-day Saints,* ed. B. H. Roberts, 7 vols. (Salt Lake City: Deseret, 1964), 3: 175.

2. James B. Allen and Glen M. Leonard, *The Story of the Latter-day Saints* (Salt Lake City: Deseret, 1976), 139.

3. Several hundred documents also provide evidence of Mormons testifying of mistreatment by the hands of Missouri citizens in formal redress petitions as noted in Clark V. Johnson, *Mormon Redress Petitions: Documents of the 1833–1838 Missouri Conflict* (Provo, Utah: Brigham Young University Religious Studies Center, 1992).

4. This prayer was given in Kirtland, Ohio, on March 27, 1836, at the dedication of the Latter-day Saint temple. This sentence, an excerpt from this dedicatory prayer, may be found in Latter-day Saint scripture known as *The Doctrine and Covenants of the Church of Jesus Christ of Latter-day Saints,* section 109, verse 50.

5. *History of the Church,* 5: 211.

6. The "Platt Country" refers to the region along the Platte River between modern day Omaha, Nebraska, on the eastern border and Casper, Wyoming, on the western border.

7. Autobiography and journal of Nelson Whipple Wheeler, August 17, 1850, Church Archives for the Church of Jesus Christ of Latter-day Saints, Salt Lake City, hereafter cited as LDSCA.

8. Reminiscences of James Madison Fisher, LDSCA, 9.

9. "The Life of Thomas Steed from His Own Diary, 1826–1910" (privately printed, 1935), 15–16; "Mormon Pioneer Overland Travel 1847–1868," http://www.lds.org/churchhistory/library/pioneercompanysearch/.

10. Recollections of James H. Humphreys, Bancroft Library, 2, 5.

11. Journal of Albert King Thurber, Bancroft Library, 23. This account also explains that shortly thereafter, Thurber "left his company and joined the church, intending to remain" (1).

12. Recollections of Leonard Babcock, August 13, 1849, Bancroft Library.

13. "To California in 1850," recollections of Isaac Julian Harvey (Bancroft Library), 45–46. There appears to be some truth in Harvey's statement, as evidenced by a Missouri reverend named Alvin Mussett, who in the summer of 1850 objected to the charge that his cattle had trampled the grain field of a local Saint. Mormon lawyer Hosea Stout, who was then working his craft in Salt Lake City, noted that the angered minister "was fine[d] ten dollars & costs & to pay for the grain destroyed. He is a perfect specimen of the Missouri ministry." See John D. Unruh, Jr., *The Plains Across: The Overland Emigrants and the Trans-Mississippi West, 1840–1860* (Urbana: University of Illinois Press, 1993), 313–15; Juanita Brooks, ed., *On the Mormon Frontier: The Diary of Hosea Stout, 1844–1861,* 2 vols. (Salt Lake City: University of Utah Press, 1964), 2: 377, for the diary entries for the date August 12, 1850.

14. Aylett R. Cotton, "Across the Plains to California in 1849 and After: An Autobiography," recollections of Aylett R. Cotton, typescript, Bancroft Library, 25.

15. Journal of Dan Carpenter, July 24, 1850, LDSCA.

16. As part of the spirit of the bicentennial commemoration of the birth of the United States, the extermination order was officially rescinded in 1976 by Missouri governor Christopher S. Bond.

17. Fred E. Woods, "Gathering to Nauvoo: Mormon Immigration 1840–46," *Nauvoo Journal* 11, no. 2 (Fall 1999): 50. For a more detailed account of St. Louis Mormon history, see Fred E. Woods and Thomas L. Farmer, *When the Saints Came Marching In: A History of the Latter-day Saints in St. Louis* (Salt Lake City: Millennial Press, 2009).

18. Jenson, *The Contributor* 12 (1891): 445–46.

19. Ibid., 446.

20. *Autobiography of Parley P. Pratt* (Salt Lake City: Deseret, 1985), 285.

21. Jenson, *The Contributor* 12 (1891): 450. Matthias Cowley indicated that the previous year, his father James was offered ten dollars per day to stay and work in St. Louis. His father emphatically said no. He added, "I started from home to go to Nauvoo, to see the Prophet of the Lord, Joseph Smith, and I'm going, bless your souls. I would not stop here for all of St. Louis" (reminiscences of Matthias Cowley, LDS Church Archives, 1).

22. However, Stanley B. Kimball, "The Saints and St. Louis, 1831–1857: An Oasis of Tolerance and Security," *BYU Studies* 13 (Summer 1973): 489–519, presents a broader picture of St. Louis in recounting how this city was used as a Mormon refuge, in spite of the 1838 extermination order. He also points out that many Saints fled to St. Louis following the Nauvoo exile (1846) and demonstrates how this inland city was an important stop for poor Mormon migrants who, after receiving needed employment, continued their journey on the Missouri River from 1846 to 1855 to the West. Sheri Slaughter, "'Meet Me in St. Louie': An Index of Early Latter-day Saints Associated with St. Louis, Missouri," *Nauvoo Journal* 10 (Fall 1998): 49–108 provides a useful resource for a study of the Saints in St. Louis during the mid–nineteenth century.

23. Journal of Hiram Clark, excerpt quoted in *Millennial Star* 4 (February 1844): 147.

24. [Autobiography of] Thomas Wrigley, *Our Pioneer Heritage,* comp. Kate B. Carter (Salt Lake City: Daughters of the Utah Pioneers), 5: 496.

25. Kimball, "The Saints and St. Louis," 497.

26. Joseph Fielding to Parley P. Pratt, January 1842, *Millennial Star* 3 (August 1842): 77.

27. Journals of Joseph Fielding, vol. 5, LDSCA, 2.

28. Evidence also suggests that the possible threat stemming from the extermination order was more of a concern during the years Mormons migrated through St. Louis to Nauvoo (1839–1846) than what is evidenced following the Nauvoo exodus in 1846.

29. Richard E. Bennett, "Mormons and Missourians, the Uneasy Truce," *Midwest Review* 2nd series, 9 (1987), 14.

30. Ibid., 13. In addition, he lists the principal northwest Missouri cities where these migrants sought employment. He notes, "Hundreds of Latter-day Saints lived and worked in Savannah, Westport, St. Joseph, and in various other towns and in such formerly unfriendly territory as Clay, Davies, even Jackson County" (17).

31. Richard E. Bennett, "'We Had Everything to Procure from Missouri': The Missouri Lifeline to the Mormon Exodus, 1846–1850," 3, paper delivered at the Heritage Conference, Independence, Missouri, September 15–16, 2000, in possession of author. Bennett maintains that whereas the Mormon Battalion actually brought in only five thousand dollars, he estimates that about fifty thousand dollars was probably brought in by about two hundred Mormon laborers during this period (pp. 7, 19).

32. Juanita Brooks, ed., *On the Mormon Frontier: The Diary of Hosea Stout, 1844–1861,* 2 vols. (Salt Lake City: University of Utah Press, 1964), 1: 222, entry for January 2, 1847.

33. Kimball, "The Saints and St. Louis," 507. Kimball notes that Felt was replaced in 1850 by his first counselor, Alexander Robbins (509).

34. Ibid., 508.

35. Autobiography of William Booth Ashworth, LDSCA, 2.

36. Autobiography of John Martin, LDSCA, 35.

37. Autobiography and journal of Charles Sansom, LDSCA, 43–44.

38. Reminiscences and diary of Charles Dutton Miller, LDSCA, 19.

39. Autobiography and diary of David D. Bowen, LDSCA (July 18, 1849).

40. Journals of William Gibson, 1852, LDSCA, vol. 3, 194.

41. *Conclin's New River Guide: A Gazetteer of All the Towns on the Western Waters* (Cincinnati: J. A. and U. P. James, 1853), 80–81.

42. *Missouri Republican* (May 8, 1851), cited in Kimball, "The Saints and St. Louis," 509–10.

43. Kimball, "The Saints and St. Louis," 510. Kimball further notes that the stake only lasted three years, inasmuch as "the threatening 'Utah War' of 1857 pretty much killed it. To strengthen the Church's defense against the U.S. Army advancing on Utah, Brigham Young called [LDS St. Louis Church Leader] Erastus Snow, and all others who could to leave St. Louis that summer" (516).

44. St. Louis Luminary, February 3, 1855, cited in Kimball, "The Saints and St. Louis," 489.

45. For more information on the 1854 Mormon emigration experience, see Fred E. Woods, "The 1854 Mormon Emigration at the Missouri-Kansas Border," *Kansas History: A Journal of the Central Plains* 32 (Winter 2009–2010): 226–45.

46. Conway B. Sonne, *Saints, Ships, and Mariners* (Salt Lake City: University of Utah Press, 1987), 97. In an article titled "Items of News from Council Bluffs," *Latter-day Saints' Millennial Star* 11 (August 1, 1849): 233, George A. Smith noted that this Welsh company "suffered extremely from the cholera while passing up the Missouri river." The Mormon Immigration Index CD published by the Church of Jesus Christ of Latter-day Saints in 2000 lists dozens of accounts of Mormon emigrants who died from cholera as they journeyed on the Mississippi and Missouri Rivers during the mid–nineteenth century. See also Pat Rushton, "Cholera and Its Impact on Nineteenth-Century Mormon Migration," *BYU Studies* 44, no. 2 (2005): 123–44.

47. The Saints only used Keokuk for one year due to the fact that they did not like the extra three hundred miles of land travel across Iowa.

48. William G. Hartley and Fred E. Woods, *Explosion of the Steamboat Saluda* (Salt Lake City: Millennial Press, 2002), 43–53. See also William G. Hartley and Fred E. Woods, "Explosion of the Steamboat *Saluda:* Tragedy and Compassion at Lexington, Missouri, 1852," *Missouri Historical Review* 99, no. 4 (July 2005): 281–305.

49. Andrew Jenson, "Fifty-sixth Company—*Kennebec*," *The Contributor* 13, no. 9 (July 1892): 414.

50. In a letter dated August 2, 1854, Brigham Young instructed Elder Franklin D. Richards, a Latter-day Saint emigration agent at Liverpool, as follows: "You are aware of the sickness liable to assail our unacclimated brethren on the Mississippi river, hence I wish you to ship no more to New Orleans, but ship to Philadelphia, Boston, or New York, giving preference to the order named" ("Foreign Correspondence," *Millennial Star* 16 [October 28, 1854]: 684). A secondary factor may have been Young's awareness of the advancement of the eastern rails, which would soon prove to be a more effective means of transportation. On this topic, see John F. Stover, *Iron Road to the West: American Railroads in the 1850s* (New York: Columbia University Press, 1978), 176–85, and Louis C. Hunter, *Steamboats on the Western Rivers: An Economic and Technological History* (New York: Dover, 1993), 481–519.

51. The best source for an in-depth study of Castle Garden is George J. Svejda, *Castle Garden as an Immigration Depot, 1855–1890* (U.S. National Parks Service, U.S. Department of the Interior, 1968). On the Latter-day Saint immigration experience through Castle Garden, see Don H. Smith, "Castle Garden, the Emigrant Receiving Station in New York Harbor," *Nauvoo Journal* 10 (Spring 1998): 41–52.

52. For more information on the role of New York church immigration agents, see the forthcoming article by Fred E. Woods, "The Knights at Castle Garden: Latter-day Saint Immigration Agents at New York," in Alexander Baugh, ed., *Regional Studies in LDS Church History: New York*, vol. 3 (Provo, Utah: BYU Religious Studies Center, 2001), 103–24.

53. Stanley B. Kimball, "Sail and Rail Pioneers before 1869," *BYU Studies* 35, no. 2 (1995): 21.

54. Letter from George Q. Cannon to Brigham Young, April 23, 1859, 1–2, Brigham Young incoming correspondence (LDSCA). Kimball, "Sail and Rail Pioneers before 1869," *BYU Studies* 35 (2000): 23, points out that "riding these two railroads [CB&Q and the H. & St. Joe] in sequence made immigrating much easier and faster. Saint Joseph, then the westernmost point on the national railway system, was about 240 miles farther west than Iowa City." He notes that it took about fifteen hours to ride from Chicago to Quincy (23, 26) and another eleven hours to go from Hannibal to St. Joseph (39, n 57).

According to W. W. Baldwin's official *Corporate History of the Chicago, Burlington & Quincy Railroad Company and Affiliated Companies* n.p., n.d. [1917], 223–24, the H & St. Joe Railroad was opened for service on February 15, 1859, and the total distance from Hannibal to St. Joseph was 206.41 miles. For an excellent article on this railroad, see Perrin Kent Hannah Jr., "The Hannibal and St. Joseph Railroad 'The Joe Line,'" *Railway History Monograph* 8 (1978): 1–61. See also Howard F. Bennett, "The Hannibal and St. Joseph Railroad and the Development of Northern Missouri, 1870: A Study of Land and Colonization Policies" (PhD diss., Harvard University, 1951), for a study of the impact of this railroad on incoming settlers immediately following the Latter-day Saint transmigration period through Missouri.

55. For example, during the period from 1859 to 1861, the established rail route from New York to Chicago was a direct line that traveled within the boundaries of the United States, although the lines sometimes varied. Yet beginning in 1862, other Mormon immigrant companies chose (for economic concerns, rail availability or the threat of the War) to follow a route that took them through Canada on the Great Western Railway of Canada, commencing at the Suspension Bridge at Niagara and ending at Windsor, Canada, where the migrants returned to United States soil at the Detroit River. From Detroit they traveled on the Michigan and Central Railroad to Chicago. See Fred E. Woods, "East to West through North and South: Mormon Immigration during the Civil War," *BYU Studies* 39, no. 1 (2000): 6–29, for a more detailed discussion of this issue.

56. *LDS Church Almanac 1997–1998* (Salt Lake City: Deseret News, 1998), 173–76.

57. These statistics are calculated from the *LDS Church Almanac 1997–98,* 162–63. There may have been as many as ten additional voyages, as noted in the *Mormon Immigration Index* CD (published by The Church of Jesus Christ of Latter-day Saints, 2000), but the information is scarce. Both the *Almanac* and the *Mormon Immigration* CD agree that between 18,000 to 18,500 Saints made the voyage. However, it must be understood that these figures include several hundred returning missionaries who often served as company leaders in order to watch over their new foreign converts on each of the Latter-day Saint chartered voyages.

58. These issues were first treated in Fred E. Woods, "Two Sides of a River: Mormon Transmigration through Quincy, Illinois, and Hannibal, Missouri," *Mormon Historical Studies* 2, no. 1 (2001): 119–47.

59. According to the 1860 U.S. Census Records, the total population of Hannibal was 6,505 residents, while West Quincy was so small it was not even listed. The *Quincy Daily Herald,* July 30, 1861, 3, carries an article describing West Quincy, which states, among other things, that it contained "not less than one dwelling house, a hotel, and a railroad depot."

60. At the time the Mormon migration commenced, Quincy was the largest city in Illinois, and it, like St. Louis, included many immigrants. In contrast, Hannibal did not have the large influx of migrants that we find in these metropolitan cities.

61. Thomas H. Bacon, *Mirror of Hannibal,* including biographies and portraits of two hundred Hannibal citizens of 1905, compiled by C. P. Greene (Hannibal, Mo.: C. P. Greene, 1905), revised by J. Hurley and Roberta (Roland) Hagood, and reprinted in 1990 by Jostens printers, Topeka, Kansas, 92.

62. Henry N. Stone, comp., *Stone's Hannibal City Directory 1897–98* (Hannibal, Mo.: H. N. Stone, 1897), 35.

63. *Hannibal Daily Messenger,* May 3, 1859, 2.

64. Ibid., May 7, 1859, 3.

65. *Hannibal Weekly Messenger,* May 12, 1859, 1. For a history of the contentious relationship between the Latter-day Saints and the United States military during the Utah War, see Norman F. Furniss, *The Mormon Conflict 1850–1859* (New Haven, Conn.: Yale University Press, 1966); Donald R. Moorman and Gene A. Sessions, *Camp Floyd and the Mormons: The Utah War* (Salt Lake City: University of Utah Press, 1992).

66. *Quincy Daily Herald,* May 21, 1859, 3.

67. *Hannibal Daily Messenger,* May 21, 1859, 2.

68. It should here be noted that Missouri chose to be a neutral state during the War of the Rebellion. Yet her land was stained by much bloodshed as a result of federal troops being forced to deal with Confederate sympathizers in Missouri who launched continuous series of guerrilla assaults. Not only were the lives of the Mormon migrants in danger as they traveled through this state, so also were the lives of local Missouri civilians. For an excellent treatment on this topic in general, see Michael Fellman, *Inside War: The Guerrilla Conflict in Missouri during the American Civil War* (New York: Oxford University Press, 1989).

69. For articles treating polygamy, the Mountain Meadows Massacre, and the Utah War, see, for example, "What Utah Has Cost," *Hannibal Weekly Messenger,* June 2, 1859, 2; "Latest from Salt Lake," *Hannibal Weekly Messenger,* June 2, 1859, 3.

For Brigham Young's negative view of the federal government during a portion of the Civil War, see "Brigham Young's Loyalty," *Daily Quincy and Republican,* May 29, 1863, 1. His position of not wanting to support the government during the War of the Rebellion was heavily influenced by President Lincoln's 1862 decision to replace Young's Mormon troops (who had faithfully helped guard the mail route) with soldiers under the direction of Colonel Patrick Connor. Furthermore, Connor had established a military post (Fort Douglas) that overlooked Salt Lake City. Young suspected that the purpose of this military surveillance was to keep a thumb on Latter-day Saint activity. Young therefore determined from that point on not to send men to fight for the Union, if called upon, although the Saints in general were thought to be Union sympathizers. For more information about the history of the controversial relationship between the Mormons and the United States military during the Civil War era, see E. B. Long, *The Saints and the Union: Utah Territory during the Civil War* (Urbana: University of Illinois Press, 1981).

70. *Hannibal Weekly Messenger,* July 4, 1861, 4.

71. In the summer of 1857, a similar matter had taken place when a group of westbound migrants had stopped to graze their cattle in southern Utah en route to California. According to Kenneth H. Godfrey, "Mountain Meadows Massacre," *Encyclopedia of Latter-day Saint History,* eds. Arnold K. Garr, Donald Q. Cannon, and Richard O. Cowan (Salt Lake City: Deseret, 2000), 799, "it appears that some of these emigrants told a few Latter-day Saints that when they had transported their families to the Golden State they were going to return, join the army, and subdue the Saints." This resulted in the infamous tragedy known as the Mountain Meadows Massacre. Such hostile reactions seem to have been evoked by an ever-present war hysteria com-

mencing at the dawn of the Utah War and continuing until the end of the Civil War (1857–1865).

72. *Quincy Weekly Herald,* August 1, 1864, 2. Kay's declaration of faith was no doubt bolstered by the deliverance he and his company of Saints had experienced aboard the *Hudson* crossing the Atlantic in 1864. On this voyage, sailors aboard a Confederate warship had pulled alongside the *Hudson* and taunted the migrants by yelling, "Say your prayers, you Mormons, you are all going down." Fortunately, nothing came of the boastful threat. For more information on this encounter, see Woods, "East to West Through North and South," *BYU Studies* 39 (2000): 9–10.

73. *Hannibal Daily Messenger,* May 22, 1861, 2.

74. *Hannibal Weekly Messenger,* May 30, 1861, 3.

75. For more detail on Mormon transmigration through Missouri during the Civil War, see Woods, "East to West through North and South," *BYU Studies* 39 (2000): 13–23.

76. "The History of Mary Ann Ward Webb and Her Diary of the Journey to Utah (1864)," in Robert R. King and Kay Atkinson King, *Mary Ann Webb: Her Life and Ancestry* (McLean, Va.: American Society for Genealogy and Family History, 1996), 108.

77. Autobiography of Andrew Christian Neilson, LDS Church Archives, 5.

78. Collection of Joseph Coulson Rich, vol. 4, part 2, LDS Church Archives, 19. As noted previously in this paper, several Latter-day Saints recalled statements made by Joseph Smith regarding the suffering the Missourians would be called to pass through due to their harsh treatment of the Saints. See footnotes five through seven wherein prophecies of doom are remembered.

79. J. Hurley Hagood and Roberta (Roland) Hagood, *The Story of Hannibal* (Hannibal, Mo.: Standard Printing, 1976), 53.

80. Journal of Thomas Memmott, vol. 1, ed. by H. Kirk Memmott (privately printed, 1976), 47. *The War of the Rebellion: A Compilation of the Official Records of the Union and Confederate Armies,* 70 vols. (Washington, D.C.: Government Printing Office, 1894), 1:188, notes that according to General Order No. 4 issued from Brigadier-General S. A. Hurlbut (the commander who oversaw the H & St. Joe Line), this railroad was divided into two divisions and four sections. Strung out across the entire distance of the northern portion of the state of Missouri from the Mississippi River to the Missouri River, the first division extended from St. Joseph to Brookfield and the second from Brookfield to Hannibal and Quincy. Regiments were stationed at each of these sections along the rail route from Hannibal to St. Joseph. The fourth section (which was part of the second division) covered the area from the Salt River to Hannibal and Quincy, and it was guarded by the Fourteenth Illinois Regiment, which had its headquarters in Palmyra, Missouri. Although Quincy was also considered part of this fourth section, there is no mention by Latter-day Saint migrants of federal troops being stationed in Quincy during their transmigration throughout the Civil War.

81. Reminiscences and journals of Jens Christian Andersen Weibye, LDS Church Archives, 285.

82. Autobiography of William Wood, LDS Church Archives, 105.

83. Journal of Peter Nielsen, LDS Church Archives, 357.

84. Diary of William Ajax, LDSCA, 109.

85. Autobiography of Mary E. Fretwell Davis, LDSCA, 1.

86. Mary Charlotte Jacobs, "The Story of my Life," LDSCA, 12.

87. Journal and autobiography of Barry Wride, BYU Special Collections, 14.

88. Journal of Ove Christian Oveson, LDS Church Archives, 23.

89. Some Latter-day Saints viewed the raging effects of the Civil War (especially in Missouri) as fulfillment of a portion of the "migration revelation" received by

Brigham Young at Winter Quarters in 1847 after the Saints were forced to leave the Union: "And now cometh the day of their calamity, even the days of sorrow, like a woman that is taken in travail; and their sorrow shall be great unless they speedily repent, yea very speedily. For they killed the prophet and them that were sent unto them and they have shed innocent blood which crieth from the ground against them" (D&C 136: 35–36).

90. Joseph A. Young, "Journal of a Mission to the Eastern States [1864]," holograph, Manuscripts Division, J. Willard Marriott Library, University of Utah, 15–17 as indicated by Craig S. Smith, "Wyoming, Nebraska Territory: Joseph W. Young and the Mormon Emigration of 1864," *BYU Studies* 39, no. 1 (2000): 31, 34.

91. Diary of William H. Freshwater, *Our Pioneer Heritage,* comp. Kate B. Carter (Salt Lake City: Daughters of the Utah Pioneers, 1964), 7: 250.

92. *History of Barbara Sophia Haberli Staheli,* LDSCA, 2. Even after the bloody conclusion of the Civil War, other conflicts tormented the passing migrants. Andrew Jenson, *History of the Scandinavian Mission* (Salt Lake City: Deseret News Press, 1927), 193, related that the Scandinavian Saints who crossed the Atlantic on the *Kenilworth* (1866) en route to Zion had "a very disagreeable ride through the State of Missouri, where the inhabitants at nearly every station did all they could to insult the emigrants."

93. Reminiscences of Charles Henry John West, *An Enduring Legacy* (Salt Lake City: Daughters of the Utah Pioneers, 1982), 5: 241–42.

94. Journal of Mary E. Fretwell Davis, LDSCA, 1.

95. The name "Josephites" is another term for members of the Reorganized Church of Jesus Christ of Latter-day Saints (now known as the Community of Christ) who were led by Joseph Smith III, commencing in 1860. For more information on this topic, see Richard P. Howard, "Reorganized Church of Jesus Christ of Latter-day Saints (RLDS Church)," *Encyclopedia of Mormonism,* ed. Daniel H. Ludlow, 4 vols. (New York: Macmillan, 1992), 3: 1211–16.

96. Autobiography of Thomas Henry White, LDSCA, 1.

97. The threat of bridges being destroyed was very real. For example, one immigrant mentioned that in Missouri, "Squares of soldiers [are] at all the bridges to [stop] destruction by rebels" (journal of John Henry Barker, June 21, 1862, LDSCA, 30).

98. Autobiography of Christopher Alston, *Our Pioneer Heritage,* compiled by Kate B. Carter (Salt Lake City: Daughters of the Utah Pioneers, 1965), 8: 37. See also History of Ole Amundsen, 2 in the Breinholt Biographies (LDSCA), wherein Andrew Amundsen also mentions that the immigration route took his company north across Niagara Falls. A more compelling reason may be that the migrating Saints went into Canada not because of the incidents relative to war, but rather because rail cars were not then available through the normal railway route which went from New York to Chicago, which was not an active war zone. He also points out that the threat on the normal "northern" route was not from a warfare threat, but rather the confiscation and availability of passenger trains (correspondence from William G. Hartley, August 1999).

99. Reminiscences of Mary Ann Rawlings Aveson, *A History of the Richard Rawlings Family,* compiled by Gladys Rawlings Lemon (privately printed, 1986), 100. During the years 1864 to 1866, the designated LDS frontier outfitting post was Wyoming, Nebraska. One reason Wyoming was selected by church leaders was to avoid the influence of apostates who had multiplied in Florence, Nebraska. There were also practical reasons. For example, the transcontinental railroad tracks had moved father west by 1864. Additionally, the distance was shortened for river steamers that commenced

from St. Joseph. The move also made fording the Missouri River much easier for ox trains, since Wyoming is on the western side of the Missouri River. See Fred E. Woods, "East to West through North and South," 21–22.

100. "The History of Mary Ann Ward Webb and Her Diary to Utah" (1864), in Robert R. King and Kay Atkinson King, *Mary Ann Ward Webb: Her Life and Ancestry* (McLean, Va.: American Society for Genealogy and Family History, 1966), 96.

101. Autobiography of Thomas Henry White, LDSCA, 1.

102. White, autobiography, 1, that he also adds, while at St. Joseph, White also learned the Union soldiers could collect one dollar for each man or boy on whom they could pin a ribbon on—a successful ribbon pinning designated that the recipient was now in the army.

Contributors

Alexander L. Baugh is an associate professor of church history and doctrine, Brigham Young University. He received his BS from Utah State University, and his MA and PhD from Brigham Young University. He is a member of the Mormon History Association and the Mormon Historic Sites Foundation, and a member and past president of the John Whitmer Historical Association (2006–2007). He also serves as editor of *Mormon Historical Studies.*

Richard E. Bennett, a native of Sudbury, Ontario, Canada, is a professor of church history and doctrine at Brigham Young University. He has a PhD in U.S. intellectual history from Wayne State University. He is the author of several books and articles, mainly on nineteenth century LDS history. He is presently church history editor for *BYU Studies.*

Richard O. Cowan received a doctorate in history at Stanford University in 1961. He then joined the faculty at Brigham Young University where he is currently professor of church history and doctrine. He is the author or coauthor of thirteen books, including *The Latter-day Saint Century, Joseph Smith and the Doctrine and Covenants,* and *Temples to Dot the Earth.*

Jean A. Pry (formerly Hamilton) is an associate professor emerita of textiles and apparel management at the University of Missouri. Her scholarship has focused on the cultural system as the unit of analysis in behavioral investigations of ethnographic, historical, and contemporary dress. Her publications include "'The Silkworms of the East Must Be Pillaged': The Cultural Foundations of Mass Fashion" in *Clothing and Textiles Research Journal.*

Michael S. Riggs is a professional public historian. He is a past president of the John Whitmer Historical Association and has written and lectured extensively on topics relating to LDS studies. Riggs holds a BS in organizational behavior from the University of San Francisco, an MA in religion from Park University, and did doctoral course work in history/religious studies at the University of Missouri–Kansas City.

Ronald E. Romig is the Community of Christ archivist (formerly the Reorganized Church of Jesus Christ of Latter-day Saints) with world headquarters in Independence, Missouri. He is a past president of the John Whitmer Historical Association and an active participant in the Mormon History Association, having served as a council member and 2003 program chair. He has published many articles in the *Journal of Mormon History,* the *John Whitmer Historical Association Journal, Mormon Historic Studies, Restoration Studies,* and other academic journals.

Thomas M. Spencer is associate professor of history and director of the honors program at Northwest Missouri State University in Maryville. He is the author of *The St. Louis Veiled Prophet Celebration: Power on Parade, 1877–1995* (Columbia: University of Missouri Press, 2000) as well as a contributor to and editor of *The Other Missouri History: Populists, Prostitutes, and Regular Folk* (Columbia: University of Missouri Press, 2005), an anthology of essays about Missouri social history. He is beginning work on a monograph about Mormon-Missouri conflict during the 1830s.

Grant Underwood is professor of history at Brigham Young University. He has written or edited a number of books and articles on Mormon history, including the prize-winning *Millenarian World of Early Mormonism.* He serves as cochair of the Mormon Studies Consultation of the American Academy of Religion and is the lead editor of the first two volumes of the Documents Series in the *Joseph Smith Papers* project.

Dale A. Whitman is professor of law and dean emeritus at the University of Missouri. His scholarship deals primarily with real estate and mortgage finance law. He is the author of numerous journal articles and five coauthored books, including *Real Estate Finance Law* and *The Law of Property,* and is the former president of the Association of American Law Schools.

Kenneth H. Winn is the former state archivist of Missouri. He has taught history at Washington University in St. Louis and is currently an adjunct professor of history at the University of Missouri–Columbia. He has written or coedited numerous works on Mormon and Missouri history, including *Exiles in a Land of Liberty: Mormonism in America, 1830–1846* and *The Dictionary of Missouri Biography.*

Fred E. Woods is professor of church history and doctrine at Brigham Young University and a Richard L. Evans Chair of Religious Understanding since 2005. He compiled and edited the Mormon Immigration Index CD, which is used globally, and has written several books as well as numerous articles on Mormon migration.

Index

About the Editor

Thomas M. Spencer is associate professor of history and director of the honors program at Northwest Missouri State University in Maryville. He is the author of *The St. Louis Veiled Prophet Celebration: Power on Parade, 1877–1995* (Columbia: University of Missouri Press, 2000) as well as a contributor to and editor of *The Other Missouri History: Populists, Prostitutes, and Regular Folk* (Columbia: University of Missouri Press, 2005), an anthology of essays about Missouri social history.